no

M000239404

SKATEBOARD,
ROLLER SKATING
AND
BICYCLE
RIDING
PROHIBITED
SEC 96 & 100 TRAFFIC CODE
W5
3RD ST
MR
DONUTS
RAGE
Go Skate
DAY
JUNE
21st

productions

compiled, edited and published by **Chris Long & Travis Jensen**

artist in chief **Dale Dreiling**

the storytelling of

**Airto Jackson Anthony Pappalardo Brian Tucci Brock Essick Brown Chris "Wez" Lundry Clarkie Corey Daniel Dave Miller David Wallace Erik Olsen Frank Atwater Garet O'Keefe Greg Lang Ismael Benhamida Jeff Knutson Jeremiah Liebrecht Jessie vanRoechoudt Jim Gray Joey Young Joshua J. Feldman Karl Watson Keir Johnson Kevin McHugh Lee Smith Leland B. Ware Lizzie Lee Marc Johnson Mark Whiteley Matt Derrick Matt Goodwin Michael Brooke Mike York Nate Sherwood Nimal Paul Cote' Richard Hart Rob Brink Rory Parker Rudy Bazorda Satva Leung Scottie Vosburgh**

with illustrations from

**Darin Bendall eThos Ferris Plock Jay Hakkinen JTRD John Rodriguez Nate Hooper Paul Urich Steve Kang**

and photography by

**Ando Caulfield Blair Alley Bob Kronbauer Dave Franklin Isaac McKay-Randozzi Ken Goto Mark Whitaker Yong-Ki Chang**

stencil work by **Skater Dave**

# No Comply: Skateboarding Speaks on Authority.

*Volume One in the **Skateboarding Speaks** series

**No Comply: Skateboarding Speaks on Authority**
Volume One in the Skateboarding Speaks series.

**Funnotfame Productions**
P.O. Box 2020
Ventura, CA 93002
online: www.funnotfame.org



ISBN 0-9740729-2-3
Series Creator / Publisher / Editor in Chief: Chris Long
Volume One Compiled / Edited / Published by: Chris Long & Travis Jensen
Book Layout / Cover Design: Chris Long
Artist in Chief: Dale Dreiling

Funnotfame Productions is a skateboarding based collective, committed to showcasing creative excellence within the skateboarding community. We welcome correspondence from skateboarding's creative class and are constantly on the lookout for emerging talent in literary, artistic and scholastic endeavors. We are an affiliate of the Writer's Guild of America, west.

Published annually, *Skateboarding Speaks* is an ongoing anthology series intended to explore the intellectual depth and diversity of skateboarders. Skateboarders of all types are encouraged to contribute and guidelines are available online. Future topics include the Reason Why, Public Skateparks, Religion and the Paranormal, Science and Technology, the Corporate Dollar, Art, Music, Creativity and more.

Publishing and production inquiries can be made via our address above, or online: editors@funnotfame.org

First edition printed in the United States of America by John Fleming, Albert Cole and Chris Long at the Vintage Press. www.vintagepress.net



**www.funnotfame.org**

*Funnotfame would like to thank Travis Jensen, Dale Dreiling and the entire list of No Comply contributors.*

## no comply: the breakdown.

**illustrations and art:**



**photography:** Front cover: Huf by Ken Goto. Back cover: Ken Goto and Dave Franklin. Inside cover / inlay: Ando Caulfield, Blair Alley, Bob Kronbauer, Dave Franklin, Steve Kang, Ken Goto, Isaac McKay-Randozzi. Mark Whitaker and Yong-Ki Chang.

## FORWARD.

When somebody treats you like a subhuman, the natural response is resentment.

We all know the story: It's a democracy - *a land of the free.* Thomas Jefferson's proposition that all are created equal forms the philosophical basis of traditional democracy, and in theory the formula is simple: a citizenry of good standing and similar virtue agrees to a general code of behavior based on common respect, allowing for the maximum amount of freedom with the minimum amount of restriction.

But everything looks different on paper.

On paper we are ostensibly free to pursue any interest so long as the life, liberty or property of no other citizen is violated in the process. In immediate reality, a group of teenagers practicing flatground tricks in an empty parking lot poses absolutely no encroachment to another individual. Similarly, tax-paying skateboarders enjoying a Sunday afternoon at the local abandoned swimming pool pose no immediate threat to anybody, except possibly themselves. Yet time and time again police, security guards and standard heroes deny these freedoms, even when they pose no immediate encroachment to the freedom of another.

While traversing the path of a skateboarder one can't help but notice the subtle ironies of everyday life: we work, legislate and tax ourselves to death proclaiming that we are free the whole time, yet we frown upon street performers, skateboarders and other outcasts who often embody the very essence of freedom. When an individual challenges the social norm by being different, it can create psychological pain in people around them. This pain is called *cognitive dissonance.* People do not like how cognitive dissonance makes them feel, so they work very hard to eliminate it and, if necessary, you.

Although the law that proclaims no skateboarding posted boldly atop the grocery store parking lot is there for several stock reasons, the root of all of them is the protection of assets. People don't want skateboarders at their businesses because the customers can get intimidated, which may result in a loss of profit. Some skateboard tricks (by far the minority of them) cause damage to curbs, ledges and handrails, which incur 'unnecessary' expenses, resulting in a loss of profit. If the person doing the skateboarding should incur any injuries the business owner can get sued, resulting in a loss of profit. The protection of money, wealth and property is the true spirit of anti-skateboard laws.

Authorities generally feel that order and routine are the measure of all things and they typically give little value to needs or desires that fall out of these bounds. Although making generalizations is always a bit unfair, generally the police of today cater to the interests of the money holders in society. The homeless and poor are classified as impediments to business and money making, therefore they get legislated out of the public squares, and the same goes for skateboarders. Property is to be protected at all costs and is consistently given higher importance than enjoyment or recreation.

There are many expressions of authority layered throughout society. Good cops, bad cops, peers, preachers, teachers, legislators, security guards, judges, skatepark monitors, property owners, control freaks and plain ole' fashioned do-gooders all have their own opinion on what others should and should not do; but in a free country, at what point should their opinions override anybody else's? What about those gray areas where one person's perception of liberty is in conflict with another's, as in unconventional or non-traditional uses of public space...like skateboarding?

It's questions like these *No Comply* seeks to address.

The relationship that exists between skateboarders and authority is a rather precarious one that provides for many interesting scenarios, and although the topic was briefly touched upon in *Manifesto,* stories of conflict between skateboarders and their environments could fill volumes. Most authorities that are really disrespectful towards skaters are people who have endured skateboarding as a problem for a really long time, and the skateboarders that are the rudest and most spiteful towards authority are the ones who accumulate deep reservoirs of negatively charged experiences in the streets.

Let's face it - this whole thing is really so immature. Skaters have no right to bitch about some poor guy kicking them out of his sole proprietorship, and if you do you're a dumb-ass. Not to sound like a good little Republican or anything, but private property ought to be respected. But skating at a public schoolyard on the weekend, in a city drainage ditch, on the public sidewalks or even on those red curbs in front of K-Mart after closing that they'll repaint anyways are all, well... *different.*

The idea that democratic countries are free countries *en total* is a common misconception. Five hundred years ago Machiavelli noted the two forms of government: the republic and the monarchy. In essence there is little difference between them and freedom at the level of citizen is no more a guarantee under democracy than, say, aristocracy, feudal monarchy or even communism for that matter.

Defined simply as majority rule, democracy has no inherent moral polarity of its own but exists merely as a conduit for the prevailing national character at any given time. The current national character is increasingly one of stress, tension and paranoia - is it any wonder our laws demand rigid control of behavior in public space?

In a sense, skateboarding represents an assault; a group of teens shows up to a spot, creatively adapts it and just takes it over. Sometimes, but not always, skateboarding is an usurpation of private property, deservingly reprehensible to one degree or another. Sometimes skaters are respectful and cognizant of the other people around them, other times they are not.

This is skateboarding, and clashes with authority are pretty much a guarantee, especially amongst the street and more dedicated pool breed. Negative repercussions, however, do not have to be guaranteed, and as with any other problem of human interaction the answer is always going to be *common respect.* Whether it's a skater disrespecting by skating something he truly shouldn't be, or an officer of the law bringing shame to the badge by punching a 14-year-old in the face, disrespect always causes problems within a society, because subhuman treatment always prompts resentment.

While every skater admits that authorities can be pretty disrespectful, the concession that skaters are often equally rude to police, business owners, security guards, skatepark monitors and other authority figures they encounter tends to fall by the way side. The knee-jerk reaction in most cases is usually one of distaste, and it is quite probable that every skater has at least one story of incredibly bad treatment both to and from some alleged pillar of society.

I've often found myself in some ironic positions as a skater: working as an authority figure at the skatepark, being responsible for fifteen kids at some skatecamp or working graveyard at a gas station where I was told to report skateboarders (little did the boss know that I would practice flatground with the neighborhood kids). In all of these situations I experienced discomfort projecting the role of an authority figure, and I attribute that to skateboarding.

For some reason, skaters, hippies, party-ers, punks and other renegade archetypes tend to view themselves as superior to any and all forms of authority. These archetypical Indigo children are determined to do their own thing, but try as we might to deny the fact, authority proper is an inseparable part of life in this universe. For better or for worse there are many authorities we obey with absolutely no say in the matter, like birth, breath and death. We are all subject to the authorities of eating, drinking, sleeping and mating, and we are all most rewarded when we follow them unswervingly. We are all certainly subject to the various authorities of Nature and the Creator, however we perceive it/them/they/Him/Her/he/she to be.

If my neighbor has annoying children or a loud dog, I simply have to put up with it; but if my neighbor dislikes the occasional hour of noise our backyard miniramp makes, the police can come and tell me to take it down. America's early settlers sought liberation from religio-political tyranny imposed by authorities with little concern for individual rights; modern skaters seek to liberate themselves from athletic-artistic discrimination imposed by the same.

On most occasions, skaters are more or less in full cooperation with the spirit of a law while breaking some particular letter of it. What's the problem when somebody skates way out in an unused corner of a parking lot, where there are no customers to intimidate and no property to damage? Skating flatground or a hip or off stairs or a loading dock does absolutely no damage to the actual property in question. Furthermore, the skateboarder is often over eighteen and knows full well that he or she would never sue the property owner in the event of an injury.

Are we really free then? Well, yeah...but not exactly, and skaters would do well to remember that the police are not there to deliberate the law with you; they are there to protect the immediate needs of the majority. Like York and Lee Smith say, "Save your breath."

It should be understood that minority groups are defined by much more than race; a minority is anybody whose interests run counter to those of the majority; in our situation, those who pursue the classical American Dream. Comprising roughly four percent of the United States population, recreational skateboarders are definitely a minority group in this country, and like any other minority they are frequently subject to discriminatory treatment from the majority. Skateboarders can and should do much more as well, and that brings us right back to *common respect*.

The introduction of firearms, cyber-warfare and nanotech weaponry into a society drastically empowers any and all authority. Culturally evolved humans find ways to adapt and coexist amidst their differences, be they religious, political, recreational or otherwise, and if *homo sapiens* are to survive even another century we must learn this. Some authorities are cooperative with skaters, and some skaters are equally mindful, even to the point of periodically repairing damage, respecting boundaries and cleaning up trash. Some security guards and cops simply look the other way because they know there is much more dangerous crime going on in our cities than skateboarding. This commitment to common respect must transcend unfair laws; one can consider looking the other way once in a while.

The most convincing evidence for the authenticity of skateboarding is its tenacity. From an anthropological point of view, skating has proven itself a viable subculture, and it is here that a statement must be issued to society: you will never stop it.

Literally nothing in a free society can stop people from picking up skateboards and riding them. Whenever society enacts anti-skate laws or measures, the creative and determined skater will simply improvise. True creatures of adaptation, like social parasites we flaunder about searching for interesting new hosts in the streets, pools, ditches, pipes and every other nook and cranny of the concrete jungles we incubate in; and despite pathological mainstream resistance we have not only survived, but *flourished* to the point of emulation and influence.

Skateboarders have survived the senseless war waged against them, not necessarily coming out victorious in every battle, but something notably more valuable. The masses tried to stop us but they fell in love with us.

The title of this book is not a call to defiance or distrust, and any real skater learns those during their first year on the street anyway. Sure, *No Comply* has the obligatory animosities and f-bombs you might expect from a title of its nature, but the well-articulated treatment of a sociologically sensitive subject from over two dozen degree-holding graduates and professionals comes as an unexpected, legitimate and most scholarly surprise.

*No Comply* did not set out to be a blaring middle finger extended towards authority or the system it's designed to protect; rather an open hand. If any authority will be positive, respectful, trustworthy and fair then under all circumstances that authority should be respected; but when any authority has become cold, blind, corrupt or untrustworthy, a person of good conscious encounters grave difficulty in respecting it.

Aside from the goal of assembling an incredible anthology written by skateboarders, my goal was to persuade any and all forms of authority, anyone who calls any shot in this world be they a cop, security guard, parent or whatever. Hopefully this book will help them better understand their role in the skateboarding equation, and if you're a skater, realize that you, too, have a circle of responsibility and influence; highlight key passages as you read and pass the book along to that over-critical parent, relative or associate who simply cannot let up in their intolerance of your skateboarding.

Thanks to stunning peformances from Travis Jensen, Dale Dreiling and the entire list of over sixty contributors, *No Comply* went from idea to finished product in thirteen weeks. This summer I conceived of the title while brainstorming for *Skateboarding Speaks* installment concepts. I then contacted one of the hardest working writers I know - Travis Jensen - about contributing to an anthology project by skateboarders that was to be part of a series. I later told him the title; he enthusiastically accepted the offer and it quickly became evident that Travis possessed skills and drive far beyond the realm of your standard contributor; after all, Travis does come into this project as an already-well-established author in skateboarding culture. In fact he put his current title, *Welcome to San Franpsycho,* on hold for three months just to come through for this project. We think the reader will also agree that *No Comply* could not have possibly been the same without the professional committment and talent of our artist in chief, Dale Dreiling.

A few contributors mysteriously dropped off after giving an affirmative nod to the project, and that explains any discrepancies between what you heard and what is. For the most part, during editing Travis and I attempted to retain as much of the writer's original voice as possible.

In the end I had to endure another near-24-hour day copy editing this beast, and at the end of a project any publisher or editor knows that's never fun. Apologies are in order to all the contributors who spent their precious time providing a list of footnotes for their work; I lost all the footnotes for the project at the last second, and we will publish them online along with all the stuff that arrived too late to make the cut.

Most of the contributions were really solid, a few needed to be trimmed around the edges and some underwent major surgery, but all of them accurately and eloquently conveyed an experience that is as much the essence of skateboarding as rolling: authority.

So welcome to Volume One of the Skateboarding Speaks series; compiled, edited and published by Funnotfame Productions with Travis Jensen. Whether you are a skater, authority figure or uninitiated reader, we hope you find the work meaningful and relevant.

May all world citizens realize that the common denominator of right human relations is respect.

-Chris Long
November 10, 2005
Ventura, California

## FIRST AND GOAL.

I just got off the phone with series creator Chris Long. He informed me that his computer just crashed and the entire *No Comply* book is missing in action. We are currently less than two hours away from passing the file. I feel like I'm about to have a damn heart attack and my hair is turning gray as I type.

At this point, it looks like we're not going to have the book in time for our December 3rd release party in Ventura. We might have to start over again from scratch. The thought of that makes winceÖall that hard work down the toilet.

This whole situation reminds me of a story I once heard about Ernest Hemingway. As the story goes, Ernest was vacationing solo somewhere in Europe after finishing a novel that had completely drained him. He had made arrangements for his wife to come meet him by train. She had the manuscript with her. It was the one and only copy. As it turns out, his wife accidentally left the manuscript on the train and it was forever lost. Hem had to rewrite the whole book over from scratch. I have a pretty good idea now how he must have felt.

Regardless of whether of not Chris is able to recover the file, I would like to take a moment to tell you the story of how this book manifested.

Three months or so after the release of my first book, *Left-Handed Stories,* I received an e-mail from Chris stating that he had picked up a copy of my book from FTC skate shop while visiting San Francisco. He said that he traded the guy working at the shop (Ando Caulfield) a copy of his own book, *Manifesto,* for mine. Attached to Chris' e-mail was a nice review he had written on my book for SLAP Magazine, which ended up running in the very next issue.

Chris and I then began e-mailing back and forth and he later sent me a copy of his book to read. I was very much impressed with the content and recommended it to a handful of my friends to check out. He did the same for mine.

This past summer Chris and I began discussing the idea of collaborating on a title. Since we are both lifelong skaters, a book about skateboarding was only fitting. Chris had some ideas about a book on authority and skateboarding. We figured every skateboarder had an opinion or good story to tell on the subject. Once the theme was established, all we needed was a title.

Chris called me up the first thing the following morning. He was very excited.

"I got the perfect title," he said.

"*No Comply!*"

I thought the title was brilliant and from there things just sort of took off. Chris and I made an incredible team. We were like Joe Montana and Jerry Rice, a real force to be reckoned with. Sure we had our setbacks along the way, which was only to be expected, but we charged right over those obstacles and continued pushing towards the goal-line.

I'm proud to say this book went from idea to nearly a finished product in approximately 13 weeks, which in my opinion is nothing short of amazing. Let's just hope Chris is able to recover the file and crank out all the copy-edits in time. I have my fingers crossed. If not, that's the breaks. We'll survive and I'm fully prepared to start over again from scratch come sun-up.

And on that note, my friends, when this book eventually does make it to print, I really hope you enjoy it, because Chris and I sure had an adventure compiling, editing and publishing the damn thing.

Yours Truly,

-Travis Jensen
November 15th, 2005
San Francisco, California

*(Editors Note: Miraculously, the file was recovered, Chris discovered and corrected over 350 copy edits and the book made it to the printer in a 24-hour period, just in the nick of time. Travis did not have a heart-attack.)*

W/S
3RD ST
MR
DONUTS

## *ON CULTURAL HOSTILITY**

A Primer by Rudy Bazorda
*revised from *Manifesto*, 2003

"If we turn to those restrictions that only apply to certain classes of society, we encounter a state of things which is glaringly obvious and has always been recognized the neglected classes will grudge the favored ones their privileges.and do everything in their power to rid themselves of their own surplus of privation. Where this is not possible a lasting measure of discontent will obtain within this culture, and this may lead to dangerous outbreaks...if a culture has not got beyond the stage in which the satisfaction of one group of its members necessarily involves the suppression of another, it is intelligible that these suppressed classes should develop an intense hostility to the culture; a culture, whose existence they make possible by their labor, but in whose resources they have too small a share..."

It was Valentine's Day. I had been skating all day long and I was tired. Putting skating first, which is the usual measure, I had forgotten all about what I needed from the store to make a little dinner for the lady. She's awesome and definitely well worth it, so I drove over to Trader Joe's and the place was a madhouse.

There were pedestrians everywhere, newspaper peddlers and quite a few people attempting to dock their oversize Suburban's and Tahoe's in the compact stalls while checking their bank accounts on their palm pilots. So naturally I set my scope on a parking space way out near the edge of the lot. I knew it would be quicker to walk, and I really wanted to avoid the frenzy this whole lovey-thing had become. As I turned to enter my stall, I caught a glimpse of an old slappy curb I grew up skating. Since Trader Joe's was on the east side, it had been years since I gave that little two-inch slab of love any punishment. Instantly I knew I had to give it a ramming. Exhausted and really just wanting to take care of business, I hesitated. I looked at her again, and there she was, oozing with lustrous red gloss no less inviting than a hooker's sin concealing lipstick. I grabbed my board out of the trunk and rushed it.

A rich lady in a Lexus cut me off without even realizing it. I was determined. I made a loop around the lot and tried again, to no avail. This time the overflow from the Carl's Jr. drive-thru foiled my plans. I circled the lot again, attracting the attention of some guy standing outside his truck looking odd. I could tell he was wondering why I pulled up in a car, hopped on a skateboard and proceeded to skate circles around the particular section of parking lot we were in. I ignored him, as this time there was a definite clear shot between myself and the object of my desire. I shralped as hard as I could into the curb with a violent frontside assault. 'AhÖthere we go,' I thought to myself. I went back for a better one and luckily the slappy gods paid up twice. I pushed off in the direction of the store when I noticed that guy again. He was staring at me like I was from another planet.

'What the heck is this guy doing on a skateboard in a lot packed full of cars?' He probably wondered.

Huh. If only he knew.

The vast majority of non-skateboarders have no idea what drives us. The overwhelming bulk of them have never experienced the joys of skating, or accomplishment in any physical art for that matter. Contentment to the average non-skateboarding adult consists of a few sappy television shows at home after work with a decent meal. Maybe a movie follows that, and don't forget the dessert.

I pulled that Freud quote from his *The Future of an Illusion*, written some thirty-five years before society witnessed any measurable interest in the phenomenon of skateboarding. A prominent psychologist generally credited with the development of psychoanalysis, Freud knew absolutely nothing about skateboarding and its related counter culture. In fact, chances are he never even saw a skateboard in his entire life, as he died in England around the start of World War II. So far as we know, modern skateboarding did not appear on the scene until the early sixties in the United States.

Freud began to extend his methods of psychoanalysis to culture as a whole, viewing its mass of ideas and behaviors as a collective unit open to study and critique. The patterns and trends of a society reflect its intellectual, moral and spiritual values or lack thereof. *The Future of an Illusion* presents itself as, among other things, Freud's hypothesis on the nature of religious ideas. One particular sub-topic explored in the beginning of the book is the notion of what he terms *cultural hostility*.

Modern society is based on compulsory labor and instinctual renunciations. Every industrial system imposes mandatory work upon its members in an attempt to secure stability. Furthermore, all societies demand that certain behaviors of the masses be suppressed in a continual state of compromise between the individual and the culture they live in.

Cultural hostility forms when the individual realizes that the system is more concerned with securing his conformity than facilitating his freedoms. In short, the individual comes to recognize that the demands of society, which are increasingly represented by corporate and political dictation, override the demands of the individual. The natural response is resentment, or hostility.

An extreme example would be the society that outlawed all forms of art, music and intellectual pursuit. Such a society would be forcing its members to abstain from activities they deem healthy and important while simultaneously demanding that by labor, taxation, trumped-up civic duty and countless other obligations they support the very same system that refuses to acknowledge their interests. The obvious conclusion for the members of such a society would be to ponder amongst themselves, 'Why should I support a system which ignores my needs?'

I have not heard a better description of the relationship that exists between skaters and authority.

It just tickles me to entertain the probability of Freud rolling over in his grave with condemnation at the uptight adults who oppose skateboarders so adamantly. Consider the countless millions of contributing citizens who have spent the majority of their teens, twenties and often thirties as skateboard enthusiasts. Most of them begin skateboarding in pre-teen childhood, a time of life when pages of experience undeniably shape impressionable minds. Teenagers constantly make deductions and observations in their attempts to understand the adult world that demands their compliance. Parents, pastors, teachers, coaches, peers and other authority figures all impose separate and often conflicting expectations upon them. Though usually rooted in good intention, the guidelines intended to matriculate the young adult into society provide a semblance of direction for the teenager at best. At worst, they confuse and drive them to angst, often smothering natural creative expressions and encouraging this 'cultural hostility' or resentment Freud wrote about.

One can understand the tendency of kids to react with fear, confusion or outright rebellion to this foreign increase in both obligation and instinctual renunciation. It is antithetical to the bliss of childhood, the only frame of reference any kid really has. Though they don't realize it, with the exception of parents and immediate superiors, kids whiz through life with relatively unchecked freedom.

Adulthood and it's associated responsibilities, many of which would be more accurately labeled personal choices or social dictums, invite resistance. They do not, especially to a teenage skateboarder, appear comfortable or as things to be embraced. Very few teenagers, indeed very few individuals, have taken the time and introspection necessary to render a definite decision as to who they are and what they really need or want out of life. The chances of this self-realization seem to get progressively thinner as cultural obligations increase. It is an arduous task to merely engage in self-exploration, let alone effect corresponding changes with action while simultaneously jumping through the hoops of modern culture. If one is not careful, self-imposed circumstances will begin to control every facet of life.

Though some handle the expected transitions with little or no difficulty, a substantial and increasing amount find the process too burdensome or flat out unappealing. The former are content to start families, begin a long ascent up the corporate ladder or take a trip through some other prefabricated career: becoming a doctor, playing professional athletics or engaging in the arts and music. However, without a strong resolve to succeed, the latter often become the flotsam and jetsam of society. What about the kids who don't seem to fit nicely into any of society's little categories? What happens if a community not only fails to provide sufficient outlets for unconventional interests, but also reprimands those who participate in such interests?

Cultural hostility magnifies greatly for individuals with interests such as skateboarding because they quickly realize that outside of a skateboard park society has no place for such interests, save the creatively sterile 'extreme' phenomenon and its cheapened, corporate derivatives.

Skateboarders, especially of the late eighties and early nineties and even continuing into today, often receive punishment for their individuality in many ways. While the skateboarding industry employs tens of thousands of citizens in the state of California alone with even average riders making decent money, skaters are told to 'get a real job.' Though skaters perform amazingly technical feats of coordination and grace often surpassing that of Olympic athletes, police respond with insults to those of us in our twenties when encountered in the streets. Parents proclaim that we are 'too old to be playing on that toy.' Every corner we turn reveals another teacher, do-gooder, police officer or other member of society telling us that our actions and interests do not fit in with their expectations. This constant disapproval not only results in the slow and steady formation of cultural hostility, it also tends to destroy the confidence of youth in their creative pursuits. Back to the words of Freud: '...it is to be expected that the rejected classes will grudge the favored ones their privileges and do everything in their power to rid themselves of their own surplus of privation.'

Privation is frustration. Isolated skateboarders are frustrated because they are neglected and singled out. In Freud's equation the 'favored ones' are the kids who happen to engage in activities that are deemed appropriate by society and provided for accordingly, i.e. traditional sports and activities.

Since local governments and authorities typically spend exponential amounts of energy and resources trying to stop skateboarding while making only minimal efforts to accommodate it, amongst skateboarders 'a lasting measure of discontent will obtain...and this may lead to dangerous outbreaks.' In this case, the dangerous outbreaks usually do not take the form of violent revolutions or social uprisings. They manifest in subtle, more potent forms of anti-social attitude and apathy towards society as a whole.

When skateboarders, members of one of the top participant activities in the United States, see an unused horseshoe pit or tetherball court in a park where they are getting kicked out or ticketed for skating a bench, they justifiably get a little angry. When they're repeatedly told to 'go somewhere else' while almost every other interest is at least marginally provided for, they justifiably get a little more angry, perhaps to the point of ridiculing the local system. When they get arrested, fined and jailed their anger turns to sharp bitterness, and when they realize that corporate interests and white-knuckled control over public space takes priority over their needs, the potential for an optimistic and healthy assessment of society wanes entirely.

When the kids of Philadelphia watch Mayor Street destroy Love Park and open-handedly welcome the multi-million dollar X-games, how can they not see the hypocrisy and begrudge both their community and authority in general? If you were a skater living in Philly would you want to participate in the local elections and affairs?

The following is a speech made by Edmund N. Bacon, father of actor Kevin Bacon and former city planner of Philadelphia. Ed was the mastermind behind the famous Love Park, and was apparently pretty outraged with Mayor Street's plan to end skateboarding there.

"I conceived Love Park as part of my architectural thesis at Cornell in 1932...Rebecca Rimel of the Pew Charitable Trust spent two million dollars to come up with a slogan for Philadelphia, 'The city that loves you back.' Today we set an addendum, [to the slogan] '...unless you are under the age of thirty and like to skateboard, in which case we kick you in the butt.'"

"This is discrimination of the worst sort, Philadelphia against the youth of the world! It was here, in Philadelphia in 1776, that the leaders of our country stood up to the King of England and told him to go to hell. I make no claim to our leader, but by God I am a person and I stand up to Mayor Street and tell him to go to hell and stay there until he sees the light and changes his ways by going to Love Park each day with a smile on his face and a warm welcoming handshake, to greet the skateboarders of the world. Then, once again, the beautiful sounds of 1776 will ring out across the hills and valleys of our city, and again I will be proud to be a Philadelphian."

Ninety-two-year old Ed read this speech minutes before he skated in protest through the park with the intention of getting arrested in front of local authorities and media. Longtime friend and Love Park architect Vincent Kling stood by his side. Evidently the elderly skater aroused quite the fear, as officers were called in for back-up! Ed was neither arrested nor tackled by undercover agents; the usual treatment dished out to skateboarders at Love Park by the city of Philadelphia.

Coupled with the knowledge that such treatment extends to skaters across the country, it is not hard to understand why many have become what they have. The idea of equal opportunity is commonly understood in terms of employment or political life, but in a true democracy the notion of equal opportunity must extend to include education, housing and other public accommodations, i.e. recreation.

The simple, straightforward truth is that the skateboarder, graffiti artist and anybody else with an oddball interest is just as deserving of the basic rights of expression as anyone else in America. Isn't that part of what's inferred in the Constitutional guarantee of 'life, liberty and the pursuit of happiness?'

For skateboarders, the widescale disallowment of their interests leaves two options: working within the system to acquire their objectives, or continuing to do what they do in spite of social unacceptance and restrictions. For a hardcore skater, the idea of quitting is not an option.

Most skateboarders are at a disadvantage as far as working within the system goes. The majority of them are boys in the six to fourteen-year age range, hardly old enough to even comprehend the enormous energy, determination and resolve necessary to effect any change in our local red-tape beaurocracies, let alone actually do so. Unfortunately, by the time they become old enough to vote or understand what little power they do possess, all interest in doing so has fizzled, long ago beaten down by condemnation from authority.

'Why try to do anything? People don't listen. . ."

This is the subconscious dialog of a skater. Many feel helpless and that government and authority are there to make life more difficult. As a result of their experiences with authority in the streets, most of which are not encouraging and borderline fascist, they develop mistrust and distaste for our culture altogether; in the case of taxpaying skaters, 'a culture whose existence they make possible by their labor, but in whose resources they have too small a share.'

So, as could be expected, most take the latter route, continuing to skateboard in spite of heavy efforts against it that are typical of nearly every community. Ignored and spited by society up until the late 1990's, skateboarders introverted and formed a tight-knit family as do other groups the majority attempts to disband. We are literally, by default on the part of authority to accommodate us, 'driven to rebelliousness' as Freud theorized. We face police, tickets, chases and the like on a daily basis, all for riding a skateboard, a skateboard that equals one less environmentally polluting car on the road at that.

I have personally listened with disgust while a heroin overdose and violent crimes flooded the dispatch radio of the Ventura patrol car that was being used to detain me for skateboarding in an empty parking lot late at night. I would attempt to expose such things to police officers and security guards, only to have them insult me and give me the nickname of 'the lawyer.' More recently, we have been ticketed and threatened with thousand-dollar fines by the Ventura County Sheriff's Department for skating an abandoned pool cited for demolition that we spent time and money repairing. I have also had police escort me home for skateboarding and lie to my parents about my actions. Do you think for a second that any of this provided me with a healthy outlook on our culture?

Why is it criminal to view architecture and public property as open to creative interpretation, especially when there is no property damage or measurable problem? What's the problem of riding an empty pool at an abandoned house in the middle of nowhere? What about those few occasions where the laws are unfair? If a city had not one basketball court in it, could ten guys who made hoops and drew a court with chalk in a parking lot be considered criminals deserving of tickets, disparaging comments and jail? The obvious solution would be to build plenty of adequate basketball courts. So why does the process get so complicated when a board with four wheels replaces the ball?

Everything looks like a big joke in school when they tell us to stand up for what we believe in and contribute to society, yet at the same place we get busted for engaging in our preferred form of physical art while other kids get a full playing field, shower and opportunities for scholarships for engaging in theirs. When I'm getting kicked out of public spots four times a week or chased out of a skateboard park for not having full body armor, it makes me not want to vote or do anything for my city or state because they consistently insult me and neglect my needs. As skateboarders over the age of eighteen, we are expected to pay taxes, endure jury duty or go to war, all the while being punished for our interests.

This is the poorly articulated side of the story that every teacher, security guard, cop or hero needs to understand. Every time skateboarders are treated as criminals and delinquents, our view of authority as the enemy is reinforced. Every time our civil liberties are infringed upon by some testosterone-charged idiot with an inferiority complex, we learn to despise establishment that much more. Every macho rent-a-cop makes authority that much more of a joke in the eyes of the skateboarder. Every time one of us pays a fine or loses a board for merely doing something we enjoy that keeps us away from real crime, the words of politicians, police and other so-called pillars of society are taken with less interest and urgency.

Modern American society generally spites skateboarders, and they learn, naturally, to resent 'their' society. To taint them is to taint our future. The more they reprieve us, the more they drive us from them, and the larger the gap between 'us' and 'them' becomes. So naturally, just as Freud theorized, the more alienated, apathetic and culturally hostile we become. Hopefully people will eventually realize that the chastisement of skateboarders is tantamount to civil and social self-destruction; that the skateboarders in the streets today are the adults and decision makers of tomorrow.

Maybe mainstream society should consider reforming its treatment of skateboarders in public spaces.

After all, it's our world too...

"After all, it's our world too..."

## *HE DIDN'T SMILE BACK*

By Ismael Benhamida

The goal was to conquer the infamous golden rail that runs sideways down the twenty-six sharp, brick stairs in front of the Grand Hyatt in San Francisco. There remained a slight problem, though: the hotel had skate-proofed this gem of a handrail with steel knobs, but that didn't stop the crew. The night before they made a covert visit to the Hyatt, grinder and saw in hand to perform a minor surgery on the handrail. The operation was successful. The next day a 50-50 was slapped down the rail. The trick was impressive in its own right, but the story would never be complete without mentioning the prep-work: a bold message to the authority.

When I saw the call for submissions on a book about skateboarding and authority I was thrilled. Read through virtually any issue of *Transworld* or *Thrasher* and one is bound to find mention of a skater's run-in with police, security guards or someone.

This underlying issue with authority has long been an important subject for skateboarders and the skateboarding culture. The clash is so ingrained in the heart of the skateboarding community that one cannot seriously discuss skate history and culture without considering authority. A book on this topic is long overdue.

Because the interests and desires of skateboarders and authorities are diametrically opposed, the clash between the two makes for an interesting bout. At first glance this might seem to be due to the actual act of skateboarding but it is more due to a clash between what skateboarders and authority figures value.

When people see a skateboarder go down a handrail they usually respond in one of three ways: 1) Oh my God. That is amazing; 2) Oh my God. That is so dangerous; but most commonly the response is 3) Oh my God. You are trespassing and vandalizing the property. Stop it now and get out of here you little punk.

The first two responses usually come from civilian passers-by who are amazed and appreciate what they see. The third response usually comes from those in positions of authority. The claim is always the same: money, materials, and liability.

I grew up in the faraway land of Boise, Idaho and attended Boise High School. Mike Moczygemba, Chard Rincover and I used to skate at the side of the school when class would get out. I still remember the trash can we used to ollie over. It was old and weathered from the cold Idaho winters. I predict it would have brought a dollar or two at a Boise School District inventory sale.

One day the vice principal came out and told us that we could skateboard but that we could not ollie over the garbage can. It is useful to consider the thought process of the vice-principal. The school had no problem spending $18 million building new basketball courts, tennis courts and an inside gymnasium when they renovated a year later. This enormous amount of money doesn't even cover the cost of the coaching staff, the athletic gear and the facilities maintenance that each team sport requires. But in the end the risk of a dent in the school garbage can was far too great! Despite the fact that we were improving our coordination, getting physical exercise and enjoying ourselves, skateboarding remained unacceptable. When I think about this I can only smile and shake my head.

Let's be honest here - a peace officer is given incredible authority with little educational requirements. Minimum Standards for Police Officer Employment requires a GED (see State of California Title 11, Division 2, code 1002 of the California Code of Regulations). Now take a person who lusts power, give him a GED, a pair of buck tight pants, a gun, some handcuffs, and a black and white to cruise the streets "to serve and protect" and sure enough those lights will flash when he sees a session at Pier 7 (RIP). The officer sees these "delinquent youths causing noise pollution and a public nuisance." I have seen police confiscate skateboards, be very hostile to skateboarders, and I've even read of SFPD officers punching skaters.

My first run in with the law was a skateboarding ticket I received from an officer on horseback in Boise, Idaho, in August of 1994. I was skateboarding on the bricks at 10th and Main. Apparently it was an infraction to skateboard on the bricks. It was legal to skate on the concrete in downtown but the bricks were a no-no. Confused, I asked the officer why it was illegal and he replied with an haughty air of superiority, "because it breaks the bricks." I remained confused, and so I pressed on; "Your horse is a lot heavier than me, your horse's shoes are metal and my skateboard wheels are rubber. I bet your horse is responsible for most of the broken bricks around here." He replied by handing me a ticket for $47 and went on his way.

I set up a court date to contest the ticket. As it turns out I went to court and he didn't show up on time so the case got dismissed. As I left the courthouse in my shirt and tie and skated down Barrister Street to catch the bus, I saw my issuing police officer driving into court. I caught his attention with a victorious wave and gave him a smart-ass smile.

He didn't smile back.

Score: skateboarders one, authority zero.

I will never forget the scene in *Menikmati* when security guards were drinking beer while watching Eric Koston skate a ledge over a set of stairs in his native Thailand. These Thai authority figures were not so concerned about marks on the concrete. They were enjoying themselves watching an athlete perform some amazing tricks. I think American police could take a lesson from the Thai's on when to escalate a situation.

Police officers, building owners, city council members and school administrators - I have news for you: acid rain and the natural environment will have a far more destructive effect on handrails and concrete than skateboards do. Don't believe me? Go paint a handrail and then come back in a few years. Thermodynamics has got you beat on that one. Don't get me wrong, I support the concept of private property - a person in their home should not have to deal with a group of kids crooked grinding the curb along their driveway if they don't want to - but I am referring to property that is public domain or close to it, like Pier 7 in San Francisco or Pulaski Park in Washington D.C.

Cities, the police officers who are employed by them and the corporations that own the large business buildings that we love to skate are not taking losses because of us. We're not affecting their bottom line. They have a vested interest in a generation of happy and healthy youth who will enter the work force in their upcoming years. To value garbage cans, concrete and handrails over the creativity and contentment of our youth is to be cold, rigid and heartless.

"I will never forget the scene in *Menikmati* when security guards were drinking beer while watching Eric Koston skate a ledge over a set of stairs in his native Thailand..."

"...the ideal authority would appreciate and embrace all forms of cardiovascular pedestrian transportation; not give me a $250 citation for skating from the grocery store with groceries in my bag."

## *A SHORT DISCOURSE ON THE MAN*

By Brock Essick

I purchased my first skateboard in 7th grade at Dave's Cave in Ventura; a Lance Mountain Coat of Arms with Cutter trucks and Mini Ratbones. Serious skating started to happen in 1992, and nearly fourteen years later I am still skating strong, for fun, and looking forward to many more years of skating in the future.

Democratic society is allegedly based on freedom of choice. All choices come with consequence; the choice of riding a skateboard is no exception. The authority, which claims to be present to protect and serve the public, made it very clear that I have no right to ride my skateboard on public property. Further sickening, the same authority came and told me that I was in violation of city ordinances for having a skateboard ramp on my residential private property.

The next possible solution in my search for a skateboard sanctuary was the idea of a park built with the intentions of its sole purpose being skateboarding. This plan has been the solution of many skaters oppressed by the authority in our society. The results have produced a few excellent recreational facilities, and many lackluster, poorly-executed deathtraps that barely fall under the guise of a "skatepark." These parks are easy to spot because they have fences like prisons and careless construction that is the result of people who do not understand skateboarding or the laws of physics. The fences show me that we are perceived as animals and criminals, while the careless planning and shoddy construction illustrates how little the authority is concerned with the safety of our children.

In an ideal world, people would respect and value all types of personalities. Cities and their citizens would embrace the beauty of a switch backside tailslide on a planter ledge. A person would realize that it is an act of beauty and physical expression committed in the essence of fun, not hate. In a fair society, the authority would be oblivious to skateboarding because they would be too busy pursuing true evil. The authority would recognize that we are not criminals. If there were no baseball and football fields would kids stop playing? Of course not, the games must go on, and thus we skate in the streets or anywhere else that looks fun. In times where there are wars being fought over oil and Americans are fat and getting fatter, the ideal authority would appreciate and embrace all forms of cardiovascular pedestrian transportation. The ideal and fair authority would not give me a $250 citation for skating from the grocery store with groceries in my bag, and they certainly would never take away my emissions-free vehicle in this polluted world.

My adventures in skateboarding have led me to meet a most diverse group of people. Since there aren't any tryouts you find all types of participants, and because of that we have quite a *menagerie* of unique characters. The ratio of good to bad seems to be about the same as in other groups, but the mainstream is sensationalized to the point that what they remember the most is the shocking and horrible, and not the mundane and ordinary. It's sad to see skateboarding lumped into the same undesirable group as the homeless, prostitutes, drug addicts, and such. Society has typecast skaters as these characters, and our own commercial skateboarding industry has not made much progress in reversing these images.

The insidious devices known as "skatestoppers" may stop skating at a spot or they may not. They are basically like a band-aid for a hemophiliac; no matter how many you apply they won't stop the bleeding. Skatestoppers only force us to find a new favorite spot, or use some tools and make the spot happening again. Guerilla tactics may be called for in this war on skateboarding, because public space is endangered. Aldous Huxley was on to something when he wrote Brave New World.

The phantom menace of liability accounts for the general trend of city reluctance in accommodating skateboarding (or at least that is usually the first response). I teach middle school students and they wanted a skate club for their physical education class. The district said there is no way we can skate at school because it is a liability, and it is against school rules. The kids don't understand; it's what they are interested in. The truth of the matter is that the sports we are forced to play in P.E. classes are statistically more dangerous. The municipalities are constantly living in the past, in an era where baseball was the most popular pastime of children, and the automatons are reluctant to support the pastime of skateboarding because their programmed response is NO! Dispel the myths.

All over this country impressionable young minds are being labeled as outcasts because of a simple recreational preference. Then they are left to skate on the streets, where they are virtually guaranteed to encounter irresponsible authorities. They are lied to and also lied about by the authorities, and threatened with fines and possible incarceration. They are stopped even when not skating and harassed about their mere possession of a skateboard. They are presumed guilty until proven innocent, based on the actions of others. The illusory ideals of freedom are quickly dispelled and the newly formed outcast recognizes that justice is neither free nor blind; and certainly not equal. Skateboarders do not intend to commit crimes in the act of riding, but over time, children begin to own the identity they have been given. What once was a young child just trying to have some fun often turns into an adult that has contempt for authority and the society it supports. Trust that is lost is not easily regained.

Contrary to the cries of popular media and education, discrimination and ignorance prevent us from being truly free. Although this country has many aspects of freedom, the days of personal accountability are gone. We all must suffer for the mistakes of the few and the stupid. Pointless lawsuits have driven any semblance of freedom from our democracy, and now the actions of the thoughtless keep us from access to public space. I can understand being told to leave private property, but being kicked out of a park while others participate in more statistically dangerous activities illustrates clearly that we are not truly free.

I don't trust the authority; the authority doesn't trust me. I assume that the majority of Americans value the authority and the purposes it purports to serve. I do not. My rights have been violated repeatedly simply because of my choice to ride a skateboard.

If the authority reacted differently to skateboarders, wouldn't skateboarders react differently as well?

"What once was a young child just trying to have some fun often turns into an adult that has contempt for authority and the society it supports. Trust that is lost is not easily regained."

NO SKATEBOARDING
CYCLING
SKATING
ON SIDEWALK
P.B.M.C.
10.24.02.
NO SKATE
PRIVATE
NO SKATEBOARDS
ALLOWED
POLICE

## *A PICTURE WELL WORTH 3,000 WORDS...*

by Dale Dreiling

Growing up, I was never a great skater. Decent would've been a compliment. Goofy foot 50-50 grinds on waxed curbs and ledges to shove-its out, 180 ollies, ten feet worth of manual, rolling out of six stair ollies. These are the highlights of my time spent on a deck. I have no claims to having landed any hammers or stoking the bystanders. When it came to skateboarding, I just rolled along; but not to be understated, the highlights of my skateboarding experience are the truly genuine friendships that I made and dare to top still to this day. I feel these to be truly blessed gifts.

Of course, along with the good times came the bad, and both molded me equally. Having had a very strict and confining childhood where freedom from the judging eyes of well-intended but controlling parents was a sigh of relief, I grew up in the streets. This isn't a claim to a rough life; just a fact.

When you get no peace at home, you find it elsewhere. My childhood suburbia took the form of a small southern California beach city, San Buenaventura. Ventura for those who know. Also for those who know, Ventura has an excessively heavy handed, wild-west mentality of a police force whose numbers are double the country's national average.

Sure, this is Ventura, home to the Hell's Angels. It's also a literal playing field for middle-class white drug-dealing gangsters and their lower-class minority counterparts, and an epicenter of the meth pandemic explosion with localist, thug surfers who throw bowling ball size rocks through the car windows of regular dudes who dare surf their beaches, bro!

Ventura gets crazy at times, but remains a sleepy little po-dunk compared to its urban megalopolis neighbor an hour to the south, Los Angeles, where hard crime happens daily. Being who I was and who I hung out with in Ventura, we all should have been non-existent blips under the legal radar. Ironically, this was never the case.

Despite many run-ins with the law while immersed in daily skateboarding, my most defining experience with the police took place not in the midst of a session, but in a random encounter en route to the session. The lessons it taught me have forever affected my outlook on authority.

My buddy Paul took me along with him on a drive to the San Fernando Valley one Friday afternoon. Our mission objective was to grab a pair of concert sound monitors he saw in the Recycler Classifieds. They were for a good price and his band was ambitious. I was attempting frontside pop shove-it's to no avail as he tested, approved and purchased the cabinets. He lugged them out of the bungalow and towards the truck. The session ended with my Powell Peralta Frankie Hill deck being used as a pack mule dolly. A minute later we were back on the 101 and heading north towards home.

Our loosely sketched plan was to break paths once back in town. I would head towards the west side where the night would inevitably end up with me joining friends at California 66. Skated by many from Gershon to Salman, this was the current "as good as it gets" spot in town, which was not that bad actually. A typical but perfect Friday night for a bunch of eighteen-year-old high school grads without fake ID's. With this in mind and Ragin' Full On in the tape deck, we exited the 101 at Victoria and headed into Ventura.

Two miles up the road, at the Victoria-Telegraph intersection, the car in front of us made a freak stop in our lane midway through the intersection. To avoid a rear end collision, Paul quickly looked in the rear view, shifted down, threw on a blinker and slid into the next lane, pulling us out of the confusion and back into our lane.

"Nice work there, Captain!" I chuckled as Paul smiled.

With that the cry of a police siren and the roll of the red and blue danced behind us.

"Christ's Sake!!!" Paul moaned when his glance back affirmed that this wail was for him.

Paul drove up the street a pace and pulled into a cul-de-sac off of Foothill Road where a new construction project was just breaking ground. He knew the routine. Remove the sunglasses, turn the music off and have license, registration and proof of insurance ready for request. We both had our hands outside of the truck for the approaching officer to see.

"Do you know why I stopped you?" the linebacker-sized officer asked as he peered into the cab. I distinctly remember the image of us looking at him reflecting back at us in his mirrored sunglasses.

With all honesty and no kidding Paul replied, "No."

"You don't recall that reckless lane change you made back there? Don't you know it's illegal to make a lane change in an intersection? Didn't you pay attention in drivers training class?!" the officer snapped. His sense of unprovoked disrespect for us was already more than apparent.

"What was I supposed to do?" Paul asked. "The guy in front of me slammed on his breaks!! Should I have hit him...slammed on my brakes and had the guy behind us hit me?!"

"License, registration, and proof of insurance, please," was the officer's rebuttal.

Five minutes passed. We both glanced into our rearview mirrors as the officer bounced glances back at us between dispatch conversation pauses.

Despite being in a ghost town cul-de-sac, the officer came back to my side of the car to hand Paul his documents. As they exchanged paperwork, the officer said, "Look, I won't give you a ticket this time. Just don't let me catch you doing this kind of thing when I'm around again, ok?"

"Yes sir," sighed Paul with as much politeness as he could muster at the moment.

"Can I see your ID, son?" the officer said as he peered down on me.

"Um....ok?" I said, bewildered as I calmly gave him my driver's license. His cocky shuffle back to the cruiser was the receding image in my mirror. I had no record of any kind so what was I to fear? It was that confidence you can only possess when you have done no wrong and have nothing to hide. So, when the officer returned and asked me to step out of the car, I felt as if a Punk'd-style practical joke was being pulled on me.

"Keep your hands where I can see them!" the officer barked as I undid my seat belt. Thinly veiled aggression drew his hand back to his holster as I grabbed the door handle and stepped out onto the sidewalk.

"Stay there! Don't step closer!" he demanded as we shouldered off about five feet from each other. The difference in our height was dramatically exaggerated by the uphill grade the street gave him: my 5'8" on a good day pitted against his 6'1", or 6'2" with a crew cut; a visual joke in no need of words.

"Do you have a fucking problem with me...?" he cursed.

"What?" I asked with God-honest questioning. I had avoided making eye contact with him earlier in the car but had no choice now.

"I don't know what you mean.." I said.

"I saw you dogging me earlier! You hate me?! Or do you just hate all cops?!" I had never had the rug pulled out from beneath me so hard in all my life. I seriously had no idea what he meant but he continued to elaborate.

"Come on, you think I'm stupid? You were dogging me when you went up Victoria, and I was at the Moon Drive light..."

What!? This man was out of his mind. To better explain, Moon Drive is a cross-street to Victoria, a block up from the 101 freeway in the direction we exited as we entered town. This Dirty Harry wannabe had been shadowing us for over three miles, just waiting for a reason to flex his muscles. Paul's driving deal was just an excuse. For whatever reason he had in his mind, it was about me, and for the life of me I couldn't figure why.

To set the record straight, when riding as a passenger in a car, as most people do, I check out the scenery but I did not recall dogging anyone or anything. Why would I? It was Friday. I had Saturday off. I had my skate and plans for the night.

"I didn't dog you, sir. I don't even remember seeing you. I've never seen you before in my life." I said, trying to stay calm while being offended, well aware that he was the cop and I was just a kid. Who would society believe?

"So, you wanna fight me?! Kill me, huh!!?" he punched. "You like Body Count? I bet Cop Killer's a cool song to you..." Ice-T's music wasn't in the car with us! Not even on the radio. This was getting really weird. All I could say was, "No, I don't wanna kill you. I don't know you."

"So, you'd kill a cop though!?

"No."

Who was this guy!? When would he just shut up and let me go? Paul was now turned around and looking back at us. This had gone on for over ten minutes. Remembering we had an audience to my benefit, not his, he decided to reinforce his power one last time.

"I'm gonna let you go this time but I have my eye on you!" he huffed, knowing he had nothing on me. He threw my ID back at me.

"Get lost!" was his last jab.

"Whatever..." I sighed and turned around, getting back into Paul's truck.

"I heard that!!" he bitched. He sat in his car and watched us pull out of the cul-de-sac and drive off towards Paul's house before leaving to go his own way. Unbeknownst to me, this incident was only part one of the story. Part two was soon to follow.

Three months later, despite mine and the protest of others, a good friend enlisted in the Army. Disagreements aside, we threw Jerry

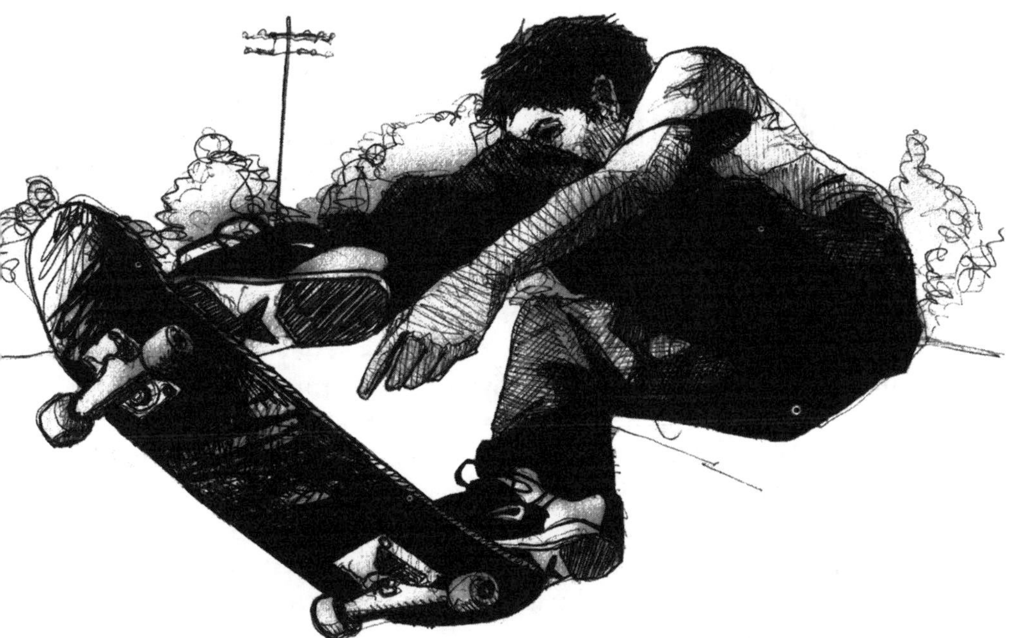

a going-away party. Being kids, we marked the occasion with beers and barbecue. On the walk back up from the park to the nearest friend's house, we saw a cop car cruising the street. I unfortunately had an open can of Budweiser in my hand.

The neighborhood had its hood elements. To say the least, it was a bit rough around the edges and colorful all the way through. A few kids with beers should have been the least of an officer's concerns. Try as I did, dropping the can behind a parked car was in vain pursuit. The cop let the siren go and got out of the car.

"You," the cop said, pointing to me. "Stay there!"

Damn it! I recognized this guy. It was the cop that pulled Paul over and harassed me! As much as I tried to play it off that I didn't know him, he knew that he knew me. His grin said it all.

"What's going on?" he asked as his flashlight spotlighted the beer can half in the gutter, contents pouring into the street.

"Just gettin' back from a friends enlistment barbecue party," I said, trying to appeal to his patriotic side. No dice.

"Drinking beers? You twenty one?" he asked.

As he put me in cuffs and laid me over the hood, he patted me down. Reaching into my pants pockets, he pulled out my wallet and its contents. His question now had an answer. Per standard procedure he continued. No, I'd never been arrested before. No, I wasn't on parole. No, I wasn't on probation. No, I wasn't in a gang. No, I wasn't on any other drugs.

"Haven't we met before?" he beamed with earnest glee.

"No, I don't know you." This was all I could protest although I knew it was hopeless.

"I think you do," he said, as if to emphasize his personal feudal victory. His prize? Winning the privilege of being the officer to write me my first ticket: minor in possession of an open container of alcohol.

This wasn't driving under the influence, this wasn't even public intoxication. This was a situation that almost every adult in this country has, in their youth, either been faced with or has dodged by the skin of their teeth. Admit it: kids drink. They drink now, they drank in the past. Even grandma drank before her twenty-first birthday. But this cop had a grudge to carry and I wasn't allowed a slap on the wrist. My punishment went as follows: a $180.00 fine and the suspension of my driving privileges for a year.

I feel that skepticism is as much my genetic inheritance as my hazel eyes and brown hair. Somewhere between having been born a blank slate and waiting to die a byproduct of society, my nature was being nurtured.

From first to last encounter, this story spans the length of my post high school graduation summer. There was much more to it than these incidents but needless to say, they were the huge mile markers. As California mandates of all high school students, I took American History and American Government. These classes are requirements for earning the right to walk away free with diploma in hand. But what I had been taught in school wasn't what was happening in the streets. I never really expected it to be, but comparatively, first hand experience was blunt, ugly and very confrontational.

At face value, reading the First Amendment of the U.S. Constitution makes it clear. We are, as American citizens, guaranteed a birth right to speak our minds; the freedom of speech to express our opinions amongst peers and critics, in the press, in the electronic media and in public without concern of persecution by authority.

There is a fine line of spider's thread width that reality weaves and anyone who has ridden a skateboard has experienced it. When someone who works a low paying, hourly wage job has their $150 deck taken away by an officer for practicing their creative hobby, are they being protected? Are they being served or just plain getting served? Who, then, is being protected? If not the skater, the curb? A step? A building? A civilian who could be injured by a runaway skateboard? The owner of the property? The public?

"To Protect and Serve."

When branded on the door of a patrol car, it doesn't state in the objective to protect the public. It also doesn't imply that the police are more the protectors of the financial investments and physical properties of the rich. When a skate session is cut short either on public or private property, what is the most likely reason to be cited for this interruption? Litigation? A lawsuit? Even to this day, I don't know one person or family who has sued a corporation, city or individual for skateboarding injuries as a result of their own actions.

When property owners, corporate employees and security guards call the police to report skateboarding on their premises, the police respond quickly and with much presence. Does this make them servants to personal property? Isn't the average skater the public? Is the public, then, being protected?

If a skateboarder called the police to report a threat made against them by a security guard or by a corporate employee, how long would it take for the police to respond, and if they did respond, who would they be there to serve? Who would they protect?

With a fat stack of banana pancakes all cozy in my stomach, I had my hopes on a tall glass of iced coffee and a few rounds on the laptop. As I walked down the hill towards the cafι to finish this piece, my eyes wandered from curb to ledge. From trash can to sign post. From bike rack to staircase. As they've been the downfall of me, my eyes roam and I can't help but to notice the smallest of details. After all these years of city sidewalk navigation, skating or not, my visual surroundings are my favorite entertainment. It's better than television.

A sticker slapped up on the back side of a crosswalk sign caught my eye. I love street art; I always have. The visuals were strong, even at twenty feet away. It was the silhouette of a cop surrounded by text. At arm's reach the text became clear. With a minutes worth of labor, I peeled it off of the sign. It was unexpected but all the same, an incredible visual exclamation point to my little literal ditty:

"I was almost to Metro Center when this big, crazy linebacker guy clotheslines me after I ollied up on the curb. I was like, 'these crackers are going to hang me!' The linebacker guy turned out to be Secret Service; earpiece, the whole nine yards..."

## *BANNED IN D.C.*

by Brian Tucci

I've been skating since 1986, and during that time, I've watched myself be transformed from a normal kid with respect for authority and property to a social outcast and renegade with no concern for either law or government.

I look at everything different now-for instance, when I see a new building go up, I think, "is there something new to skate? What's security like? When are the guards off?" Not a second thought about its residents...like I'm casing the joint for a robbery.

I guess it's a crime to some people, and I will admit I've fucked some things up - like skating on office windows while people sat inside at their desks, looking on in shock. Or had the same guard chase me from the same spot four times in one day, saying the same thing each time: 'next time I'm going to call the cops.' I've seen people chased and tackled into cars, or hit with nightsticks. Sometimes the cops try to talk shit, like, 'you're older than me, why are you still doing that?' I usually just don't say anything, but think to myself, 'you're just a park police bike cop...you're not going into the hood to clean any of that up. For the most part, your job is to kick out the bums and skaters from downtown to make it cooler for tourists.' Funny thing is, usually the tourists are stoked to see us and stop to watch. Their kids are like, 'we wish we had a place like Freedom to skate...'

As skaters we learn to adapt to our environment and make the best of what's around us. I remember before any of us had cell phones, you could call someone on the payphone across the street from a hot local spot; sometimes a bum would answer and yell, 'yo pooch the phone's for you!'

Sometimes when the cops came, if it was just one or two of us, we would hide our boards in the secret stash spot. When the cops got out of the car, but didn't see any boards, just some sweaty kids in skate shoes, they would search the spot and find nothing...lecture us and move on.

I've learned the importance of politics when it comes to skating, like days when the President is around or in transit, days when the cops come or when news crews are filming. If there's a large street festival with road blocks, the chances of the cops coming for skating are slim.

My favorite spot at the time was the MLK library, but Freedom...that's the fort. One Friday after a shift at the local skate shop, I went down to Freedom. It must have been Memorial Day weekend. I remember there were a lot of people around town - tourists, a typical Washington weekend.

I was just going down there to see a few friends and move on. I guess I should mention the grudge I had going with the local park police officer. He had stopped me a few times, gave me a ticket, took my board, told me I was a smart-ass and lectured me about my nose ring and dreadlocks.

One time I was chilling at the dugout, he tried to sneak up on me and snatch my board, but I saw him creeping so I grabbed the video camera with everybody's footage on it and broke real quick. As he starts to chase me, he drops his gun and I get away. No joke, I never pushed so hard in my life. I got lucky that time but I knew the cop was pissed. After that escape, I knew next time would be life or death.

So back to Memorial Day. It was a crowded session, I can remember twenty or thirty of us just hanging out and skating. I had not been there long enough to warm up; in fact I'd just gotten there. I remember standing next to the three steps next to the big white wall in the center of the plaza and hearing someone say the magic code word for evacuation.

I was in a real bad spot; I guess the wrong place at the wrong time doesn't even apply here. The cop chose me to make an example of that day because I shook him the last time, but I was not going to let him take me without some resistance.

I took off across the plaza towards 14th Street...there were a lot of skaters there; everyone scattered, but he could have grabbed any one of them. As soon as I got to the corner of 14th, he turned on the siren. So I'm like, 'I can't go jail for no dumb shit.' So I jet down 14th Street against traffic, and the cop is cold flipping. I had him doing donuts in the street like Starsky and Hutch. Later my friend jimmy said I looked like the video game 720 when the bees were chasing. I zigzagged through traffic, down Pennsylvania Avenue, past the district building, past the Reagan building, left up 13th and then right down E. I was not gonna let Officer Lame get me.

I was almost to Metro Center when this big, crazy linebacker guy clotheslines me after I ollied up on the curb. I was like, 'these crackers are going to hang me!' The linebacker guy turned out to be Secret Service, with an earpiece and the whole nine yards. All of a sudden, the park police cop shows up, gets out of his car and is flipping mad. He puts me in cuffs, the paddy wagon comes and I get taken to the park police substation at Haines Point.

Friday night, Saturday and Sunday I was locked up there. It was a holiday weekend (no court on Monday) so I was looking at some time. When I got there, I went through processing and found out that I was being charged with assault on a police officer and a rack of other shit. I was transferred to the central cell block after two days; this is the main jail for all DC crimes and it was sketchy...I was shitting my pants. Two days in and I'm with the real criminals! I guess I blended in because nobody even really talked to me.

After that I was taken to another cell to meet the public defenders. The lawyer told me that the charge was serious but if I plead guilty there was a chance the judge would throw it out. Court was the next day.

I was moved to another cell, your typical lockdown. There I waited until court the next day. I was thinking I was going to go to jail on federal assault charges, just for wanting to skate without getting busted. How was my job going to feel about me missing work? I thought I was going to get fired as well. I could not sleep the night before court; I actually don't remember sleeping at all in central cell. I didn't think I was going to skate for a really long time. By the time the marshal came I was so paranoid I had convinced myself it was all a trick and I was going to get the gas chamber or the electric chair.

When I was called before the judge, I was feeling like a piece of death; the same crusty-ass clothes for four days, no food...I was a mental wreck. I didn't want any part of this, but I was in front of some strict judge who didn't understand why I was in court on assault charges, when really I'm just some skateboarder who ran from a cop. I plead guilty to some bullshit charge; it was suspended but I was told that if I was caught at Freedom again, it would be six months in jail and a thousand-dollar fine. When I got out, I heard that the cop had gone to Freedom and said to the skaters, 'we got your ringleader, Brian Tucci, locked up and you're going to be next.' Needless to say, I was cool off Freedom for a minute...but it's so perfect, I knew I'd be back. For now it was time to lay low.

I moved to Frisco in hopes that there would be less harassment, so I could just work, skate and live. There wasn't much difference; cops are the same all over. I thought out west it would be more accepted. I guess old habits die hard, because I managed to amass a grip of unpaid tickets, some just for skating down the street.

Time went by and wouldn't you know it - busted again, this time at Pier 7. Of course it was a Friday. This time I had to be at work in two hours. The cop didn't even see me skating that day; I walked away easily because I was skating the end block. I saw her coming and stashed my board across the street in a bush, then went back for my phone that I left on the bench. I should have just taken the loss. The cop asked me where my board was; I told her I didn't have one. She was like, 'you're full of shit - I'm not going to give you your phone unless you give up the board.' I was like, 'hell no!' So she ran my name and took me in on a warrant for unpaid skateboard tickets - off to 850 Bryant - again. I got out later that night, but I was so pissed. I don't ever want to see another cell for skating again.

After these experiences I have come to realize there are two different worlds when it comes to skating: how we see it and how people on the outside see it.

Being a skater not only made me think for myself, but also shaped how I think. I have had to, and still have to, adapt to blend into society, but still maintain my personality and identity as a person who skates. The act of skating factors into most of my decisions; it's like race - it's always there. There is never a time when just rolling down the street isn't fun for me.

Yet I see this freedom has a price. Skating has shaped my feelings toward society, as I am being frowned upon or judged for who I am or what I do. I have had to recognize my enemies and avoid them. Skating has made me more aware of the hypocrisy in law and the people in power.

There is also another side, the side that can't be held back. Like when I got locked up, I knew there were gonna be more people like me going to the same spot when the cops were gone. They really can't stop us all at once. That's one thing I love about it: we find more spots when they cap them, change our schedules to remain low-key, some of us even work within the system to implement change. We might have to mask our intentions or tone down our actions, but it won't stop because it's who we are.

I want to be able to just cruise if I feel like it. Parks are fun, but for me, streets are the biggest thrill: bombing a hill in traffic, timing the lights, weaving through cars, blasting over manhole covers, potholes, dead rats and pigeons...whole streets. I look at objects that have definite, designated purposes - a bench, picnic table, handrail, tree box, wheelchair ramp, etc. - completely different from a normal person. When I see a new development go up, I'm instantly thinking I could do a trick on that dumpster on the side of that loading dock. To me it's more than just a trash can; it's opportunity.

There are many types of cops in DC, far too many to list, but we know the ones who bust us. We remember how we are treated, who the rookies are, who the dicks are, who says, 'I used to be just like you...' or 'come back after six when I'm off, my superiors are on my ass...' Sometimes I say what's on my mind, but that's if I know I'm gonna get heard (which usually winds up in a ticket). Usually it's just a lecture and they let us go. My rule is, when you have to talk, show respect for authority even if you don't really give a shit. I used to think, 'they can keep taking my boards...I have ten more at home and ten more in the mail,' but my criminal record was building, so there was a time when I couldn't just talk my way out. Three strikes, you know what I'm saying?

We build and we destroy. Cops are helping us by keeping us on our toes. The least we can do is to not distract them from the real crimes committed by the people who run the authorities.

"One time I was chilling at the dugout, he tried to sneak up on me and snatch my board, but I saw him creeping so I grabbed the video camera with everybody's footage on it and broke real quick. As he starts to chase me, he drops his gun and I get away. No joke, I never pushed so hard in my life..."

"I began to notice how people were being treated unfairly on a daily basis, whether by a cop harassing kids hanging out at the park or a Circle K employee asking us to leave the front of the store, even after we bought merchandise..."

## *CRIMINAL MINDED*

by Joshua J. Feldman

I was first introduced to what society would call a criminal activity in the year 1989.

My neighbor was a sponsored skateboarder who was always out in front of his house practicing freestyle and street tricks. Dave Tucker was an intelligent young man who was not only a respected skater, but a very responsible role model for many youngsters.

One day out of nowhere Dave handed me a board and told me to just roll around. I had ridden a skateboard only a hand full of times, and never in the presence of a real skater. He showed me a couple of simple tricks and I started to catch on. Dave and his girlfriend sat and watched me learn these tricks and told me I was a natural. They were so excited that this ten-year-old neighborhood kid was catching on.

As I skated more and more, Dave began taking me out to different spots. He took me to several schools around town to street skate and eventually started bringing me to backyard mini-ramps. Dave built over fifteen backyard ramps for kids all over town, including a couple of vert ramps. He even built a small ramp in my garage! The whole skate community looked up to him for his genuine personality and his dedication to skateboarding.

Said to be his prodigy, he made it a point to introduce me to everyone wherever we went. I met a lot of good people during this time. Dave made me feel special about being a young skateboarder, and that drove me to dedicate all of my time to doing it.

At the beginning of seventh grade I moved to a different area of Ventura. I didn't see much of Dave anymore, but I met so many friends through skating that I was never alone when I wanted to skate. I was starting to get really involved in the street skating scene around town. Skating was becoming very popular and it was common to see groups of kids skating from spot to spot. I skated a lot with Sonee Frazier and Adam Fuscaldo. They were both troublemakers, but we always rode together. Chris Larsen, Tim Preble, Greg Pike and Brian

Stemson were a crew from across the way that I knew as well. There were times when I'd see another crew of skaters around. We referred to these guys as the Five Points brigade. Harry, Joe, Chad Schroeder, Eric LeMonde, Chris Long, Caleb Seavey, Erik Scott, Gary Cease, Josh Bruce, Eric Potts, Steve Kang, Burrito, Pee Wee and Peter Polis were among a few. Peter was like a pro. He was doing tricks back then that nobody could touch. These guys were raw skaters who meant business and ruled every spot they skated. I was intimidated by this group. They were polite guys, but they let their skating do all the talking, and there was a lot to be said.

Time goes by and you become friends with people after seeing them so often. I would go skate with some of the Five Points guys, and it would give me butterflies in the stomach every time. They had so much skate energy that it overwhelmed me. There was such a positive vibe with these guys that it was damn near impossible not to learn a new trick every time we skated.

However, times were changing around Ventura. We would go skate at the credit union, or the mall, or at any number of schools and were being screamed at by people. One day at the credit union there were about fifteen of us skating a curb in the parking lot. We were not in anybody's way. An extremely angry banker came out and was immediately yelling at all of us. A few of the guys ran off, but the rest of us stayed. This guy sat us down, like he was a cop, and told us that we were outcasts and to never come back again. The anger in this man's face was unforgettable.

Being run off by people for skating was becoming a usual occurrence. At first people weren't sure how to deal with us. It was rare, however, that we were politely asked to leave. We would question people as to why they couldn't just simply speak to us in a respectable manner. Most of our questions were met with further disrespect. Slowly but surely the police were involved. Some people would just call the cops and not even bother talking to us. This made us so angry; like we were less than human and weren't worth the time of day because we rode skateboards. Cops would roll up on our spots and treat us like criminals. Here we are on the weekend, at a school or bank, and someone calls the police. We are practicing tricks that take more skill than any sport I've ever seen, yet we have to be aware at all times of who's watching us. If we'd see a cop, we were out of there in a flash. If we were taken by surprise, we were either ticketed or given the FBI interrogation. This is how I learned to hate authority.

My view of authority was forever changed one weekend at a local underground bank parking lot. It was a great skate spot that we had been going to for a long time. There was security off and on, and occasionally cops, but there were several exits to vanish through. There was a large group of skaters down there this particular weekend. We were filming some tricks when suddenly a security guard rolls up. Nobody really ran because there were so many of us.

This security guard got out of his car and walked right past all of us to where my friend was standing. They had met each other the previous weekend, and there was instantly an argument. There were threats of jail coming from the security guard, and a nothing but a question of respect and morals coming from Chris. The security guard became angry and was starting to threaten him with violence like the previous weekend. Chris made a comment about not wanting to fight anyone with a gun, and it was then that the guard took his gun out of the holster and placed it in his car. There were now real threats of violence coming from the guard, whose job was to uphold the law, not break it. A few more words were exchanged, and then we all left. We couldn't believe what happened! The security guard was in such a fit of anger that he failed to notice the video camera that was capturing the whole ordeal, and we never saw him again.

That event not only opened my eyes to corruption in security and law enforcement, but to authority in every sense of the word. I began to notice how people were being treated unfairly on a daily basis, whether by a cop harassing kids hanging out at the park or a Circle K employee asking us to leave the front of the store even after we bought merchandise. It seemed like people with any sense of authority were going overboard and forgetting about real morals.

When people came down on us for skating, we weren't surprised anymore. We all eventually became used to it. What we never got used to was people treating us like hoodlums when we weren't skating. Skating opened my eyes to the way people treat each other. We'd go walking through the mall and have security guards following us the whole time. We would be places without our boards and be treated differently because of our clothes, or because of the way we talked.

There were other people like us that also saw through authority and had the same opinions on people that we did. I'm referring to street performers. You can go to Venice Beach and see people off the streets doing amazing feats. They, too, are liked by some, hated by others and harassed by the authorities, but they always put on a good show, and when you give them some change for their entertainment, they are always eternally grateful. Spending time on the streets can be humbling and really sharpen your senses to the way people treat each other. I realize now that as skateboarders, we are people from the streets.

Skating exposed me to the craziest people, the nicest people, and everyone in between. These incidents, as well as countless others, have forever changed the way I look at our society. When I see a police officer I feel intimidated and threatened. Authority fails to have me feeling protected. When a janitor at the high school becomes a potential threat to your personal freedom, you know that something is not right.

It feels like people want to harass us or sometimes erase us from existence. Skateboarding irritates some people, so we are often treated like criminals. Some people consider us to be the same as vandals or thieves. We are far from that. We have been trained by society to analyze the way people act and react. We are aware of what's going on around us. We see the corruption in our world and feel compassion for those who struggle. We know the true moral differences between right and wrong. We are a very realistic, humble and giving breed. Sadly, most of society considers us to be nothing more than criminals on wheels.

"You can go to Venice Beach and see people off the streets doing amazing feats. They, too, are liked by some, hated by others and harassed by the authorities, but they always put on a good show, and when you give them some change for their entertainment, they are always eternally grateful."

MEX

## *SO COMPLETELY WRONG*

by Jessie VanRoechoudt

It's amazing how your life can go from being 'better than you ever could have imagined' to 'so completely wrong' in a matter of minutes.

I was on a Vans tour in Mexico City, we'd done a few demos in the previous days and were on our last day of tour - I'd just gotten a couple of street photos and was stoked to be finishing the tour on a good note. We were driving back to the hotel when someone spotted what seemed like a photo-worthy skate spot on the side of the road.

The distributor, being the accommodating fellow that he was, pulled over, parking in a grassy area next to the off-ramp. A few of the others trekked back to try to get a photo on the potentially skateable guardrail. I'd just gotten a few photos and was exhausted from skating all afternoon in the Mexico City heat, so I decided to stay in the van and wait with the others.

Sometimes getting a skate photo can take longer than one would think, especially when factors such as traffic are taken into consideration. After we'd been waiting a while, someone asked if the distributor had any water. He pointed to a cooler in the back of the van, unfortunately no water, but it was stocked with beer on ice. No complaints. I asked if it was cool if we sat in the van and had our beers, or if we need to have them in brown paper bags. To which they made some kind of joke about Mexico not being America, "you're free to drink here." Okay, I felt kind of ridiculous asking - I knew that would be their answer. Looking back on it - it almost seems as though it was just a detail for setting the scene, a little jab to build the plot and reinforce the irony of what was about to take place.

So we each get a beer in hand to accompany our conversation as we wait for the others to get the photo and return to the van. Obviously - the next thing that happens is that cops pull up. They pulled over just ahead of the van, first trying to give a ticket for parking in an illegal spot, and from there it just became one of those bad-to-worse scenarios.

At one of the demos in the previous days, the rearview mirrors had been stolen off the van. In a resourceful attempt to remedy the situation, the distributor had stopped by a pharmacy and bought little replacements and surgical tape to affix them to the now-empty metal arms that protruded from the base of the front windscreen. It was a totally functional solution - though the cops didn't see it as such, at least not as long as there was money to be made on their part. The distributor's initial monetary offering for the "parked in an illegal spot" accusation was no longer sufficient now that the new accusation of "no rearview mirrors" could be waged.

The haggling over an adequate pay off continued. To show their disapproval of the distributor's current offer the cops began a more thorough investigation of the van. Upon realizing that there were foreigners inside, the bidding price was immediately elevated. After another few minutes of haggling, and taking the distributor's ID, the cops pointed at me. Though I know a little Spanish, and was aware that everything seemed to be going in a 'worse than you could have imagined' direction, the kid next to me translated more thoroughly. "They said that they need to take you to jail because you are drinking," to which I replied, "but everyone is drinking, why me?" I was temporarily oblivious to the gender politics of the situation - the choice to take me to jail was not completely at random, as I was the only female in the van. Perhaps through some messed up gender politics I was perceived as making for better bribe collateral.

On the brief drive to the police station I was having trouble coming to terms with the situation. How did I just go from being in a totally perfect moment, basking in the glory of a successful, fun tour to on my way to a Mexican prison? Worse things have happened, and I'm not the first to be unfairly persecuted. Nevertheless it was still hard to accept the fact that in a few minutes I was about experience the unpleasant reality of a Mexican prison. I was baffled at how my life had just gone completely to shit in the matter of only a few minutes, and trying very hard to keep my imagination from spiraling uncontrollably with thoughts of the potential horrors that were quite possibly about to ensue.

We pulled up in front of the police station and the cops opened the van door. My legs were shaking and I felt a bit as though my body was working against my brain as I stood up and stepped out of the van. There seemed little other choice than stepping out of the van, as they didn't seem to be asking politely anymore - there was now a guard motioning for me to do so with a machine gun. After I got out of the van the guard pressed the barrel of the machine gun against my temple. We stood there like that for what seemed like quite a while to me, though time has the sensation of taking on a slow-mo effect in these types of situations. I stood there listening, though not understanding, as the negotiations continued between the distributor and cops. I was still in a state of shock at how my life had gone so completely to shit in such a short time span.

The cops were still not pleased with the bribe offered and at this point became more overt about showing their disapproval. Two guards ran out through three lanes of stopped traffic to a park and grabbed some poor guy who was sitting there on the grass reading and dragged him by the arms back through the stopped traffic to the sidewalk in front of the police station. The guards pushed the guy up against the wall and started to beat the shit out of him. This guy definitely must have been taken aback by the whole situation, perhaps thinking the same as me: "What the fuck? I was just sitting there not doing anything wrong; how did my life just go so completely wrong?"

The two guards continued to beat the guy until he fell to the ground at which point they kicked him until he stopped moving, then one of the guards followed up by pummeling his face with the butt of his machine gun. It was quite an attention-commanding performance. I was certainly enthralled by the whole display, as I stood there with the machine gun still pressed against the side of my head. The display of brutality had the desired effect and the distributor thankfully sorted the situation out quickly. I never asked how much he paid them, but whatever it was I was thankful. They let me go, I got back in the van and we left. I don't know what happened to the random guy that they beat up, or perhaps he wasn't random, perhaps it really was a performance - maybe he was in on the deal, under cover and just waiting there on the grass outside the police station for such a scandal - but I don't think so, they hit him pretty hard in the face with the machine gun - you could hear the noise of the impact.

Though my little anecdote includes skating and authority figures it might not seem to fit exactly within the confines of going to jail specifically for skating, but the Mexico City cops' reasoning in my scenario is similar to how allegations are made against the act of skating. The allegations are deemed to be legitimate, despite lacking substance at their core. My getting taken to jail for being a woman (as it appeared was the logic in this allegation by the Mexico City cops) was in a sense the same as getting ticketed or arrested for skating. My presence in the van in this instance - like skaters' presence at spots - is not understood. It doesn't fit in with people's understanding of how things ought to be. Your presence not being understood fuses with stereotypes and perceptions of what is considered socially acceptable.

Then somewhere in this unarticulated zone of undefined right and wrong in people's (in this case the cops') bizarre world view come bullshit claims masquerading as legitimate allegations - based on social stereotypes and a lack of understanding.

After I got home I was talking with a knowledgeable lady at the café by my place. I told her my story and she explained that often in Mexico referring to a woman as 'a woman who drinks' is akin to saying 'prostitute' - as far as I understood from the café lady it was not a universal metaphor, but a cultural notion that existed to some degree, which sort of explains the cops' allegation that I needed to go to jail because I was drinking even though the others also had beers in hand. Still a messed up concept of justice, but it makes a bit more sense as far as the cops attempting to stretch this claim to a somehow socially acceptable allegation.

Everyone sees the world through their own personal filter, and if they don't skate they don't see why you might be standing around for an inordinate amount of time, visually measuring up some architectural oddity. Your presence isn't understood and it doesn't fit well with the established categories in people's brains. That lack of understanding combined with an increasing amount of fear in public spaces, and a social stereotype of skaters that my friend and I jokingly refer to as the 'hooded sweatshirt ticket' freak people out.

It is more so the skaters than the act of skating that is threatening to people. Skating is not allowed in certain places because of what it is associated with and represents, not because of what it is. If you want to see how transparent the substance of anti-skate rhetoric can get, just go look at the plaques on the banks at the Federal Building in San Francisco; there is one that reads, "these anti-rolling devices have been placed here for your safety" - which is obviously the captain of bullshit claims.

## *TIME SERVED FOR $25*

by Frank Atwater

One time we had a pool going in Camarillo up in the estates at a big house that was being restored. We'd sneak in on the weekday afternoons, you know, after the workers had all taken off...we knew the trespassing rules; we knew the deal - show up late, in and out.

This one was a really sick peanut pool we had been skating off and on for three or four months; Senn even skated it once when he was am I think. The pool was getting remodeled, too, so there was no coping and the hips were unskateable because of these rocks.

One day we ran into this kid who said his mom owned the pool, and that it was all cool if we were skating. That was killer; now all of a sudden we're talking permission pool!

This one particular day Jesse Pilgram got us a ride out there on a Saturday. We show up with the chicks that gave us a ride, cruise in the backyard, business as usual except there was some lady in the kitchen, which kinda alarmed me until she said, "Oh, my son skates, you can skate the pool...no problem." We only skated like twenty minutes because Jesse wanted to leave; the girls were getting bored.

A week later me, Jesse, this guy Brian and another kid named Jason went back and no one was home or skating so it was on. Everything seemed cool, we were skating, having a good time and all that but it was back in the small wheel era, and Brian had these really super-gnarly flat spots; just sounding like a machine gun. I guess the neighbors heard us skating and called the police, and they must've called the owner of the property because soon enough the lady from the kitchen the week before was right there with two County Sheriffs.

So I'm thinking it's all good; she was just showing up to let the police know that she had given us permission to skate the pool the week before. It was quite a surprise when she told the officers she wanted to press charges.

"Wait a minute...what are you talking about?

"We were just here last Saturday and you gave us permission to skate; you said your son skates, remember?

Despite the fact that she had looked me square in the eye while saying it, she denied every bit of it.

"You're lying...I don't know what you're talking about."

We spent the next two and a half hours handcuffed in the back of the patrol cars, which was pretty harsh because the cops were far from friendly. I thought they were going to take us into booking and the whole nine yards; but we ended up just getting notices to appear for our newly acquired trespassing citations.

So we all show up at the arraignment, and the public defender was this surfer friend of mine named Jim and he found some fine print in the trespassing statute which said something to the effect of "first offense, no priors...maximum fine $25."

The judge gave us thirty days to pay, but at the time I was pretty much couch-surfing and homeless; so instead of paying into the system I clogged it by putting myself on the calendar to see the judge about doing work release or time in lieu of the fine.

I hate public speaking; I get sweaty palms in the courtroom and all that. A month later when I got up to the podium, the whole room just got silent.

"Um...I'd like to serve time in lieu of the fine, your honor?"

He looked at me like I was from another planet.

"You mean to tell me that you can't afford a $25 dollar fine?"

"No sir, I'd like to do time."

The whole entire courtroom broke out in laughter. Ten days later I went in at 8:00 o'clock p.m. I was out by midnight, with two hours left for Coors.

All in all the experience taught me that those in authority are by no means perfectly honest. When I went back to court later people even recognized me as 'the guy who served time for $25'.

"So instead of paying into the system I clogged it by putting myself on the calendar to see the judge about doing work release or time in lieu of the fine..."

"We were still up top skating the banks and had no idea the cops were down there. To get from the lower level where Maldonado was to the top, you can take an elevator that opens up in front of the banks..."

## *FIFTH GRADE INTERROGATION TO THE CHINA BANKS*

by Satva Leung

Fifth grade in Mendocino, 1985 was the first time I encountered the phenomenon of police harassment.

As I walked into the playground that morning the first thing I noticed was the strong smell of smoke. The school's gym burnt down the night before. The middle school was right next to the grammar school (school was just about to let out for the summer). My first thought was, "cool, maybe we won't have to go to school next year because the school burnt down."

The day goes by and I am about to leave for home when one of the teachers pulls me aside and tells me that some people want to talk to me. They escorted me into a room, and then asked me about what I had done the day before. The day before basically went like this: school, got home, rode my bike, took out the trash, homework, TV, bed. They recorded the conversation on a big, 80's style tape recorder. Ghetto-ass Mendo cops.

So a month goes by and everything is cool until one morning the teacher says, "those guys want to ask you some more questions." Great....I walk into the room - you gotta remember I am in 5th grade - and I see two fat-ass cops, dark lighting...straight out of the movies. I'm thinking I am definitely in trouble, but for what? I didn't do anything. They ask, "So what did you do the day the gym burnt down?" I told them my routine for the day just like before but I switched around taking out the trash and riding my bike.

They flipped out.

"We got you! You think you can lie to us?!" One of the cops then laid his .357 magnum on the table right in front of me and said he had a statement from someone saying they saw some skateboarders skating down the hill by the school that night. Just because I skated they thought it was me that the witness saw.

"You ready to go away for a while?"

I am flipping out, thinking they are just going to pin this on me. A couple more hours of this went on and they finally let me go. They never did catch the people that burnt the gym down, but they tried to pin it on me because I skated and lived close to the school.

Fast forward a decade or so and I'm at the China Banks - gotta love the China Banks in San Francisco. That place is raw; especially when you get tackled by a cop.

So here is the situation - we were filming for the Toy Machine video *Welcome to Hell.* We had the van parked on the street in front of that super high marble ledge where Mike Maldonado was trying to 50-50 the beast. The rest of us went up to skate the banks. We skated for a good forty-five minutes before the cops showed up and tried to bust Mike skating the ledge. We were still up top skating the banks and had no idea the cops were down there. To get from the lower level where Maldonado was to the top, you can take an elevator that opens up in front of the banks.

Basically I am super close to getting my trick, so I am pushing full force towards the bench blazing right by the elevator. There is a cop in the elevator and as it opens all he sees is me pushing as fast as can right by him. He thinks I'm running from him, so he begins to chase me. I don't see any of this because I had already skated past the elevator, so all I'm thinking is frontside wallride to fakie over the bench. Jamie Thomas, who was filming at the time, gets up from his filming squat because he sees the cop running towards me. The cop catches me and wraps my sweatshirt around my head.

I'm thinking, "Am I getting jacked right now by some thugs?" I seriously did not know what was going on so my natural reaction was to fight back. We scuffled around for a second and then the cop handcuffs me, and writes me a ticket.

The whole time he was convinced that I was running from him. I kept telling him, "Why would I go and try to hit the bank one last time before running?" and his response was "You're such a bad liar! You should go to lying school!" Okay.

A lot of cops are on some power trip when they arrest kids skateboarding. They say we don't have anything better to do than destroy public property and my response to that is, "Don't you have something better to do than tackle kids and fine them for having fun?" You can see a clip in the *Welcome to Hell* video, but unfortunately you can't see the whole thing. The cop running behind me without me even knowing it looks crazy! I need a copy of that. I doubt I'll get it though. Jamie probably has the tape locked in his safe.

## *THE INTERSECTION OF TWO SUBCULTURES*

by Garet O'Keefe

I don't really have anything good to submit on the topic of skateboarding and authority because I'm a good white boy who never got in much trouble with John Q. Law.

My run-ins have been because of too much booze, not because I occasionally skate the streets at night.

I suppose, if anything, I've observed that the conflict is frequently on the intersections. That is the intersections of cultures, races or stereotypes, to name a few.

If a non-skating police officer sees a skater creating on the pavement burning off frustration, anger or other less-than-productive human emotions and experiences that each must face in order to develop more fully as a person, the officer might simply see a threat to society, a stoner or whatever.

The officer may not appreciate what is going on and thus he or she may not see the real person on the board. On the other hand, the skater when confronted by the officer may challenge the officer's authority, in a similar failure to recognize that the officer may be ignorant or even jealous of the skater.

At that intersection of two subcultures (the skater subculture and officer subculture), conflicts inevitably arise because of myopia in both directions. But, we have choices and I think even if someone is irresponsibly wielding authority, the question of who really has the authority in the interaction remains to be seen. I suggest kindness and love have more to do with it than people think.

"At that intersection of two subcultures, conflicts inevitably arise because of myopia in both directions."

"This really pissed the lady off because then, without saying a word, she knelt down and released the dog from out of her arms. The dog ran over to the bottom of my feet, barked a few times at me, and then sunk its teeth into the calf of my right leg."

# NO EASY WAY OUT

by Travis Jensen

In June of '93, my mom bought me a one-way ticket from Milwaukee to Boise, kissed me on the cheek, and sent me off to live with my dad and step-mom for a year.

I had just finished 8th grade. My mom needed a break. I was more than a handful. My grades were lousy and I was constantly in and out of trouble. The only thing I cared about was skateboarding. Nothing else mattered.

The skate scene in Boise at the time was small, yet thriving. There were approximately thirty hardcore skaters in town. There were no public skate parks or backyard ramps in Boise back then, so we were restricted to skating street.

That year of living with my dad and step-mom couldn't have gone by any slower. It was like serving time. The rules at their house were much stricter than those at my mom's. It was nearly impossible to sneak anything past the two of them. Their iron-fisted approach to parenting only provoked me to rebel even more. I figured I had nothing to lose. Being grounded was no big deal to me. I was used to it and had mentally conditioned myself to do the time.

When I wasn't grounded, I spent most of my time skating at the Park Center Mall, which was about a mile down the road from my dad and step-mom's place. It wasn't much of a skate spot, but I made due. There was smooth flat ground, a few manual pads, two decent curb cuts and a handful of slick red curbs.

On Memorial Day of '94, I met up with my friend Rubin Grimes in the K-Mart parking lot of the Park Center Mall to skate. Rubin lived on the other side of town. The two of us went to different schools. I remember being in a particularly good mood that day, because I was consistently landing all of my tricks. On top of that, I was scheduled to move back to Milwaukee in two weeks, to the day.

As luck would have it, less than an hour into our session, Rubin and I were rudely interrupted by some screwball, heavyset lady exiting K-Mart. She was carrying a scrappy Yorkshire terrier in her arms that was barking uncontrollably.

"You're not supposed to be playing around on your skateboards here!" She yelled at us from afar.

Rubin and I ignored the lady and went about our business.

"Did you boys not hear me?!" The lady yelled again, huffing and puffing towards us. "You're not supposed to be riding your skateboards here!"

"Excuse me," Rubin replied, "but do you work here?"

"No, but..."

"Well then," he said, stopping her in mid-sentence. "Who are you to say we're not supposed to be skating here?"

This really pissed the lady off because then, without saying a word, she knelt down and released the dog from out of her arms. The dog ran over to the bottom of my feet, barked a few times at me, and then sunk its teeth into the calf of my right leg. Before realizing what happened, the little shit had already scurried back into the safety of the lady's arms.

"What the hell's your problem, lady?!" I yelled.

"That's what you get for skateboarding where you're not supposed to!" She scowled, then turned around and charged back towards K-Mart.

Rubin and I decided it was best to just leave. We didn't want any problems. The two of us skated off to the other end of the mall to skate the manual pad next to the Hallmark Store.

A half-hour or so went by and Rubin and I had pretty much forgotten about the whole incident with the screwball lady and dog.

I remember I was in the middle of doing a nose-wheelie on the manual pad when out of the corner of my eye I saw a cop car pull up and park next to us.

The officer got out of his car and instructed Rubin and I to take a seat on the curb. We did as he said. The officer was a spitting image of Ivan Drago, the Russian boxer from *Rocky IV.* I wouldn't have been surprised if they were related. He was blonde, sporting a mean flat-top, and ridiculously buffed. The only thing he was missing was the thick Russian accent.

"Let me see some identification, boys..." he said to us.

Neither of us had any ID. We were both too young to have a driver's license.

Drago informed us that since we were fifteen he could still issue us citations.

I asked Drago what we did wrong. He said he was responding to a complaint he received about us harassing a lady in the K-Mart parking lot. Apparently the crazy lady had lied to the dispatcher. She said we were calling her foul names and that one of us even kicked her dog. I tried to explain our side of the story; Drago wouldn't listen.

"Save it," he said, pulling out his ticket book and pen. "I don't wanna freakin' hear it. Bottom line is skateboarding is illegal on private property and therefore I'm issuing you both citations."

I was very nervous. I knew my dad would flip on me if I brought home a ticket. Not only that, but I was pissed that Drago wouldn't hear me out. He was being an ass about the whole thing. Since he didn't respect me, I wasn't going to respect him.

"What's your name?" He asked me.

"Timothy Crockett," I lied.

Tim Crockett was the quarterback of my school's football team. The two of us didn't get along. I then proceeded to give Drago a fake address. Once he finished filling out my ticket, he then asked Rubin for his info. Following my lead, Rubin told Drago his name was Steve Rocco and made up some bogus address.

Just as Officer Drago was handing us the tickets, I shit you not, my English teacher, Ms. Day, walked out of the Hallmark store and saw what was going on.

Ms. Day was in her late 20s, foxy as hell, and fully supportive of skateboarding. She used to let me base all of my papers around skating. I did well in her class.

"What's going on, Vince?" She asked in a worried voice. "Is everything okay?"

Fuck, I thought, I'm really screwed now.

"Wait a freakin' minute," Drago said.

"Did you just call him V-I-N-C-E?"

Before Ms. Day could respond, Drago grabbed me by my arm, raised me to my feet, and slapped handcuffs on me.

"You're under arrest for delaying and obstructing a police officer, buddy."

Hearing those words made me feel like I was going to be sick to my stomach. I couldn't believe I was actually being arrested. My dad was really going to kill me now.

"Wait a minute!" Ms. Day said. "Vince is good kid! There's no need to arrest him!"

"Bullshit!" Drago snapped. "He's a damn liar!"

Drago then demanded that Ms. Day give him Rubin's real name or that he would arrest her for delaying justice.

Ms. Day said she had never seen Rubin before in her life.

This was true; he went to another school, but Drago then turned to me for an answer, and I kept my mouth shut.

There was no way I was going to rat out my friend. Drago was forced to let Rubin go. Rubin and Ms. Day watched in shock as Drago guided me into the backseat of his patrol car, and then put my board in his trunk.

I was in a daze as we pulled out of the Park Center Shopping Mall, heading for the police station downtown. Along the way, I tried not to think about how much trouble I was going to be in with my dad and step-mom.

At the station, Drago led me through booking and into an interrogation room, which looked almost identical to those you see on TV. The room was dark, and with the exception of a medium sized metal table and two chairs, completely empty. It even had one of those two-way mirrors in it where the person on the other side could see you, but you couldn't see them.

"Sit down," Drago demanded.

I took a seat. Drago shut the door and left me alone in the room for a good forty-five minutes. When he returned, he took a seat in the chair across the table from me, pulled out his pen and pad, and said, "Now let's try this again. What's your full name and address, Vince?"

I told Drago everything he wanted to know. Surprisingly, he didn't even ask me about Rubin. I still wouldn't have snitched on him anyway. Drago then stood up from his chair and left the room again. I must have waited for well over two hours until he finally returned.

"Okay, let's go, Vincent." He said.

Drago escorted me back through booking and into the main lobby of the station. My dad was standing there waiting for me when we arrived. He had his arms crossed and the look on his face scared the fucking shit out of me. I knew I was really in for it.

After removing the cuffs, Drago handed my dad the skateboarding ticket, and released me into his custody.

I asked Drago, "What about my board?"

He laughed and said, "Your father's asked that we donate it to charity. They'll probably use it for firewood next winter."

Damn, that's harsh, I thought.

My dad smacked me a couple of times upside the head as we walked through the parking lot to the car.

"You're goddamn lucky all you got was this skateboarding ticket," he said, waving the pink slip of paper up in my face. "What the hell were you thinking lying to that cop like that? Are you fucking stupid, boy? If there's one thing I can't stand it's liars!"

Before even putting the key in the ignition, my dad belted me a few times in the stomach and chest. It hurt like hell, but I took it like a man.

My dad didn't speak to me the whole ride home. He smacked me around a few more times at the house, but for the most part left me alone in my room for the rest of the evening.

I apologized to Ms. Day at school the next day for putting her on the spot like that with Drago. She told me not to worry about it. She said she didn't think any less of me.

I spent my last two weeks in Boise confined to my room. I had no TV. No magazines. No music. No nothing. It was like being in the hole. The only time I left my room was to go to school. It was rough, but I stuck that shit out. Thankfully my move back to Milwaukee was already set in stone prior to my arrest. Otherwise, I probably would've been grounded that entire summer and off to military school in the fall - no joke. Who knows where I'd be now. I sure as hell lucked out that time around.

Although my arrest at the Park Center Mall was my first significant skateboard related run-in with the law; it certainly wasn't my last. Since then I've been arrested several other times for skateboarding and have received more tickets than I can count on both hands. I'm not complaining. It goes along with the territory, and will forever be a part of skateboarding culture.

"I've been arrested several times for skateboarding and have received more tickets than I can count on both hands. I'm not complaining. It goes along with the territory, and will forever be a part of skateboarding culture."

"Rebellion to tyrants is obedience to God."
—T. JEFFERSON

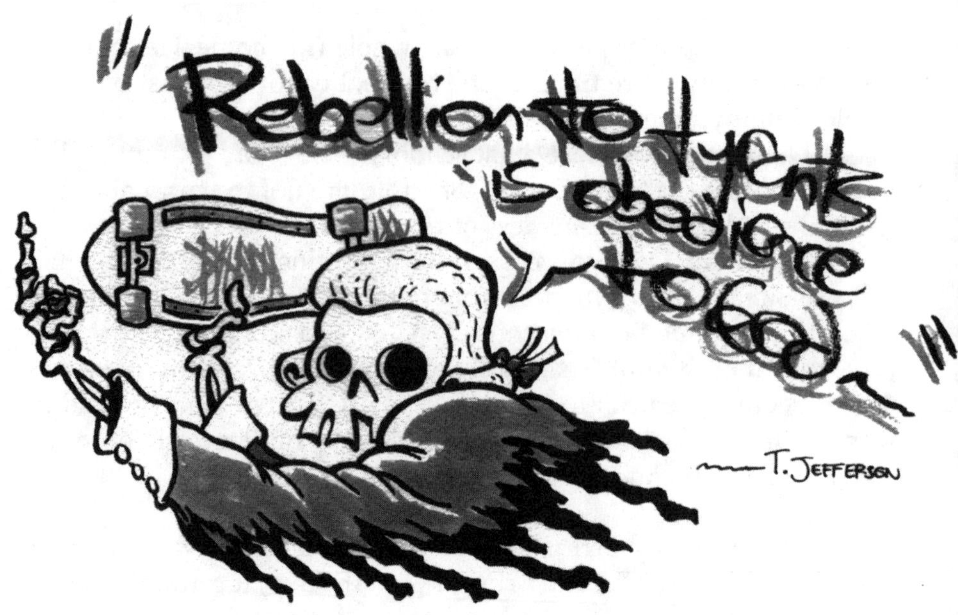

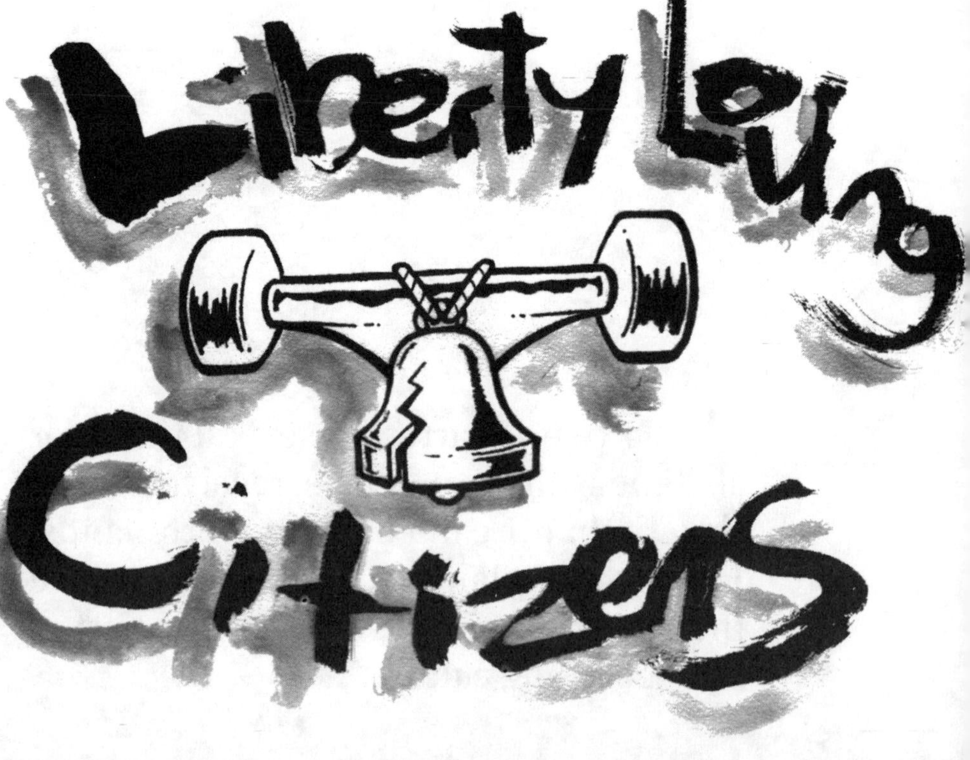

Liberty Loving
Citizens

# *FRAMER'S INTENT?*

by Mark Whiteley

I've often wondered how the founders of the U.S.A. would react to the state of their nation if they were able to see it in modern times.

Obviously their intention was to form a nation in which every resident could live life in as unfettered a way as possible, free from persecution and tyranny. Their ideas were sound, and though their wording was somewhat flawed regarding their long-term interpretation, the principles our country was founded upon were noble and philosophically just at the time of their inception.

I can only assume, then, that the founding fathers would be saddened to see that in 2005 the current interpretation of their basic societal framework included the green-lighting of acts such as the bum-rushing of a 13-year-old skating alone in a public park in the middle of the biggest city in the nation by unidentified plain-clothes park enforcement officers not even sanctioned by the city police department that resulted in an $1,100 ticket and the confiscation of the kid's private property. I imagine men like Thomas Jefferson, who said, "Rebellion to tyrants is obedience to God," would be dismayed.

Of course the problems between skateboarders and law enforcement officers in all their forms pale in comparison to many of the other issues that could be brought up when talking about the disgusting ways the leaders of our towns, counties, states, and country have bastardized the intentions of the men who drafted the Constitution, but those problems are symptoms of a larger sickness infecting our society. Throughout society there is general lack of respect by law enforcement officers for the personal freedoms of those living a divergent or non-typical way of life, and that lack of respect causes people who come in contact with those agents to lose respect for them, creating a vicious cycle in which both sides become more and more hostile and disrespectful towards each other. The main problem here in regards to the intentions of the founding fathers is that it homogenizes the population of the country into a typical existence as defined by a *de facto* ruling class, which then forces people who don't meet (or care to meet) the definition further and further towards the edges of society, turning them into "outcasts." The American ideal that the founding fathers established, of all men being created equal, goes out the window when the man varies from the contemporary model of normalcy.

Enter the skateboarder.

The average skateboarder varies from the contemporary model of normalcy because he or she thinks about and uses his or her physical environment in a different way than the average citizen. This is the basis of the difference between 'us and them' and what causes the ongoing problems between skateboarders and law enforcement, pushing us toward the edges of society and into a mentality of disliking and distrusting law enforcement agents.

To be honest, I can understand why skateboarding upsets people. It's loud and noisy, it's physically dangerous, and it often involves trespassing. But I don't think these are really the things that bring down the wrath of the law on us-model airplanes are loud and noisy, but model airplane enthusiasts aren't targeted by the law; riding a bicycle on a public street is physically dangerous, but bicyclists aren't usually targeted; adults playing basketball on grade school courts are trespassing as much as skaters who are skating at the same school, but the basketball players aren't targeted. It's the fact that skaters are using objects in ways that they weren't intended to be used that brings down the wrath of the law-what we do stands out as obviously different and therefore draws unwanted attention. Because a bench was made to sit on and not slide along, because a set of stairs was made to be walked up and not jumped down, because wheelchair ramps were made to be slowly traversed and not launched off-these are the source reasons we are targeted. We are singled out, harassed, and punished as burgeoning criminals because we are able to see and use common objects in multi-purpose ways.

Sadly, as we have all seen, it does not end there. Countless municipalities over the last three decades or so have outlawed even the possession of a skateboard in a public space. In these towns, simply rolling on a skateboard in front of your house is a punishable offense. For most kids who find skateboarding, the unjust treatment they receive as a result of wanting to take part in a largely harmless activity forms a negative association with law enforcement agents they will carry for their entire lives. As skateboarding and other non-mainstream activities gain popularity, the number of young people who take part and then receive the same unjust treatment will grow, and thus the percentage of the population with a general mistrust for the law will grow as well, which can only lead to further and more intense trouble down the line.

How else are liberty-loving citizens supposed to react to the treatment we receive? When you're a young, impressionable kid and four cop cars come flying into an empty parking lot where you and a few of your friends are trying to learn how to kickflip over a parking block, make you sit down, take your names, threaten you, ridicule you, take your skateboards, and tell you to never let them see you skating in "their" town again, respect is not the first emotion you feel for the police. As similar interactions continue to repeat themselves in various forms and locales, the less you will take police officers seriously and the more contempt you will harbor for them. By the time a skater has reached adulthood and been treated to years of verbal and physical abuse at the hands and mouths of various law enforcement agents, the chance of the skateboarder ever respecting or trusting any of these agents in almost any situation is virtually non-existent.

Beyond that, once the seeds of law enforcement injustice and inequality have been planted in your head, you begin to see it in other sections of the population aside from your own: police kicking the homeless guy off the bench he's trying to rest on, racial profiling, illegal searches and confiscations, and general abuse of power all running rampant through all sections of society that don't fit the model of the general population's *modus operandi*. Before too long, people who have been subjected to this kind of treatment will feel a widening gap between their way of life and their experiences and that of the society the law favors, further marginalizing them and causing deeper tears in the fabric of a society designed and purported to be fair and equal for all of its citizens.

Not to be overly dramatic about it, but authority figures exercising their powers in an unjust way only serve to erode the societal foundation their power is built on, in the same way that the current war on terror only serves to motivate future terrorists who have seen the terror caused by people who claim to be fighting terror. One day, the growing mass of abused and marginalized citizens may rise up and strike fear back into the hearts of their oppressors, as has happened countless times throughout history. Thomas Jefferson would probably approve. Until then, a little civil disobedience and "Skateboarding Is Not a Crime" stickers seem to be our only tools.

We'll gladly use them.

"When we'd rather grind the handrail in front of the gov't building or corporation than enter and get involved in any of the myriad evils that perpetuate inside, they become alarmed." -Bazorda

## ITS FUN SHAKING THE STATUS QUO

by Michael Brooke

One of the most unique aspects about skateboarding is that it can be done anywhere. Unlike surfing or tennis, skateboarding is something that has no real boundaries. This is both a blessing and a curse.

My first board had clay wheels; it was obviously leftover stock from the 60's and I soon graduated to a FibreFlex with Bennett trucks and Road Rider 4's. I tend to dwell on the freedom that skateboarding offers, but over the past thirty years I have encountered a number of people who are hellbent on enforcing "the rules." Some are security officers, some are police officers and others are just interested in dictating their ideas on "safety" to me.

There are times when I wonder about society's priorities. There are a large amount of serious crimes being committed each day and yet, skaters seem to be continually harassed. For example, when I hear that cops are busting kids at skateparks for not wearing elbow pads, I figure something is a little whacked. This is not to say that elbow pads aren't important, they are. But my gut tells me that if you build a skatepark, let skaters skate. Don't use it as another way to enforce more rules.

Over the years, I have had a number of run-ins with security officials. Perhaps the most memorable was the time when I was shooting a segment for the Concrete Wave television series. We decided to film at a shopping mall since it offered an underground garage. I had been skating for about five minutes when a security vehicle arrived. The security guy rolled down his window and asked if we had a permit to film. I replied that we didn't, since we didn't know we needed one. I told him we were just finishing up and would leave in a few minutes. He wasn't interested and promptly told me to get in my car and get out. What was funny about the situation is that it was all caught on videotape (and I was wearing a mic). The finished TV segment actually incorporated me getting kicked out. My mother saw it and was both amused and embarrassed that her then 35-year-old son had been kicked out of a shopping mall for skateboarding.

In 2005, I conducted an interview with skate legend Stacy Peralta. I asked him if he felt that skateboarding was still remarkable, given the fact that it has become so mainstream - in essence turning into snowboarding. His answer parallels what I spoke about at the start of this piece: "Skateboarding has something that surfing and snowboarding will never have, which is that you can and always will do it where you're not suppose to...there is something inherently sublime about doing your own thing where you're not really supposed to." Too right, Stacy, too right!

This 'inherent sublime-ness' doesn't just manifest itself with skateboarding. I also enjoy challenging preconceived notions wherever I may find them. Take for example, the idea of creating variety within skateboard magazines. Since the late 1980's, most skate mags have focused on one type of skateboarding: street. Sure, the occasional vert shot may have found its way in there, but by and large, it was young, male street skaters. The notion that it might be worthwhile to cover other types of skateboarding or skaters (females, older skaters) seemed to be thrown out the window. In 1999, I had enough myopia to last a lifetime. I decided that the skate world needed a magazine that was focused on something other than street. The three years I worked on International Longboarder prepared me for my next venture: Concrete Wave Magazine. So far, the response has been excellent. Some folks hate the mag; others love it. By challenging what is presented in the other skate media, we are helping to move skateboarding forward by offering an alternative voice.

Make no mistake; however, pushing boundaries or resisting authority can be a painful experience. Those in authority don't like change and they certainly don't like to see their power challenged. When you butt heads against what is perceived to be the established order of things, you may find yourself in situations that are very unfamiliar and uncomfortable. However, there are huge rewards in knowing that you helped to facilitate change within society.

There is a definite connection between being a skater and the ideas of questioning and/or challenging rules. I think this is built into many skaters who have run-ins with authority. Whether it's a question of where you are skating or your reaction to what you see in the media, I always follow one simple rule - "choose your battles wisely."

- bonus part -

The folks at Fun Not Fame have pressed me for more words. Man, do they crack the whip. It would appear that while my words have passed inspection, the actual word count isn't up to par. So it's toss up. Do I tell them "NO WAY" and challenge their authority and submit nothing extra? After all, isn't that what this whole book is about? Sure, they make the rules about word count, but damn, I was pleased with my submission. I wasn't worried about numbers...I just wanted to write a compelling piece. I want so much to say "Enough! I can't write any more!" But I can't - I am compelled for some unknown reason to keep pushing forward to meet their word quota. Note to self: must take assertive training class this fall.

While it would be great to just defy them and hand in nothing, I think it's best to pause for a moment and do a word count. Let's see here...they want another three hundred words, eh? Well, it would appear that the above paragraph brought me closer to my goal. Perhaps it's best just to end here.

I mean I would love to start a whole new story on Canada's philosophy of peace, order and good government and how that relates to questioning authority but I can't see that happening at this stage in the game. Sure, it would make a great submission for the book, but then I'd be over my word quota, defying their authority once again.

And we can't have that, can we?

"Make no mistake; however, pushing boundaries or resisting authority can be a painful experience. Those in authority don't like change and they certainly don't like to see their power challenged. When you butt heads against what is perceived to be the established order of things, you may find yourself in situations that are very unfamiliar and uncomfortable..."

"I was a punk rocker, not some shitty hippy; and this was still at the time when punk rock was considered a reaction to the hippies and the disco-fueled suckiness of the late seventies..."

## *OBSERVATION, CONTROL, AUTHORITY, ACCEPTANCE? ASSESSING THE STATE OF SKATE*

by Wez Lundry

Skateboarders today really have it so much better than cohorts my age did when we were younger.

A lot of the issues still exist, issues that help us to define who we are and where our place(s) exist in and amongst society, but to a large extent huge changes in perceptions, demographics, politics, history, popular culture and other indicators have made things a lot easier for today's skateboarders.

Believe me, I am well aware of how much that may suck for someone to hear (and consequently how much I might suck for saying so), because nobody likes to hear how much better they have it when they still feel as though there is a lot of change that needs to occur (as I still believe). I am conscious that I may be accused of sounding like dad (or grandpa?) when he said, "When I was a boy, I walked seventeen miles uphill both ways in knee-deep snow to get to school..." What I have, and what grandfathers and fathers have that younger skaters don't have is the luxury of hindsight, which establishes a baseline for comparison. Now, after alienating most of my readership, and establishing myself as an untoward, irrelevant Barney, hopefully what comes next will prove to be valid and remind everyone that the more things change, the more they stay the same.

I have been given a list of questions to answer that revolve around my experiences with and perceptions of authority. In the hopes of not sounding too narcissistic I'll try to answer them while providing some insight into how I assume others must feel, or attempt to connect related themes to those who go through the same sorts of things I did (and still do; I still skate pretty often). "Why me?" and "Who cares?" are the two questions that first pop into my mind, but I'll ignore them for now.

Skateboarding was never on TV when I was younger, except for the occasional broadcast of the '70s stalwart skateboard movie

*Skateboard Madness,* which we laughed at as a total hoot given its psychedelic theme that had a long-expired shelf life (even only a couple years after it came out). I was a punk rocker, not some shitty hippy, and this was still at the time when punk rock was considered a reaction to the hippies and the disco-fueled suckiness of the late seventies. Nowadays I am surprised that people don't find it ironic to place a Phish sticker next to a Sex Pistols sticker, or by the fact that punk rock has "broken" into the mainstream and now sounds as shitty (or even shittier) than the worst disco.

I was a skateboarder too, and skateboarding and punk rock went hand in hand. People didn't like either, so I had two strikes going against me, and neither world was welcome in the suburb in which I lived (Bellevue, Washington, just outside of Seattle), or anywhere for that matter. I am sure you've either experienced or heard about life then (early '80s): people yelling shit at you from their car, cops fucking with you for no reason other than riding your skateboard, jocks wanting to fight you, girls (well, luckily not all of them...) wanting nothing to do with you, etc. I already knew I was different, and there was this circular effect of expressing my difference that made people hate me that made me want to express my differences more, which, in turn, made them hate me more, ad infinitum, ad nauseum.

So it was rough: I got beat up, I got picked on, I got harassed by the cops, and it was work to find girls. My only salvations were skateboarding, music and my friends. My parents or anyone in my family didn't understand me, especially at one of those life defining moments of mine in 9th grade: my friend brought hair clippers to school and I started shaving my head in the bathroom during a break. The clippers broke, and I had a half-shaved head that looked totally fucked up. My mom shit her pants and we went to the mall to pay to get the rest shaved off. My mom looked at me different from that day forward, I think.

Pretty soon my three salvations all became one thing: my friends all skated and listened to punk rock. And it was in this environment that all of my early ideas about authority, politics, music, the way the world is and the way the world should be developed. It's like the scene in the film *Repo Man* when Otto's friends get shot while trying to rob a store and the skinhead (Duke) who stole Otto's girlfriend is dying in his arms, and says that it's not his fault - "society made me what I am today." The scene is hilarious because it sounds so stupid, and we all think it funny that he would think society turned him into a glue-sniffing armed robber, but in many ways it is true.

Our societies have a great deal in "making us what we are today." It is this assumption that is the point of departure for the following essay which, unlike Duke in *Repo Man* who sought redemption by trying to justify his criminal behavior, I am celebrating because I don't think that we're that fucked up and most of us don't have to be forgiven for anything significant. We just need vigilance.

Nowadays a lot of young skateboarders simply go to a park when they want to ride, and I completely understand; when I was younger the very few parks I did get to skate were always super fun (North Vancouver and China Creek in Canada; Soquel; Derby in Santa Cruz; later Del Mar, Upland, The Turf) but it was never the extent of skateboarding. Rather, these times were miniscule compared to the time we spent in parking garages, looking for pools, at people's backyard ramps, skating banks and ditches, etc. This is the one thing that I think is separating the generations, the access to public parks that may be suppressing the drive to find other terrain, which most often includes illegal terrain. That drive, to find illegal terrain not made for skating, is one of the things that defined us, and I'm sorry not to see more of it. I'm reminded of a sticker that *Juice Magazine* did: "Keep Skateboarding a Crime."

Parks have a side to them that most skaters don't think about, which I have written about before and will only briefly state again here. Skateparks allow cities to ban skateboarding elsewhere, and they allow for monitoring and controlling an activity that was once viewed as outside of the realm of control. Sadly, many skateparks are shoddy piles of shit that some fly-by-night contractor with no skateboarding experience built with the simple goal of making money. Although there are also a few great park building companies, most fall somewhere in the middle, leaning heavily toward the shitty side.

Has this caused the disappearance of the drive to find new stuff from the skateboarding youth of today? Definitely not completely, but it has shifted the way some people look at skating. It may help people skate a wider array of things, since at most good parks there are both simulated 'street' obstacles as well as transitioned stuff, and it may help kids progress more quickly with a reliable, constant place to skate. But it may also intractably change the way skateboarders themselves think about the activity in the larger social context, especially considering the concomitant shift in social acceptance of skateboarding, from mass media to mass marketing, consciously or subconsciously.

Before I sound like I am pining away for the 'good old days' when skating was more of a rush and condemning the newer generations of skateboarders to wimpy irrelevance and a coddled upbringing, I'll admit that there are also some positive aspects. Not only am I now usually older than the cops who bust me for skating pools, but they have now grown up watching the *X-Games,* seeing *Dogtown and Z-Boys* or *Lords of Dogtown* in a theater, and seeing the mass commoditization of skateboarding in malls and chain stores (and often their children skate, or want to).

Today I skated a virgin backyard pool with two friends after cleaning it out, and then we went to find another. We found a killer bowl, but as we were just about finished cleaning it up, we saw the cops coming into the backyard and heard the woman cop say: "Scottsdale PD." They looked at our IDs, joked around with us, and let us go, which has been the usual reaction when cops find us skating in someone else's pool. It's a far cry from fifteen years ago, when I got caught skating a pool in Seattle with one friend. The cop held his gun to my head for about thirty seconds while we were telling him that all we were doing was skateboarding. He caught us doing that, not trashing the house; we weren't armed - that was a camera in my pocket and we were cooperating. We were cuffed and stuffed into the back of his car, but let go as soon as he contacted the realtor who said we could walk. At the same pool a month or so later I got a felony trespassing ticket, and was looking at up to six months in jail. Despite the fact that pool skating still keeps me on edge somewhat, and I try as hard as possible to avoid being caught, I don't think as much today about going to jail as I did when I was younger.

Before the uninitiated reader thinks that we as skateboarders have become the star jocks and spokespeople of our generations, think again. Despite growing public acceptance of skateboarding, it is far from completely accepted. The aforementioned example of skateparks is illustrative. The implied give and take of skateparks, as far as cities are concerned, is providing a 'safe' place for the 'kids' to do their 'sport' while increasing obstacles against skateboarders elsewhere: creating fines for or banning skateboarding in public places. It serves a dual purpose of pseudo-legitimizing while at the same time marginalizing: skaters are expected to read and follow rules drafted by politicians, the hours of operation are set by the parks department, often parks are fenced in enclosures, parents supervise as do rangers or police. Skateparks are sometimes closed completely for set periods of time if they are deemed to be trouble, such as when high school and junior high kids, almost all of whom don't skate and only come to the park to cause trouble, get in fights. The state can not only give you a place to skate; it can also take it away, which is the danger of complacency in allowing the state to provide you the only spot to skate.

Comparative cases can be constructive in this regard. Having traveled a fair amount in Europe and Asia, as well as North America, I can also say with some authority that most, if not all, societies are less uptight about skateboarding (and most other things) than we are in the U.S. Some of it must do with the puritanical origins of this country, and the drive for conformity within a specifically prescribed set of norms (despite the professed goal of 'acceptance' a brief look at American history will show that acceptance has hardly been historically granted, but rather fought for: slavery, women's rights, civil rights, gay rights, struggles over religious freedom, freedom of speech, etc.). Some of it obviously has to do with capitalism, and the evolution of American capitalism, specifically the extremely litigious nature of our society coupled with the ever-present desire to always place the blame somewhere (after all, someone has to get sued). Some of it has to do with the aforementioned phenomenon of granting a park in order to take away any other claims a skateboarder might have for somewhere to ride.

Take Indonesia, for example, a country where I do a lot of work and spend a lot of time. Prior to 1999, it was a ruthless military dictatorship responsible for one of the largest mass murders in the 20th century (1965-67). Yet nobody bothers skateboarders, security guards and police generally leave skateboarders alone or grant permission for them to skate, and the public at large minds its own business. "Public" spaces, such as universities and regular parks, are fair game for skating; after all they belong to everyone. Incidental 'damage' is considered only the result of the use of an object that was made to be used (albeit often not intentionally designed for skateboarding, people are accepting of these new uses). Kids' behavior is dictated much more by traditional social interaction than by written rules and regulations. Authority doesn't seem arbitrary but rather a natural extension of timeless social interaction.

In coming full circle, if we are truly, at least partially, products of the society in which we live, it's worth taking some time and thinking about our daily interactions involving not only our skateboards but our entire lives. Despite the aggressive, litigious nature of American culture, very rarely is this questioned seriously or vigorously. And don't get me started about the current political situation in the United States: increasing fear mongering of an indefinable enemy, a war in which victory is impossible (you can't defeat an ideology), corruption and nepotism at every turn of the newspaper page, an unwillingness to acknowledge the debt with which future generations will be saddled.

In thinking about society, development and authority, it is bizarre for me to think that in some ways a repressive military dictatorship like Indonesia can allow for certain personal freedoms that are far from guaranteed in the "World's Oldest Democracy," TM, and yet if we think about the nature of efficiency in instituting social control *a la Foucault* (who looked to Jeremy Bentham's model) it should at the very least cause us to pause and think about our daily transactions and choices.

Including those made on a skateboard.

## *NEGATIVE REINFORCEMENT*

by Rory Parker

Skateboarding is comprised of misfits who banded together when no one else would have them.

After a while those sour grapes begin to taste sweet, and the semantics of denial are no longer necessary in attaining the independence you unknowingly coveted. The tattoos and scars accumulate, and you become different than you were before. After a certain point you no longer have any peers. No two wounds heal the same. It's with a species of shame that I admit I only rebel out of the pain of being rejected. How many of us have done the same?

I suffered through five years of torment at the hands of Jesuit education. Useless knowledge for knowledge's sake filled the void for many, but, in me, the emptiness always remained. I dropped out of college, simply quitting, never filling out the paper work, never telling anyone of my choice. I just stopped going. One day a letter came in the mail, telling me I wasn't welcome anymore.

Apparently no one had noticed that I'd left months before. I elected poverty over plenty, though I must admit I still hold out hope that providence will send me a comfortable existence. I sit back and look at the people in their shiny new cars, rushing from their opulent homes to work, then back again, only to repeat the same ordeal. I laugh at the emptiness of their lives, working sixty hours a week to pay the mortgage on a home they rarely see. It's a notion I've never understood, to work your youth away so that you'll be comfortable in your old age. Why give up the best years of life, only so you can coast through the worst?

Old age and infirmity creep up slowly, and the day you reach that fabled retirement your body may no longer be willing to pursue those dreams that you deferred. Days blend into each other and eventually the only joy you feel comes from searching the obituaries and finding that you outlived one more friend you never had time for.

I look on others and feel comfort in knowing that they've chosen a life devoid of chance or meaning, but I can't disregard the specter that maybe it is I who is missing something. Is it only me that feels this way? That can't be so, but, lacking an intimate working knowledge of others I have no real proof. Maybe I'm the only one, and maybe I've made a terrible mistake. Fuck it; it's too late to turn back now.

I remember being told more than once over the course of college that my writing was too immature, that no one would ever publish it. I remember being told that I had to go about it the right way if I wanted to stand a chance. Get a degree, intern, work my way up from writing ad copy. But I realized that the ones giving advice were the same ones who'd failed.

I once took a screenwriting class at the local community college. I enrolled on a whim, thinking that maybe I'd write the next great American movie and make a million dollars. Well, that never panned out, but I learned a lot from the teacher. I can't remember his name, but in all fairness it doesn't really deserve remembering.

He was a fairly young guy, so full of the self-aggrandizement that's a result of failure. He'd sit in the front of the class and ask students who their favorite authors were. Famous authors were met with derision, while obscure ones were dismissed with a snort and the opinion that they were okay, though overrated. He harangued us for a semester with his view of screenwriting, but never really taught us a thing. It quickly became obvious that he had no real intention of telling us how to write a screenplay. Instead he recommended a number of books we could buy and seminars we could attend. They'd been thoroughly vetted by him and he assured us that they could provide us with what we needed, so far as form went. His plan, as far as the class went, was to provide us with something that no class really, in his opinion, offered. He would teach us how to sell a screenplay. How to format it, package it, and mail it.

And he did so, in excruciating detail. Scripts were to be mailed in a plain manila envelope, accompanied by a one page letter, no more. He instructed us on certain typefaces that studios loved, pacing that had to be used. "I am not," he would say, as his paunch swelled over his belt and the stubble on his face made him look worn rather than rugged, "...here to teach you to write the world's best screenplay. I am here to teach you to write a movie that will sell." It seemed as though he'd missed the point. If you want to make a ton of money there are much easier ways of going it about it than being a writer. Even if the point is being in the orbit of fame, selling coke would be an easier, more lucrative way of achieving your goal.

The more I listened the more I came to despise him. Though I'm an inveterate smart-ass I've always made a conscious effort to avoid challenging college professors. I've seen too many kids reduced to piles of quivering apology by a well-placed remark against the fallacy of youth's omniscience. But, though I can usually admit a teacher knows more than me, this dude wasn't getting that luxury.

I confronted him once in class, when we were discussing the proper form for a script. A girl had suggested that rigidity is damaging to writing, and that true creativity can rarely come from a common form. It was his condescension that pushed me over the edge.

"Of course you'd say that. If you've been in this business as long as I have you'd see the reasoning behind it."

This was delivered with the biggest cocksucker expression I've ever seen, and was, of course, no real answer at all. And, I realized, after all this time in class I'd never actually heard what this guy's credentials were. All that time, and I'd never seen a thing he'd written. So, I simply asked him about it. Asked him what right he had to be teaching the class, asked him how the fuck he could have the gall to stand in front of a bunch of strangers and try to impose rules on something that was inherently rule-free. Of course, I couched it all in more diplomatic tones.

"Well," he said, expression no longer so cocksure, eyes darting about the room... "I got my PhD in film studies from USC."

Not very impressive. I don't know for sure, but studying movies in college and calling yourself a doctor seems like jerking off and calling yourself a sex therapist. It's just not very hard.

"But," I asked, going for the throat, "What movies have you written? I mean, have you sold a script?"

His answer didn't come so fast that time.

"Well, I was hired to adapt stories from *Chicken Soup for the Teenage Soul* for television."

What the fuck? I asked if they'd aired it on TBN or something.

"Actually, no..." he said, his former stridence now long gone.

"It never made it to production."

It was the last time I attended class. I couldn't believe that the only real knowledge this guy had to pass along had come from rewriting someone else's words, words which, in the end, weren't even deemed good enough for sappy inspirational television. It's like trying to coach football because you once tried out for the team and didn't make it.

You could say that his class was the last straw, though I'd been headed for collapse long before. I gave up on the normal rules, started writing what I wanted. Stories of sex, drugs, cuss words, racism; all the horrible things that are inside me, that are me. I'm sure it's harder this way, but way more fun.

Now I'm twenty-five years old. So fucking young, but, Jesus, the years do roll by slowly. Advice still comes from everywhere around me. Parents, friends, strangers, they all know better than me. "Why are you writing for a skateboard magazine? Don't you know the real money is in writing copy for instructional booklets? I know a guy who works for the LA Times, want me to get you a meeting? You know, you should really go back and finish school, you'll never get anywhere without a degree."

Fuck what they think.

One of the few things you can be sure of, in this life, is that people are going to try and tell you what to do. It may be your teachers, your parents, your boss or the fucking man on television; everyone knows how you should live your life better than you do. They set rules for you to follow, establish social norms for you to conform to, and, should you falter in your forward march to synchronicity, mete out punishment for your transgressions.

And they do this without permission. Most of the rules we are expected to follow are there whether we like them or not. Consultation isn't part of the arrangement. But why not? Birth alone isn't a sufficient demand on allegiance. Mere happenstance of conception cannot bind a man physically. My life is my own, to live as I see fit. The only problem is, most people just don't see it that way.

Why is it that most people are so eager to unite behind an ideal? Provided a general sense of well being they are content to merely eke out an existence as best they can, without too many messy questions or challenges to their masters. And, to those like me, to those whom that type of blind faith is anathema, the resulting demand on your patience can be nearly intolerable.

You see, humanity demands authority and leadership. It can come in the form of man or god, but the need for an outside force to drive and shape your life is overwhelming. It takes out the guess work. It also provides a delightful lack of accountability. It's so much easier to run gas chambers when someone else orders you to do it.

But, life can be a beautiful thing stripped of those needless accoutrements. With a sense of independence and the realization that you can play by your own rules if you want to, the world opens up.

Authority is not a real thing. It is merely an idea, a conceit granted to another that gives them power over you. It's there to hold back the freedom others mistakenly name lawlessness and amorality. Humanity fears the personal responsibility that comes as the price for true individuality. But those who retain the consent of the governed, they who keep the bellies full and the coffers ringing, they're the ones to be truly feared, because they have the unswerving allegiance of the majority which can be a mighty tool to silence dissent. Sound the bells of nationalism and they will come running, and beware to any of those who would be vain enough to think they can stem the tide through sheer force of will; they will be drowned.

Despite the terror of it, it is still possible to struggle, to put up a resistance, no matter how feeble. Because, though there are rules to a game, it is always possible to cheat. The fabric that holds together a willingly enslaved populace is necessarily weak. One small tear, one tiny glimpse at what lies on the other side, and the whole thing can fall apart.

"Most of the rules we are expected to follow are there whether we like them or not. Consultation is often not part of the arrangement. But why not? Birth alone isn't a sufficient demand on allegiance. Mere happenstance of conception cannot bind a man physically. My life is my own, to live as I see fit. The only problem is, most people just don't see it that way..."

"In America's lawsuit-phobic culture, it seems the pad-free park is becoming a rarity...in the seemingly more 'skate-liberal' city of Portland, Oregon for example, no one will harass you about wearing a helmet in the public skateparks; but go to San Diego or New York, and you can be sure you'll be buckling your helmet and strapping on those kneepads."

## *COPS, SECURITY GUARDS AND PUBLIC SKATEPARKS*

by Rob Brink

No wonder we feel cops and their less skilled brethren, the security guard, are the bane of our skateboarding existence. Both will rain on our parade at any cost. Both power trip and could most likely find something better to do than bust you. Every once in a blue moon, they might even be cool. But in the end, both are like pit bulls; you never can, and never should, entirely trust them, because they don't give a rat's ass about you and while one might be somewhat cool, chances are he was a prick to the person coming before or after you, and the next guy to come bust you may not be as cool. If you're a skateboarder, the only thing worse than a security guard is a cop, and the only thing worse than a cop is, well...nothing really.

MEDIAN AGE:

SG: 35-the true average among the (even more shunned than skateboarders?) GED-wielding, eighteen-year-olds eager for authority and the (we thought they were retired) sixty-year-olds looking for an easy minimum wage gig.

COPS: 35-that perfect post-military, post-the-athletic-dreams-aren't-happening, pre-graduating-to-office/detective age

BRIBE FACTOR:

SG: Fifty-fifty shot. Your pocket change is more likely their day's take-home pay-and that's before taxes.

COPS: Probably not a smart idea unless you're in a faraway land where you'll most likely be paying for your freedom as opposed to being able to skate a spot.

EQUAL OPPORTUNITY?

SG: You betcha! Must check more than one of the following: Caucasian, African American, Asian, senior citizen, Trekkie, illegal alien, abnormally skinny, abnormally large, bored, bitter, previous failure, other...

COPS: Predominantly white males and white tomboy females.

OUT-RUNNABLE?

SG: Hell yeah. Out-walkable, out-talkable, beat-uppable (ask Moses Itkonen).

COPS: Yes, but take the approach that skateboarding should take on: at your own risk.

YEP, THEY REALLY SAID IT -

SG: "I'll get fired if I get caught taking this bribe on tape!"-Security guard to Jayme Fortune after Jayme tried to slip him a twenty-spot for an extra five minutes. If the cameras weren't rolling, it would've been a different story, though.

COPS: "One of them actually started to skateboard in front of me."-Sgt. Charles J. Rumsey IV, Waterville Maine Police Department, appalled that someone might think riding around on a piece of wood could be harmless to the community.

IT'S REALLY ATROCIOUS THAT ...

SG: They'll radio in for the men in real uniforms because you're trespassing, yet the kids playing basketball jumped over the same fence you did and are playing freely.

COPS: Now that we have a place to skate, they're worrying about what we don't do in our own space (i.e., wear helmets).

BUT HEY AT LEAST THERE'S<br>ONE WHO'S GOT OUR BACK

SG: Big Black-Dyrdek's personal security and deal...er, neck-breaker.

COPS: Boston's very own skateboarding cop, Officer Jeff Zetalotti - he doesn't skate on the job, but if he has to kick you out, he'll let you know his secret spots.

TIMELESS QUOTES:

SG: "He said he was pissed because he's 80 years old and works for six dollars and 45 cents an hour."-P.J. Ladd, translation of what the security guard probably didn't say.

COPS: "Doesn't it suck when the cops kicking you out of the spot are younger than you are?"-Mike Blabac to Rob Dyrdek.

YOUR WORST REPERCUSSION:

SG: Getting kicked out - unless he calls for the cops, in which case:

COPS: A ticket ranging into the hundreds of dollars and beyond. The ironic part: The ticket for running a red light in California, a crime that could prove potentially fatal to your life and the lives of many others, is a mere 271 dollars.

SHUT UP ALREADY -

SG: "Do you know Tony Hawk?"

COPS: "I used to skate."

USED TO BE:

SG: A cop, ex-military or a police academy reject.

COPS: High school jock, ex-military, or volunteer EMT or Fireman.

WEAPON:

SG: Walkie Talkie.

COPS: Gun, billy club, tazer, pepper spray, K-9.

*(continued).*

FASHION ACCESSORIES:

SG: Custom security ball cap, mustache, eyeglasses, Payless utility shoes, half a uniform (shirt from the guard before him with a fresh name badge), sometimes a 3-piece suit if they work for a legit corporation, walkie talkie.

COPS: Aviators, shined shoes, mustache, police hat, flattop haircut, police uniform, helmet, and badge.

FOOD:

SECURITY: Coffee and donuts.

COPS: Coffee and donuts.

EDUCATION:

SG: Most likely less than the cops (All they need to know is how to call the cops).

COPS: High school football or wrestling team, police academy.

AUTHORITY TO:

SG: None, except to call the cops or attempt to take your board (Until you or your friends grab it back).

COPS: Arrest you, cuff you, confiscate your board, write you a ticket.

IF THEY WERE COOL THEY'D:

SG: Stay sleeping at the front desk.

COPS: Keep driving.

*afterthoughts...*

Cops and security guards only represent the microcosm of the authority totem pole - regarding American skateparks, how do municipality parks, rules and laws measure up?

Skateboarding is illegal (citations issued to the guilty parties) in the central business district of Louisville. After a failed attempt at a small skateboard facility (insufficient ramps and obstacles) in one of the local parks, the city decided it was time to meet the demands of the skateboarders.

In April of 2002, Louisville, Kentucky unveiled its first and only public skateboarding park - the Louisville Extreme Park, boasting 40,000 square feet of concrete skating surface, a 24-foot fullpipe and a wooden vert ramp. Under Kentucky state law, because Louisville isn't charging patrons to use the park, the city has recreational immunity - meaning liability for the park is fairly low. The facility has a "skate at your own risk" policy, recommending but not requiring that full pads be worn. A local ordinance only requires skaters to wear a helmet, and because this is an ordinance, it is the responsibility of the local police to enforce the helmet rule. The park is unstaffed and open 24 hours a day, and no waiver needs to be filled out.

According to Jason Cissell, spokesman for metro parks in Louisville, the city realized they would only have one chance to build a park like this. So the scope of the project changed from, "Let's build a park to satisfy the needs of the elementary users," to "Let's do this right..." As a result, the Louisville Extreme Park quickly gained national attention and attracted skateboarders from all over the world. The success of the park has Louisville working on Phase Two, which includes bike and pedestrian pathways being built around the park, as well as the addition of permanent restrooms.

With the number of public skateparks steadily increasing in the United States, the legislation and laws that go along with the building and management of these parks is quite varied from state to state. In the seemingly more 'skate-liberal' city of Portland, Oregon for example, no one will harass you about wearing a helmet in the public skateparks; but go to San Diego or New York, and you can be sure you'll be buckling your helmet and strapping on those kneepads.

In America's lawsuit-phobic culture, it seems the pad-free park is becoming a rarity. Most states require a great deal of gear to ride their parks. Whether or not these rules are enforced or that parks are truly 'full pads' is a somewhat hush-hush situation. No one wants to rock the boat, especially while they're in it.

Portland, Oregon has worked with the local skateboarders, parents and neighborhoods to implement a "skateboarders police themselves" policy at the city's two public skateparks, Burnside (originally started without permission from the city) and Pier Park. Because of this team effort, it was agreed that the parks would be free of charge; no waiver or membership is required, and skaters make their own rules and govern themselves while at the parks. As a result of this agreement, the city of Portland cannot be liable for any injury that occurs at Pier Park or Burnside. Safety gear is always encouraged by the city but not required. Neither of the parks are staffed or lit at night, however, the city does provide trash removal and bathrooms.

Burnside, one of the most famous skate spots in the world, has a reputation of being a park for advanced skaters, so Pier Park was designed by the city, parents, and younger skaters after realizing less-experienced skateboarders needed a place to go. It is the city's newest public skateboard park and was a youth-generated project built by the National Guard.

According to Michelle Harper, spokesperson for Portland Parks and Recreation, "Skateboarding has surfaced as a significant interest for the future of parks in the city, and we have nowhere near the amount of parks we need. It's definitely on our radar screen. We have more on the drawing board because the public has told us they wanted more." The "police yourself" policy, although rare in the United States, seems to be working due to the city's willingness to move forward with more skateparks. Harper also added that although skateboarding was restricted in many areas of the city in the past, the council has relaxed many of those restrictions, realizing skateboarding is a form of transportation and exercise that many people depend on and enjoy.

In 1999, following in the tradition of Burnside, many local skaters took it upon themselves to begin building the Washington Street skatepark. When the city discovered the park, efforts were made to eliminate it. The skater's fought the good fight for a few years, and today Washington Street park is a reality. The city has allowed the building to commence and has even allocated funds toward the construction of the park. Many skate companies and citizens are donating time, money, and materials to the cause.

A little heart goes a long way.

"A little heart goes a long way..."

BEWARE: Perhaps skateparks aren't ideal substitutes for your favorite local street spot, but when citations are written for skating downtown, a day of skating can cost way more than a few bottles of water and lunch. Here are some average costs for skating in the wrong place at the wrong time. Keep in mind that some cities will take your board or just flat out arrest you:

## Average cost of a skateboarding ticket in America's major cities:

San Diego: $50

Philadelphia: $25

Los Angeles: $100-150

San Francisco: $55-100

New York: $35-100

Carlsbad: $130

Chicago: $35

Washington DC: $50

"Some of the safest places to get away with skateboarding are in the sketchiest of neighborhoods, where the cops have much bigger fish to fry than the errant clack and grind of a heated street skating session..."

-Paul Cote'

## *OVERREACTION?*

by Erik Olsen

Back in 1993, our little skate crew of myself, Stein and Hathaway would skate across from my house at the Safeway shopping center all the time. There were some red curbs and not much else, but we would skate anything back then.

There were never any "No Skateboarding" signs, but we knew there was an off duty cop that was hired to patrol the shopping center and he would sometimes kick us out. One day while skating in front of Safeway, we saw the cop at the other side of the shopping center, leisurely walking our way. We decided that was a good time to leave, before we got the boot, so we headed off.

We skated to the next block where there was a post office with a really bad manual pad into the street. Just as we were skating on the sidewalk into the post office parking lot, a Mustang 5.0 screeches up into the driveway. It took us all by surprise. As it was normal for jocks and other "cool" kids to pick on skaters, I figured it was another one of those episodes where we were going to have to either run or defend ourselves with our skate weapons.

As the car screeched dangerously close to us, the off-duty cop from the shopping center a block away jumps out, grabs the closest person to him (me) and throws me onto his hood, face first. I am like, "What the fuck!?" as this all happened in a matter of five seconds. This meat-head, egotistical cop got mad that he didn't get to kick us out, give his little spiel and feel better about himself so he threw my 15-year-old frame onto his fast car as he yelled something to the effect of, "What are you doing running away from me little punk?" He was all heated up, adrenaline pumping, pretending he was on duty and doing something worth while, while really he was clearly crossing the line by attacking us on the sidewalk.

He had me pushed on his hood as he took our names; he took some deep breaths because he was all winded. As the minutes passed, he calmed down and eventually realized he shouldn't have reacted like that; just shows how peoples ego's are big and how unnecessary that is. He must have thought, "No punk skaters are gonna leave until I tell them, I'm in charge here - attack, attack, attack!!!"

We eventually flipped it on him and ended up telling him how irresponsible and inappropriate it was that he did that to us, and that we were going to report him. We took his name and badge number, but nothing ever happened. That was during the time when skaters were seen only in that one commercial smoking weed. Now that skating is cool and officer Dick has a kid that skates, I'm sure he would not react like that...or would he?

That's why I like skating in the ghetto - those cops have real crimes and injustices to make right and a skateboard is just something people ride; it's not a criminal offense.

"As the car screeched dangerously close to us, the off-duty cop from the shopping center a block away jumps out, grabs the closest person to him (me) and throws me onto his hood, face first..."

## *SATCHMO'S FALL FROM GRACE*

by Marc Johnson

The story I had in mind was something that happened in 1993 with a freelance 'bounty hunter.'

This guy called himself Satchmo after the late great jazz musician Louis Armstrong. Fat and black doesn't give you the right to assume a legendary moniker, but dipshit hadn't thought about that. What he did was roam around San Diego wearing an Army surplus security guard suit with a handgun holding people at gunpoint after he called the police. My guess is that he couldn't or wouldn't make it through proper police training, and he figured that it was the next best thing to buy a gun, wear a costume and cruise the streets in a stripped down old police car playing cops and robbers.

On this particular day, my two roommates and I were face down on the ground at gunpoint and the gun slipped out of his hand when the cops rolled up to the skatespot. Of course when it hit the ground the barrel was facing in my direction, namely at my face. In some other realm of possibility/probability, that fucker went off and a sixteen year-old Marc Johnson died in the parking lot of an abandoned bank in La Mesa. Satchmo was convicted of some degree of manslaughter, went to prison for some years, and this story came and went much like my short-lived time on the merry-go-round of third density. Blah blah blah.

What I realized while trying to recall and write about this incident was that I didn't care about it anymore. I couldn't muster up any feeling of horror anymore about staring down the barrel of that moron's gun after it hit the ground. And man did it hit the ground, barrel in my face. Guns fire when they are dropped. Satchmo was waving the gun in the air to signal the officers when they drove into the parking lot and the damned gun fell from around eight feet in the air from his upstretched arm. What a scene that was. The police actually apologized to us for taking us to jail (where I sat for four hours), but according to law, a firearm was illegally drawn and therefore paperwork had to be filed. We were 'booked.' Satchmo actually got the raw end of that deal. He didn't even have a job. This was just his little hobby, pointing a loaded weapon at teenagers and feeling like a hero. He even had a 'Satchmo' vanity plate on his used cop car. The police were fucking stunned. My roommates and I sat cuffed in the cars while the officers questioned this guy for two hours. We got out and were driven home at around 1:00 a.m., boards confiscated, the whole bit. I was a minor after all, which is why they kept me in a holding cell for so long. I can't imagine what my mother thought when she got a call in North Carolina about her son being in jail, sixteen years young and three thousand miles away. How powerless she must have felt.

I know that people take hold of anything in life that fills the potholes of the heart. Who knows what kind of walking death people go through that cause them to want control over others? That is a concept older than recorded history. It just is. Someone will always want control. Life and death come and go, centuries pass, and nothing changes in regard to authority.

I think what many people don't understand is that control never lasts. We are mortal. Officer Chumpstain might be a bigshot for twenty years on the force, but every good deed and bad passes away much like the vigor and youth with which he conducted his affairs while on the job.

I guess my only wish would have to be an awakening of people in so-called authority. You have no authority over any other soul on this Earth. You have nothing but the lessons you either learn or don't learn in your own lifetime. You have nothing, you own nothing, you take nothing away when you pass away from this place. And yes, you will pass away. But can you imagine to where?

In this idea, and in the search for an answer to it, crooked lines become straight, and badges and guns, fear and authority have no more meaning or worth than an old washing machine in the front yard. Stare at it, and know that one day you'll be out there along side it, someone playing authority all over you. And after all those years, what did authority amount to in your own lifetime? Will your gravestone read 'HERO' after a life of dictating what is right and wrong for the lives of others?

Authority is necessary and unnecessary. Why is obvious. There are unpleasant people and actions playing themselves out day after day. Sometimes there are people who can help. Not always are those people the ones that you imagine would.

I wish we were all free.

# *SHREDIQUETTE*

by Corey Daniel

"We can do this the easy way or we can do this my way..."

The cop was not joking even though Daniel and I laughed out loud. Daniel questioned, "Are you serious? I'm a citizen; I can just arrest anyone?" Daniel grabbed me by the neck the same way in which he had been grabbed by the store manager and placed me under citizens arrest. "Your under citizen's arrest, Corey!" That is when the policeman decided we were going to this his way.

Have you ever had your neck grabbed by a store manager while passing by a storefront on your skateboard? Have you ever had your board stolen? Nothing is free. Forget expression, forget motion. They've made a million imperfect perfections and they don't want us messing it up. Forget it. Skateboarding tickets plus skateboard confiscation plus two 12-year-olds equals?

Just ride your skateboard and tell everyone you're sorry.

"Sorry everyone...so sorry about your pools, schools, parks and shopping centers. Your roads and infrastructure. At least I'm not alone; at least there are millions of other skateboarders in the world. Skateboarding is taking over everywhere and I'm real sorry there is nothing I can do about it..."

Just ride your board and tell 'em your sorry.

Just don't let 'em touch you; don't touch them. You must maintain a personal circle when authority flexes it's steroid injected muscle. Seeing that manager grab Daniel by the neck made me think that authority needs a little discipline of its own! Who is in charge of who's in charge?

I just skate where it feels right. I feel the most right skating stuff made for skateboarding, by skateboarders.

Remember the golden rule. Skateboarding is art. *Shrediquette,* underground artisans!

LOVE
FREE
LOVE
SKATE

# *AUTHORITY, POLITICS AND LOVE*

by Kevin McHugh

"The need for recreation is universal...your idea of recreation may be playing a sport or watching it on television, sitting under a tree, sailing a boat - or all of these - but far from being a luxury in your life, recreation is a necessity."

Public parks are meant to cater to the recreational and social needs of the public, which may encompass many different sports or activities. When planning for public space, a combination of the spatial aspects of architecture is needed to meet the requirements of the diverse, multi-faceted client: the city and its people.

John F. Kennedy Plaza, in Philadelphia, Pennsylvania, was the subject of a political struggle between the municipal government and skateboarders, simply because the park was being used excessively for skateboarding, an activity that the park was not originally intended for. The design and physical construction of Love Park made the urban space a worldwide attraction for skateboarders, and increased the popularity of both street skating and the city of Philadelphia. The unexpected popularity of skateboarding in the park brought millions of dollars in revenue through events like the *X-Games*, and also through everyday tourism. Skateboarding in Philadelphia attracted students and young professionals, and the park became a symbol of Philadelphia's attitude towards youth culture."

In an article for the Washington Post, Debbie Goldberg said that many young academics chose the schools they wanted to attend because of Love Park: "...skateboarding at the park has become a well-known and visible part of Philadelphia's youth culture. Some college students, such as those at nearby Drexel University and the Art Institute of Philadelphia, have said they chose their school based at least in part on its proximity to Love Park. Skateboarders own several art galleries in the trendy Old City section, as well as many of the skate shops that have cropped up in Center City and the suburbs.

In 2000, a bill was passed that made it illegal to skateboard on public property, and in 2002, Love Park was shut down for renovations that would prevent skateboarding. As a result of the renovations, Love Park was closed to skateboarders, forcing many to find other spots to skate, and in some cases, leaving professional skateboarders no choice but to move out of the city. The renovation of Love Park not only made the skateboarding scene much smaller in Philadelphia, but it also created economic, political and demographic effects that were underestimated by city officials.

The indirect site placement of Love Park dates back over three hundred years, when William Penn dispatched surveyor Thomas Holme to lay the city out in 1682. Holme's final plan was to create the city within a two-mile area between the Delaware and Schuyl-kill rivers, establishing a grid of streets broken up by four public squares of eight acres each.

In the plans, there was a central square for civic buildings at the intersection of two major streets. The development of commercial space within the vicinity strengthened the area as the center of the city. Benjamin Franklin Parkway was a grand boulevard reminiscent of the Champs-Elysee in Paris, and it was supposed to connect City Hall with Fairmount Park, which was at the north end of the parkway.

The idea of building a boulevard was part of the "City Beautiful" movement, which began in the late nineteenth century. The idea of the movement was to bring "classical beauty into an urban scene that was rejected as being chaotic and untidy."

The concept of having a park in the downtown area was originally devised by Edmund Bacon as a part of a thesis at Cornell University in 1932, which was a plan for the future of downtown Philadelphia. Bacon, who would eventually become the executive director of the Philadelphia City Planning Commission from 1949 to 1970, wanted to situate the park at the downtown end of the Benjamin Franklin Parkway to help alleviate traffic congestion by breaking up the intersection. The park's architect was Vincent Kling, who made Bacon's idea a reality by creating and designing the finer details of the park. The park was finished in 1965, and dedicated to John F. Kennedy in 1967.

In *Urban Space*, Love Park was recognized as a "civic center" type of square. Out of nine possible types found in American cities, Love Park earned this designation because it is situated in the political and financial center of the city. Civic centers can also be homes to public works of art, and Love Park is no exception. The fountain was originally supposed to be chosen from a competition created by the City Hall Plaza Committee in 1964, but none of the submissions fulfilled the needs that the committee was looking for. Instead, they commissioned Vincent Kling to design a jet fountain, with the idea of adding a sculpture later, but it was never added.

The second piece of art found in Love Park is Robert Indiana's *Love*, which is the piece of artwork that gave the park its nickname. The monument was supposed to be a satire of American popular culture and its "wholesale devotion to consumerism through the advertising media." The aluminum monument was erected for the Bicentennial celebration in 1976, and it remained there until 1978. Indiana's gallery in New York tried to sell the sculpture to the city, but they refused to buy it, so it was removed. After it was taken away, citizens expressed so much anger for the city's actions that F. Eugene Dixon, chairman of the Philadelphia Art Commission, bought the sculpture and donated it to the city.

In order to be successful, parks not only need to meet city-specific rules and regulations, but they must also take into account the aesthetic and practical requirements that are demanded by the public. Project for Public Spaces (PPS) is a non-profit organization that has helped thousands of communities with the design and management of public spaces. The organization came up with four qualities that satisfy the public's needs: access and linkages, comfort and image, uses and activities, and sociability.

The first quality, accessibility, deals with convenience, ease of access and pedestrian activity. Love Park is situated in the heart of downtown Philadelphia, and is easily accessible by many modes of transportation. Ricky Oyola, one of the first professional skaters to make Love Park famous, relied on public transit to skate the park: "It was probably, like, '87...we used to take the bus on Saturdays, get dropped off and skate all day, take the bus home...that was my first experience going to Philly..." In terms of accessibility by car, the park divides five major intersections, so getting to the park by car is relatively easy. The park is also surrounded by sidewalks, which also brought in many people from the surrounding office buildings who wished to have lunch in the park.

The quality of comfort and image requires that a successful park have adequate seating, a clean atmosphere, and it must be safe. Love Park, before its renovation, had simple marble benches and ledges that could double as extra seating, allowing larger groups to meet at Love. The Park had an adequate number of garbage cans, but suffered from a severe mouse problem due to the people that would eat lunch in the park.

The issue of safety depends on from what perspective the situation is viewed from - before the ban on skateboarding, there was minimal police presence, but the park was still considered relatively safe, because it was always filled with skaters. Oyola believed that the skaters made the park safe to walk through, saying, "We made this place alive…it was just drug dealers…fighting each other all the time, every day…we made it to where people could walk by and not feel scared…" After the skateboarding ban was implemented, a heavy uniformed and undercover police presence was evident at the park; however the main purpose of the police presence was to deter people from skateboarding.

Most people didn't mind the skateboarding, and many came to sit and watch people skate the park. Daniel J. Keating, III, CEO of the Keating Group whose head office is directly across the street from Love Park, says that "[Skateboarding] created night-time life in the park. Daytime and nighttime. Ironically, what I found is the people who are living in the Phoenix, young and older, thoroughly enjoyed seeing the activity there…I'm an advocate; I think it's a lot of fun. It looks very hard to do."

In May 2003, the Philadelphia Daily News held an online poll regarding skateboarding in Love Park. Of the 1,041 people that voted, 69% of the voters wanted to allow skating in Love Park. The uses and activities of the park were clearly evident, with people sitting or skating in the park at all hours of the day and night. To a skater, Love Park was the epitome of the perfect skate spot, having the perfect combination of obstacles like continuous granite surfaces, stair sets and open areas with smooth tiles that allowed for hours of activity.

PPS believes that the final quality, sociability, is the hardest quality for a public space to achieve. In *Planning for Parks and Recreation needs in Urban Area*s, Elinor Guggenheimer stated that "Among the major recreation lacks in cities are places and opportunities for young people to meet each other and to spend time together." The sociability of Love Park before the renovation and skateboarding ban was unmistakable, and it was one of the few public places in which strangers could come together and socialize because they shared an interest in skateboarding. Whether people skated or watched, skateboarding created sociability within the park, creating a sense of community that is unrivaled by any other skateboard park in the world.

On April 25th, 2002, Love Park was closed by city officials for renovations. Despite the contradicting statements issued by politicians regarding the renovation of Love Park, the changes made to the park were an attempt to make it unskateable. The renovations to the park included the replacement of stone benches with wooden ones, grassy areas along the eastern end of the park, and the introduction of new planters. Mark Brandsetter, a skateboard videographer, commented on the renovations, saying: "They put up these pink flower planters and these pink garbage cans that now all have urine stains down the side of them…they put up all these hideous wooden benches…it's not like they really designed anything, they just kind of took a bunch of stuff and threw it in, and that's how it felt."

Many people, both skateboarders and non-skaters, strongly disliked the final result of the renovation. PPS has the current (renovated) Love Park on its "hall of shame" list, because the renovation rendered the park practically useless; the heavy police presence makes people feel on edge, the planters are ugly, and the benches are uncomfortable and small.

Despite the renovations, individual skaters, politicians, and companies have tried to put solutions forward to create a compromise for the use of Love Park. On July 22nd, 2003, the Coalition to Free Love Park made a proposal to the municipal government, with the hopes that the park would be re-opened for skating. The proposal set out to create a multi-use plaza, which would cater to both lunchtime users and skateboarders. The first proposal was to allow skateboarding from 3:00 p.m. onwards on weekdays, so that the skaters of Love Park do not interfere with the lunchtime users.

The coalition also requested that the marble benches be brought back, and for some of the pink planters to be removed to make the park more skateable. Another proposal brought up by the coalition was to put protective coating, such as steel tips or polymer, to protect the ledges, yet still allow them to be skated on. The coalition also suggested making up an organization that would raise money to repair any damages caused by skating, so the city would not have to pay for anything.

The final proposition brought up by the coalition was to have two zones strictly for pedestrians. The zones were to have corrugated material on the ground so that skateboards cannot roll smoothly over them. The corrugated ground would be used at one spot dedicated strictky to pedestrians, and the other would be in front of the *Love* sculpture, so tourists could have an unobstructed photo.

In June, 2004, DC Shoe Company offered to donate $1 million dollars over ten years if Love Park could be reopened to skaters. DC has special ties with Love Park; Love regulars such as Josh Kalis, Stevie Williams and Brian Wenning ride for their professional team. DC has also shot many commercials at Love Park, and dedicated one of Josh Kalis' pro model shoes (the "Verdict") to the closing of Love Park. Despite the generous offer, the city refused the donation, and the Mayor vowed that he'll never let skaters return to Love Park.

"Instead of treating these children like criminals, we should be welcoming them with lemonade and Tasty-cakes..." - Ed Bacon

*A 92-year-old Edmund Bacon shows his support of skateboarding at his creation, Love Park.

Jere Stuart French, author of *Urban Space,* reminds us that "Urban spaces, from any time in history or any society on Earth, can tell us much about the quality of life enjoyed by its people." The activities in a park or public space can represent the quality of life in the whole city. Philadelphia is in a population crisis, losing 4.3% of its population between 1990 and 2000. It is interesting to note that between 2000 and 2001, the same time in which skateboarding was criminalized, the population dropped 1.8% in that year alone. Although people are leaving Philadelphia, the outflow of people is much less than other large cities, like New York. The main problem is not necessarily the outflow of people from the city-it is the fact that Philadelphia cannot attract new residents to replenish the population. David Thornburgh, of the Pennsylvania Economy League, says that "...the real heart of the challenge is not keeping people here by building higher walls, but to increase the flow of people to the city...Demographers tell you that the people who are most likely to move are better-educated, younger people ages 20 to 44...They move for jobs, education and to take advantage of the vitality driven by the buzz associated with a particular place."

Now that the ban on skateboarding is strictly enforced and the park has been renovated, the city lost the interest of a crucial demographic, one that could foster the growth and development of the city. In *The Rise of the Creative Class,* Richard Florida believes that municipal leaders are catering too much to companies, and are not trying hard enough to attract the "Creative Class," a term he coined to describe the younger, creative generation. He states: "I have heard countless people across the country use the same phrase to describe the inability of their city's leadership to adapt to the demands of the Creative Age: 'They just don't get it.' In most cases, their leaders are doing everything they think they can to spur innovation and high-tech growth. But most of the time, they either can't or won't do the things required to create an environment or habitat that is attractive to the Creative Class...

In 2002, Florida gave a speech at Moore College of Art & Design, explaining how cities can succeed in the modern economy by catering to the lifestyles of creative workers rather than the financial desires of corporations. He addressed the closing of Love Park by saying: "Skate parks are very important to young people, an intrinsic part of their creative culture, part of their identity...To take the park away is to tell them that they are not valid. Big mistake."

Before 2002, Love Park was a symbol for Philadelphia's acceptance of youth culture, sending signals to the world that the city is a hip, creative place. Andrew Hohns, an investment banker, believes that Love Park is the key to attracting youth to the city, saying: "Love Park is an international symbol of youth and vitality, an image Philadelphia desperately needs to project...The park also brings life and vibrancy during the evening to an otherwise underused city block. It provides a generous amount of free publicity for the city, and generates a significant amount of tourism.

So far, over 4,000 people from over 36 countries have signed an online petition to open Love Park to skateboarding. The park is an integral part of attracting youth and tourism, but it is insignificant with a skateboarding ban, which restricts the use of the space. The park must be open to all, not just people who would like to sit down and have lunch. Closing the park to skaters, or any sort of activity, makes the city less desirable for the "Creative Class."

In addition to losing the interest of a young demographic, the city is also missing out on a huge financial opportunity by restricting skateboarding. Board sports are the fastest growing type of activities among youth in America ages of six and older. Skateboarding is the second fastest growing, bringing the total to just fewer than twelve million participants, according to the Sporting Goods Manufacturer Association's study of sports participation.

The skyrocketing interest in skateboarding also means that the revenues gained from the sport are exponential. Miki Vuckovich, editor of *Transworld Skateboarding Business,* said that the skateboarding industry created $1.4 billion in sales in 2001, up from $510 million in 1996. Philadelphia also reaped the benefits of being a skateboard haven in 2001 and 2002, hosting the ESPN-sponsored *X-Games,* which can be considered the Olympics of participant activities. The events were held at Love Park and City Hall, and generated approximately $80 million for the city's economy over the lucrative two-year contract.

Love Park was Philadelphia's symbol of youth and cultural progressiveness. Skateboarding at the park made Philadelphia one of the most popular cities in the skateboarding world, one that had the potential to be a city that could profit greatly from skateboarding, both socially and economically.

There are many reasons why Love Park is closed to skating, but there are even more positive reasons to reopen it. Edmund Bacon believes that the ban on skateboarding in Love Park is totally absurd, saying: "It's an absolutely socially unacceptable thing for these paunchy councilmen to sit there and say these kids can't [skate] when there is absolutely no reason whatsoever for it. People come to the park to see the skateboarders...for goodness sake!" Not your typical elderly, authority figure's opinion.

Erik Ellington, a teamrider for Baker Skateboards, brought up a very interesting point to the Philadelphia Daily News, which adds to Bacon's argument that there is no reason to ban skateboarding in Love Park. He comments on the connection between skateboarding and political popularity, saying: "I heard that Mayor Street, who banned skateboarding in Love Park, was named one of the worst mayors in America by Newsweek...Mayor Daley, who welcomes skateboarding in downtown Chicago, was named one of the best. You think there's a connection?"Although skateboarding does not solely impact the public perception or popularity of a cities' municipal government, Ellington's comment highlights a much broader problem: the failure of Philadelphia's authority figures to respond to the needs of the public.

The ban on skateboarding in Love Park and the refusal to make any compromises is a small example of the rigidity the Philadelphia municipal government displays towards public demands. In addition to the government's unwillingness to compromise on the matter of Love Park, the government created a stigma towards skateboarding, branding skateboarders as criminals.

Liz Kerr, a skateboarding activist, believes that Edmund Bacon's positive attitude towards skaters and skateboarders is the key to making Philadelphia a better city, saying: "This is the man who said that, 'Instead of treating these children like criminals, we should be welcoming them with lemonade and Tasty-cakes.'"

It seems a bit hypocritical of the government to turn its back on the one activity that made the city world-renown, yet reap the benefits of being home to one of the most famous (and notorious) skate spots in the world. The municipal government not only turned their back on skateboarding, but also turned their back on the thousands of skaters who are part of a generation that have the power and ability to shape popular culture.

In a letter addressed to the Philadelphia Inquirer, Kathy O'Neill criticizes the municipal government for wanting to improve the image of the city, but taking the wrong measures to do so: "Mayor Street should be doing all he can to encourage these young people to come to Philadelphia. He talks about improving the image of our city, making it a hipper place. He bent over backward to bring MTV's reality show to Old City. But the city continues to ban skateboarders from Love Park and banishes them to the hinterlands of the city under I-95, in FDR Park. This policy must change."

In a city that is so desperate to attract young professionals, the government will never win the younger demographic over with the current mentality it maintains. Without allowing for compromises to be made between the public and the government, Philadelphia will continue to work fruitlessly in improving its image. Despite all the potential benefits that can be created from the promotion of skateboarding in Philadelphia, the city believes that the negative effects from skateboarding outweigh the positive, and stand by the decisions they have made in the past.

Although skateboarders still try to skate Love Park, the police strictly enforce the ban on skateboarding, therefore restricting the use of what should be a public park, open for all uses.

"There are many reasons why Love Park is closed to skating, but there are even more positive reasons to reopen it. Edmund Bacon believes that the ban on skateboarding in Love Park is totally absurd, saying: "It's an absolutely socially unacceptable thing for these paunchy councilmen to sit there and say these kids can't [skate] when there is absolutely no reason whatsoever for it. People come to the park to see the skateboarders...for goodness sake!"

## *SCOTTSDALE'S FINEST*

by Brown

Cops. Pigs. 5-0. Po-Po. Fuzz. Heat. Donut Munchers. Assholes. There are many names for cops and authority figures as there are for skateboarders, punks or society as a whole.

Skaters in general are wary about cops. Maybe it's because of the environment they've grown up in or because there are so many useless laws on the books like curfew and jaywalking.

Authorities come in all shapes and sizes. They are easily recognized, however, because they are usually wearing a uniform or some monkey suit and barking in your face. Cops, code enforcers, tax men, city council, local and federal government are prime examples. Their only function is to keep the machine well-oiled and running, and this poses a problem because skaters can never really be true law-abiding citizens. We will always be at odds with these people. Maybe it is because we chunked up a small piece of their concrete jungle or we haven't given up some money we worked so hard to earn. We see the world different than any other humans on this planet. Who else says, "Shit...check out that ledge, its super clean?"

Understandably society has grown frustrated with authority. Every skater, young and old alike, has had run-ins with police; every skater has their stories. These can range from being stopped for speeding or ticketed for trespassing. Although I have had a few positive experiences with authority, for the most part the officers I have dealt with are arrogant and rude. Since I was young they have shown little or no respect for me, and I've had so many terrible experiences with badge-wearing idiots I've lost count. The following story is among the most memorable.

I was skating in downtown Scottsdale, Arizona when I was struck by a car. I was not injured at all because the car was slowing to a stop to make a right hand turn. The woman driving the car got out and apologized profusely. Even though I assured her I was alright, she gave me her insurance and personal information.

By the time we started to go our separate ways a small crowd had formed. Among them was an employee of a local ice cream shop who informed me that he had called 911. I explained to him that I was fine but that I would wait around for the paramedics. They dispatched a fire truck, an ambulance and of course, two squad cars because one is never enough.

From the moment the cop got out of that car I was no longer the victim. As he walked towards me I informed him that I was physically fine and no help was needed. He ignored me. I tried explaining what happened, but he didn't care. He was not out to respond to an accident; he was out to intimidate. He said something along the lines of "Skating in Scottsdale is illegal..." and I quickly disagreed with him.

"We're too busy to be dealing with punk kids like you..." he informed me.

"Look man, this is bullshit." I said.

Instantly I was in handcuffs. Before the second cuff was slapped against my wrist one of the yuppie passerby's said that he would be glad to testify against me. Among other obscenities, I started yelling, "Testify!? Testify against me for what you piece of shit!?" The cop quickly responded with "Disorderly Conduct" and I was soon on my way to jail. While I was in the cop car, I was kicking the divider between the rear seat and the front, yelling at the cop explaining to him how dumb he was. Needless to say, now he really wasn't happy with me. When he pulled me out of the car he pushed me into the wall, then tightened my handcuffs until it hurt. I was fingerprinted, jailed and finally released to my mom. I never received a ticket in the mail or an order to appear for court.

Experiences like these are bad for society, and skateboarder or not, just about everyone has had a problem with police. This tends to be because of the zero-tolerance (on anything) policy adopted by local law enforcement. No longer is there the local friendly policeman actually looking to protect the beat in which he or she may serve. Instead they look for reasons to either harass, ticket or arrest the average citizen either to meet their unofficial quota we are all so familiar with and raise money for the city. There is no concern for age or reason. In Whitman, Massachusetts, two boys, both age twelve, were arrested and shackled for skateboarding in front of their homes.

There are reasons people get pulled over for having one taillight smaller than the other. There are reasons that 97-year-old ladies are getting carted off to jail over upaid parking tickets. No longer are policemen, policemen; they are revenue agents, and the system works something like this: first officers are hired and instructed to write tickets for just about all offenses, in lieu of arresting. These tickets are then paid by the receiving party. These monies provide the city with more funds to pay for various government agencies and actions, including police departments and self-appointed raises. This in turn provides them to hire more policemen, to write more tickets, to raise more money, to hire more policemen. It is a vicious cycle. This is why skateboarders are ticketed for skateboarding, trespassing or vandalism.

In a truly free country our government would generally have no right to tell us where we can't walk or that we can't skate on public property. Everyday they pass new laws to restrict our freedoms. How long will it take before we have no rights at all?

So what can the average citizen do about all of this? There are many ways to fight the system legally. So put down your dog-eared copy of the Anarchist's Cookbook and that Molotov cocktail, at least for now. When I was arrested for being a skateboarder (I mean hit by a car) I never received a fine or did any time in jail. I did get the name of the arresting officer and his badge number, and I wrote a formal complaint against the officer to the Scottsdale City Police Internal Affairs Department. I received a reply stating they would investigate the matter. I wrote a few follow-up letters and received absolutely nothing back. Being young at the time I gradually lost interest and dropped it, but to this day I still kick myself in the ass for doing so. I firmly believe that had I pursued the matter I could have got some attention to the case. Maybe even perhaps some media coverage to show the abusive practices of the Scottsdale city police towards skateboarders.

If you should ever receive a ticket for anything, fight it. Although it can be easier just to pay it and be done with it, you can also fight it without much effort. In most states, in lieu of appearing, you can write a letter stating that you plead not guilty. Be forewarned this does waive your right to a speedy trial. However, the issuing officer must now appear in court when you do; if he fails to do so the case is dropped. This happens more often than you think. Also in most states, if you lose you are entitled to another trial. File the paperwork; most likely they will realize that it is more profitable to drop your case and move on to the next more easily manipulated person. Remember, the city in which you live operates like a corporation; treat it that way.

In the last analysis, it's not up to police to make the laws, only to enforce them. The problem is that most police officers do not treat people with respect. This only furthers their alienation from society. If they could only realize - the harder you push something, the harder it pushes back. If police were more understanding and rational they could actually connect with society. This is very important and yet they fail to recognize. If an officer of the law is patient and understanding towards skaters and society alike, they are more likely to achieve their goal. For instance, if an officer came up to me and said, "I understand that you're just trying to enjoy yourself skateboarding, but if you could just find that imaginary place somewhere else..." I would bounce. This would be far more effective than, "Hey punk, I'm sick and tired of you guys vandalizing this property. Don't you know you're trespassing? Get the hell out of here."

In general when skateboarders are treated with respect, they tend to do likewise. Unfortunately we live in a society where we may never be treated with respect by law enforcement. This has many underlying consequences. How can a skater respect the law if they cannot respect the authorities enforcing them?

All things considered, I think we live in one of the best countries in the world. We have a lot of luxuries that we take for granted. One of the best things about this country is that the people have a voice. The people that founded this country were a bunch of aristocrats that didn't want to pay taxes and stood up for themselves. So take your stand. There are 330 million people here; take a look around and do what you can, but don't forget to live.

Skateboarding keeps us young in our hearts and young in our minds. So get off your ass and go skate, while you still can.

## SKATEBOARDING IN WASHINGTON D.C.

by Keir Johnson

Ever since I first began skateboarding at the age of twelve, I've noticed that one thing has always been a consistent factor in my life: free time.

Skateboarding requires the sacrifice of free time. That is, budgeted time that is solely for the purpose of being outside riding your skateboard where and whenever that might be. While many other people participate in structured lifestyles and traditional life sequence events, many skaters live open lives...on purpose.

In Washington D.C. having this sort of free time meant that as a skater, downtown on the weekend you'd witness many things that most people would not. At Pulaski Park, on 13th & E St, we would often see presidential motorcades with secret service assault vehicles and police cars come charging down Pennsylvania Avenue. Many people would stop and watch the motorcades as they came down Penn. Ave, yet as skaters we were happy because it took the police presence off of us. In fact, any time there was a protest like the Million Man March or the March For Peace, we were always excited at skaters because we knew it meant we would have Freedom Plaza to ourselves that day.

Our free time is rewarded and aided by people who have come out of their element to joint a protest in the city. It's no wonder that some of the best days I've ever had skating downtown were due to war protests and peace marches. Washington D.C., for hundreds of years, has been the vocal point for every major protest against the government and the authority figures who represent it.

Though skateboarding has only existed for about twenty years in the city, we've now forged an unwritten pact with the protesters and marchers of the world. When they come to our city to voice their ideas and protest the authority figures of the world, they entitle us to free reign of the city. In at least a small way we are able to appreciate our day because of their sacrifice to a particular cause. To all those in the struggle out there, respect.

"Those young dweebs were really getting a kick out of this; they definitely played high school football. One of them actually focuses my skateboard...I'm left with a broken deck, tail between my legs and ready to blow."

# *READY TO BLOW*

by Dave Miller

Tap downtown over to red arrow (before they turned it into a gay-ass ice skating rink), that spot ruled...red granite ledges with enough flat to rock out anything you wanted to. That place was like a mini skate park. I know I'm taking a chance, but better at night than in the day where I might split a pedestrian's shin wide open. I'm pushing hard, building up speed, plenty of grates to bust flips over, especially when your going Bill Kaschner fast.

I've been practicing this wild-ass trick with my buddy Matt. It's like a half-heel flip to 360 wrap around the same foot you flipped with...(editors note: this trick is most commonly known as the lawnmower or front foot impossible. Mattias Ringstrom does them on vert, and they were very popular in the H-Street days). I got two shots in and low and behold, the po-lees is there, showing up in packs; honestly there had to be about five squads, and of course one of them is a hard-nosed seargent; he's got his motorcycle boots on, lookin' like a complete dweeb. The other ten blues build a circle around me, one of them confiscates my board, the Danny Way VW board.

Hardnose walks up to me...he's a close talker; right up in my grill. "What the fuck do you think your doing? This is a sacred place; this is a testament to the men killed in (some war)...I should break your board and kick your ass..."

I'm shaking for real because I've been close to and have heard stories of these Milwaukee police kicking some ass. I'm like, "sorry..." What am I supposed to say? I'm not gonna go on a long rampart about how we skaters have nowhere else to go. I'm like, "look...I'm sorry...it's late...no one's around...I didn't think it would be a big deal."

The shitheads are all laughing. Those young dweebs were really getting a kick out of this; they definitely played high school football. One of them actually focuses my skateboard; I'm not kidding. After that they leave, I'm left with a broken deck, tail between my legs; and ready to blow.

"After listening to a random lecture for about five minutes and being thoroughly embarrassed by being detained for nothing more than holding a skateboard in a fast food restaurant, I mustered up the courage to sarcastically spit out 'Thanks officer, you're doing an excellent job...keep up the good work.'"

## *COLD FISH SANDWICH*

by Leland Ware

Despite what numerous people told me throughout my life, for me skateboarding is not just a fad that I will grow out of.

It all started when I was about ten years old. My friend Frankie down the street got a banana board called "Big Red" and gave me some old relic from the 60's, a rectangular plank, with roller skate trucks and steel wheels; man I wish I still had that thing for the mantle. We went butt boarding down the hill we lived on that day. It's been on ever since.

Twenty years later, the majority of my friends are professional skateboarders. I work as a videogame tester in San Francisco, and still ride my skateboard on a daily basis. I don't see any of this changing anytime in the near or distant future.

My earliest memories of dealing with authority through skateboarding are the campus security guards at Washington University in St. Louis. I lived behind the campus. As street skating began to progress in the late 80's and early 90's, my friends and I discovered that Wash U was architecturally perfect for what we were trying to do at the time; it was filled with benches, stairs, a quad that was lined with ledges and many different-sized handrails. The campus had it all.

I began skating there on a regular basis with friends when I was in the 7th grade. The obvious problems of noise and destruction of property made us instant targets of campus security. When we were younger kids we would generally get the boot and as we got a little older the security guards would confiscate our skateboards. We quickly learned the security guard's schedules and best routes of escape through campus. After awhile it became a game. We would skate as long as possible with the full knowledge that at any moment we might have to run or skate as fast as we could to avoid getting our boards taken. As I grew older and traveled to different cities, I discovered that being ready to run at any moment wasn't a unique experience. In fact, it was pretty standard. A popular slogan from that era was "skateboarding is not a crime." Our philosophy from a very early age was "skateboarding is a crime, but only if you get caught," and we weren't getting caught.

Over the next ten years I lived in the Midwest, on the east coast and eventually settled in San Francisco partly because it was a Mecca for street skating. The one thing that seemed to be a constant everywhere I went was police and security's hatred of skateboarders. The feeling was, and still is, mutual. I think it's because skateboarding isn't something that can be controlled or contained. It will continue regardless. Society is largely based on control. We are expected to essentially do as we are told. When doing what you're told conflicts with doing what you love then there is a problem. The police and security are doing their job of controlling for money; the skateboarder is skating because they love it. Love is always a stronger motivation than financial gain; therefore skateboarders work harder and faster to facilitate skating than the cops do to shut it down.

Everywhere that I've skated there has always been a method to the madness. Skate with a large group of people, at the first site of cops or security scream "5's, 5-0, Po Po" etc., run in opposite directions, reconvene at a predetermined location and head for the next spot. This organized chaos is quite effective. Confused police or security do not know how deal with a scattering crowd therefore giving the skaters more of an opportunity to escape. If you do find yourself in a situation where you might get caught, throw your board in the bushes or a trashcan, walk away, and come back for it later.

Despite numerous close calls, unpaid tickets and warrants, I've actually never been arrested for skateboarding in over twenty years. If anything, this has clearly illustrated to me and perhaps the skateboard community as a whole, the general incompetence of most police. I mean if they can't catch or stop some kid on a skateboard, then how are we supposed to believe that they can catch a master criminal? Furthermore, if police are wasting time chasing a kid on skateboard, while a violent crime occurs nearly every minute in this country, I am lead to believe that police for the most part aren't on top of their game. This loss of faith in the basic infrastructure of society leads to a great deal of questioning of the system as a whole. If police aren't really able to successfully do their jobs, then how about the mayor, governor, or even the president?

I think on a really basic level, skateboarding conditions you to question things that the average person may not notice. You begin to wonder why things are the way they are as opposed to blind acceptance. This is probably the core of how being involved with skateboarding has shaped many a skateboarders' perception of authority in general.

One experience that really drives the point home for me happened roughly five years ago. I was living in the Richmond district of San Francisco and had taken the California bus downtown to the Embarcadero to go skate Pier 7 with my friends. When I got off the bus I was hungry, so I decided to stop at Carl's Jr. for a burger. As soon as I stepped inside the restaurant I noticed a bunch of younger skaters. I didn't think much of it at the time other than, "I hope these kids don't start asking me a bunch of questions." The kids had already gotten their sodas when I stepped up to the register to order my fish sandwich and fried zucchini. I was in the process of paying when I heard the general commotion of kids running out the door and a loud, "STOP RIGHT THERE."

I looked to my right and noticed a middle-aged man in a police uniform entering from the opposite side. I could literally see the hatred in his eyes and instantly knew he didn't like skaters.

As I stood waiting for my food, I heard him say "YOU, GET OVER HERE... NOW."

Surprised, I looked at him questioningly and responded, "me?"

"YEAH YOU, GET OVER HERE..."

At this point I could feel all the eyes of both patrons and employees on me. I walked over and he requested my I.D.

I asked, "what did I do?"

He explained, "skateboarding is illegal in San Francisco," as he wrote down my information.

"But, I'm not skateboarding," I coolly responded in an attempt to remind the irate officer that we were in fact inside of Carl's Jr. and my freshly ordered fish sandwich was waiting for me on the counter.

"Well, now I've got your information...so if I catch you again, I'm gonna take you in," he barked back.

Needless to say, I was pissed, but I managed to keep my cool. After listening to a random lecture for about five minutes and being thoroughly embarrassed by being detained for nothing more than holding a skateboard in a fast food restaurant, I mustered up the courage to sarcastically spit out "thanks officer, you're doing an excellent job...keep up the good work." He returned my I.D. and I returned to my lunch.

With the full knowledge that I work 40-plus hours a week and have taxes taken out of my wage to pay his and many other salaries, I couldn't help but wonder what other wastes of flesh's salary I was helping to pay. I am sure that there are many...

“The root of the problem with skaters and police starts with the fact that skateboarders in general have been marketed this idea that they have a right to skate anywhere they want, anytime they want, on anything they want, and that anyone who tries to stop them is the enemy.”

## *A STRATEGY FOR SUCCESS*

by Jim Gray

I think the best starting point to understand a person's viewpoint on the topic of skaters and authority is their background, because that drastically affects their viewpoint.

I personally have had few problems with authority while skateboarding, and have only received one ticket (for no pads at a skate park). I have been let off countless times when caught skating in places I should not have been (mostly backyard pools). I also grew up in an era of private skate parks, and lived in a hotbed of skateboarding. I then became a pro skater and was privileged to be aware of many great places to skate with no hassles, or was in a position to make those places for myself. I rarely found myself in need of scouring the streets for something that I enjoyed riding. I also grew up skating mostly on transition, so I don't have a lot of desire for finding a set of stairs in a public place, so I haven't been in the position that most skaters find themselves in very often.

That alone makes my starting viewpoint a little different than the average skater who only skates places he gets kicked out of. I have been around skateboarding and skateboarders for a long time. I started skating around the age of ten, was sponsored at the age of twelve, and have never stopped skating since. I am now forty-two, so that's 30-plus years around many generations of skateboarders, and 30-plus years experiencing the public's attitude toward skateboarders.

I started working in the skateboard industry in 1986, and started my own skateboard company in 1991, so for nearly twenty years I've been very involved in that side of the industry. I've sponsored many skaters and witnessed their interaction with authority as well, and I feel I have a good understanding of what is going on out there. I've also been reading skateboard magazines for thirty years and have seen how they have portrayed the clash between skaters and authority over that thirty year period.

Personally, I think the problem with authority and skateboarding is a natural clash between two groups that just don't understand each other. You can call it authority vs. skateboarding, or adults vs. youth. I see the authority side backed by the lack of tolerance currently existing in our society (at least in the U.S.) for anything not fully understood by those whose job it is to monitor and control. Then add in a few police egos, toss in a side of lawyers scaring everyone involved about their liability, and the authority side is ready to battle.

Like most things that come out of my mouth in regards to skateboarding and skateboarders, I guess my feelings about authority and skateboarders will probably piss some people off who prefer fantasy to reality. Those who think all the problems are purely the fault of the police and other authority figures are the same ones who will walk down and buy a skateboard made in China from a skateboard brand whose stock is traded on Wall Street and at the same time tell you how hardcore they are. Contradictions are a big part of skateboarding, and marketing is a bigger influence on skateboarders than most people will ever realize.

I feel most attitudes towards authority start in the pages of magazines, and on video. We react to what we are taught, and skaters are taught that authority is out to get them, and that they need to rebel against all authority.

"Hey you...got your pads?"

The root of the problem with skateboarders and police starts with the fact the skateboarders in general have been marketed this idea that they have a right to skate anywhere they want, anytime they want, on anything they want, and that anyone who tries to stop them is the enemy. On the other side of the coin, you've got cops, security guards and the like being taught rules in black and white, with little room for gray area.

Here is a simple example.

I recently met with the watch commander of our local police department to discuss the over-policing in our local skatepark. His opening viewpoint was basically "the law says helmet, elbow pads, and knee pads and that is what the city attorney has told us to enforce." Marty Jimenez and myself gave him a bit of a lesson on the history of skateboarding, showed him magazines with no one wearing pads anywhere in them, and tried to let him see the skateboarder's viewpoint of the situation both from what's being sold to them and the reality of why they hate the discomfort of pads. His biggest concern was that his job is to enforce the law - period.

We brought up the fact that probably one in every ten people stopping at a stop sign does not stop long enough, and is technically breaking the law, but that they did not have officers sitting at every stop sign in the city just picking people off one by one. We told him we felt that cops coming to the skatepark every fifteen minutes to write tickets was like fishing in a fishbowl; just picking easy targets. We seemed to at least educate each other somewhat on our different viewpoints about the issue, and since then the police have not been quite as aggressive at our skatepark. They still are coming, and while I wish they were not there at all, I am not that stupid to pretend that we will just make them go away. I just feel good that I was able to get them to sit down, and that the results will help ease the tension between some of the skaters and the local police. I think skaters have to be part of the solution if there is going to be one.

On the other side I hear skaters in the park all the time saying how lame the city is for making the law (which is actually a state law that the city had nothing to do with), and how lame it is for the cops to write tickets. I agree with the latter part, and I hate to wear pads too. I also hope to be part of a group that someday gets the pad laws changed to some extent because no one else is going to do it for us. What sucks is that the skaters don't realize that the law which allowed the city to build that skatepark without fearing being sued also contains wording forcing the cities to enforce pad laws to maintain that protection and keep the skatepark open, and they hold that against the police to start with when they had nothing to do with it.

Then, when a skater cops an attitude to the police or park rangers who come to enforce a law that they didn't make, but are told they must enforce, then they just fuel the fire for authorities' misunderstanding and/or dislike of skaters.

The sad reality is if both cops and skaters have bad attitudes towards each other, only the skater is really affected because we need them to be mellow for us to have a good time, but they don't really need us at all. That's just reality, and something skaters need to keep in mind. It's part of why cops in general sometimes have a cocky attitude. They don't have to be nice, but if you are not nice to them, then you had better watch your ass. If you mouth off to a cop when they pull you over in your car, you might be dealing with a search. If you say "sorry, I wasn't paying attention to how fast I was going," then you might get let off with a warning.

There is a lot of misunderstanding on both sides of the issue; that's just one example from my personal life. I know most clashes exist with skaters out in the streets, industrial parks and retail centers, and they happen on both public and private property everyday.

You have to put yourself in someone else's shoes to understand their view. I don't think skateboarders put themselves in the shoes of police or property owners very often. If they did they might have fewer problems with cops and get out of that ticket more often. They also might get more help in solving their problem of not having anywhere to skate, and might not have so many problems skating around town.

I think many skaters are harassed because the last time the guy whose job it is to keep people out of some big building or somewhere like that was told 'screw off' or whatever because the skaters didn't want to deal with the reality that they didn't have a right to be there. If they would have just bailed quietly, that guy might not be such an asshole to the next skaters he encountered. Skater's attitudes towards authority affect how the next person is treated.

I think skaters need to understand their right to skate vs. the right of others to protect their property. Sure, you should have the right to ride a skateboard, just like you should have the right to ride your bicycle, but what do you have the right to do on your skateboard? Most skaters would be pissed if some guy just decided to ride his bicycle over the hood of their car. They'd say "what the hell are you doing?" They'd want to kill the guy. Do you think the bicyclist saying, "bicycling is not a crime" and that you should just chill out is going to make you any less pissed and want to let the guy screw up your car?

I don't think so.

To some guy who watches a 100-million dollar building downtown with $50,000 marble benches, it's the same thing. He's thinking how could you be so stupid to think you have the right to screw this bench up, and at the same time he knows he is going to lose his job if he just lets you do it and looks the other way. The question is not whether you have a right to ride a skateboard, because you should have a right to ride your skateboard. Should you have a right to cause damage and destroy public or private property? I know what you would say if it was your property and it was not a skateboarder doing the damage.

No skater wants baseball players to throw balls at and dent the crap out of their garage door because the baseball players have the right to play baseball and they think it sounds cool when the ball bounces off your garage door, just like you like the sound and feel of grinding a marble bench. Skaters also would not like rock climbers to climb their house because they don't have a local rock climbing wall, because it's irritating when someone uses something that's yours without any respect for its value to you. It's easy to understand those examples and also easy to find them ridiculous because they seem so unlikely, but that's because those groups have a place to go, and skateboarders often do not. But, if they didn't have somewhere to go, would you put up with that?

On the authority side of things, most involved on the other end are too old to start skating now, so they will probably never know the feeling we do. That is a part of the misunderstanding. We all know that once you are addicted to skateboarding, nothing and no one is going to stop you from the incredible feeling of rolling, but to someone who doesn't know that feeling, they just hope the annoyance will go away so they won't have to deal with it. If they understood the feeling, realized it wasn't going to go away and that we weren't going to stop, then maybe they'd be quicker to assist in finding solutions to the problem. That is, if they felt we were worthy of helping, but sometimes after being told to go to hell a hundred times, you can't really expect someone to go out of their way to help you.

So, what would I like to see? I'd like to see the skateboard industry use it's power and energy and help use the statistics it has on the number of skaters in society relative to other sports to force cities to accept the fact that skateboarding is not going to go away, and work to come up with solutions to give skateboarders a place to go. I've done it myself in my local community and now we have a thriving skatepark. We've gone from the misunderstanding by some that skateboarding is a bunch of bad kids to the city now fighting over where the second park is going to be built and demanding that the second park be twice as large. We only got there by standing up for ourselves, learning how it's viewed from the other side of the fence, and working within the system to make it happen. That is what it is going to take to get skateboarders accepted by society, and it's happening all across the country, but only because a few skaters have gotten together to make it happen with little or no support from the skateboard industry itself. Take a look and see what some skaters have done to help skating progress and have places to skate. Places like Burnside in Oregon, Washington Street in San Diego, and the San Pedro project would not have happened if skaters didn't take matters into their own hands and make things happen.

Okay, so my viewpoint is mostly just about skateparks, but what about the streets? Well, if you don't want to skate in a park, fight for a plaza, a skate spot or some other alternative, but don't expect that society as it is today will ever just let you ride on anything you want, anytime you want. Realize that bicyclists can't ride anywhere and on anything they want, and that boaters can't take their boats anywhere they want, and if guys decided to play football in the parking lot of the local mall, they would be kicked out, too. They might not be kicked out as fast, but still they would be asked to leave at some point. The reason they have places to do what they want is that over time, society accepted what they do as normal, and included them in as part of the culture. Skateboarders and skateboarding are getting there, but we have a long way to go.

Also, giving in to the reality that you need to work with the system fights that very urge to rebel that has been spoon-fed to skaters by very wealthy magazine publishers who just happen to own a large stake in the skateboard business, as well as other skateboard company owners who will sell you any attitude that keeps you buying products. Your anger to authority fuels support for their brands and keeps them in charge, living a good life, and eating well off your dollar. They have private facilities for them and their teams, but you and your buddies are left to fend for yourselves. You should be as equally pissed off at the industry that could have and should have helped get skateboarding more accepted in society as you are at that jerk of a cop who is kicking you out of some spot. If all the energy used to fuel anger towards authority was used to overcome it, we might just live in a land of awesome skate spots.

So that's my dream, and I know there are a million stories of pointless skate harassment, but I believe the overall problem will only be solved if skaters stop whining about being picked on, and start doing something about it.

Whatever your viewpoint is about skateboarding and authority, I think your view is only worth as much as you've done to help get something accomplished for skaters and skateboarding. You can be part of the solution, or you can be part of the problem. It's your choice, and you can choose whatever path works for you, but my respect is for skaters who support skaters, not just those who feed off of them.

## *SKATE LAWS FROM HELL*

by Clarkie

California Assembly Bill 1296

Perhaps the biggest abuse of authority in skateboarding history stems from the 1997 California bill AB 1296 written (or poorly written I should say) by Orange County conservative and "safety bunny" State Senator Bill Morrow.

Skateboarders actively participated in what we thought was a push by the International Association of Skateboard Companies (IASC) to get skateboarding on the hazardous recreational activity (HRA) list to exempt public property owners from liability resulting from skateboarding injuries. We were under the hysterical assumption that skateparks would not be built without this limited liability law.

However, the writers of AB 1296 did not intend to put skateboarding on the HRA list as was assumed. It is written with references similar to the HRA list, indeed declaring skateboarding as a hazardous activity, but it was actually written and put through the California Senate as, "An act to amend, repeal, and add Section 115800 of the Health and Safety Code relating to liability in skateparks." The law finalized was better known as, the "helmet and pad law."

We now know they meant that skateparks could not be built unless helmets and pads were worn. This was never expressed to all of us who signed and circulated petitions and the law must have been "back room" written as skateboarding never found its way to the HRA list. The HRA list is simply a list of activities such as hang gliding, sky diving, tree climbing, mountain and trick biking, and spelunking that the respective disciplines got themselves on to relieve public entities of accident liability; no safety equipment requirements attached; no hidden catch.

The root of all evil is this from AB 1296: "(a) No operator of a skateboard park shall permit any person to ride a skateboard therein, unless that person is wearing a helmet, elbow pads, and knee pads."

The law gives cities an alternative to enforcement: "This law can be satisfied by compliance to section (a). The posting of signs at the facility affording reasonable notice that any person riding a skateboard in the facility must wear a helmet, elbow pads, and knee pads, and that any person failing to do so will be subject to citation under the ordinance required by paragraph (1)." In other words, as long as they post a sign, it's cool.

Also, more craziness; this law was only effective in unsupervised parks and only covered skaters fourteen and over, and only if they were doing a trick. What the hell were they thinking? Does this mean that to be within the liability protection clause a city would have to disallow anyone under fourteen to enter a skatepark?

In spite of its flaws and confusion this law seemed alright and something we could live with to some extent, and if it meant skateparks could exist without the threat of lawsuits and perhaps more will be built in the future, right on. We liked the idea of "unsupervised" parks, though it didn't make sense that helmets and pads were required since skateboarding is so low on the injury list and pads aren't needed for anything but vert. We were also thinking it wasn't likely that cities would choose to enforce it, taking up police time not to mention court time babysitting skateparks enforcing helmets and pads that don't really have anything to do with safety in the first place. Cities wouldn't be liable for injuries, skateboarders would be skating without cops chasing after them, skating where it was legal thus reducing the annual stack of tickets a skateboarder collects, nobody could get sued, and all the city had to do was post a sign and walk away. This would be cool, right?

Wrong!

California State Senate Bill 994

Enter good 'ole SB 994 - "An act to amend and repeal Section 115800 of the Health and Safety Code, relating to liability."

AB 1296 stayed in effect until January 1, 2003. In 2002 in spite of all the problems cities and skateboarders faced, another push by IASC was put into effect before AB 1296 sunset. Petitions flew around everywhere: in all the skate parks, skate shops, magazines, online, and door to door to save AB 1296. The catch phrase was "save our skateparks." Yup, they said all the skateparks would close unless AB 1296 was repealed and extended. SB 994 did just that.

While there were huge problems with the law, there was plenty of time to address the problems, deal with the gray areas, drop the helmet and pad requirements, get rid of the age restriction and rewrite a sensible law; or better yet let it sunset and seriously get skateboarding on the HRA list. Skateboarding should no longer be governed by cops, and skaters should not be charged exorbitant fees or get criminal records and rap sheets for doing nothing wrong. Skateboarding has come full circle and has its place in society. It deserves the respect all other activities and group sports have.

AB 1296 had to change to stop the harassment of skateboarders. Everyone was appealing and pleading to get it changed. Cities did not know what to do. Skatepark groups, individuals, cities, parents, and skate mags were up in arms. I even know of a skateboarder lawyer who wrote a published document pleading with IASC and Senator Morrow not to put it through again and in spite of all that, it was pushed through the Senate with wording UNCHANGED and to remain in effect until January 1, 2008!

Unfortunately the SB 994 whoopla got a lot of publicity and as a negative result several other states got nervous, followed in California's footsteps, and began adopting similar laws. Only 14 states actually have put skateboarding on the HRA list and have no state laws or gear requirements.

## Abuse of Authority

So here we all are, stuck with this friggen' law for another two years! While some cities such as my own, Santa Cruz, were cool about it and just posted the sign, some cities took full advantage of the law in their favor. Mostly with a financial gleam in their eye.

It was up to each city to develop a municipal code and post it at their skatepark; however, the law was so poorly written that each city came up with their own interpretation. Namely to enforce or not to enforce, but for those who chose to enforce, it brought in revenue to the general fund. Some tickets with all the added court expenses amounted as high as $400. Some chose to enforce as a way to avoid "out-of-towners." You know the type; they travel, they have fun, many are pros or very advanced skaters who teach the local kids tricks, sign autographs, toss product. For a lot of them it's a requirement of their job. They may be a professional skateboarder whose company sent them to rape and pillage your town along with a videographer to make the next company video. Easy prey, since most are street skaters they are not likely to come equipped with helmets and pads. Big ticket right there! And they're traveling; not likely to appeal a hefty ticket.

Some cities abused the law just as a form of intimidation. Recently, Berkeley city attorneys decided to start enforcing the pad law and one day sent out their riot squad to ticket skaters. (editor's note: see back cover and inlay) Many skateparks are the new donut shop for cops where they park and write their reports, or take their break, or in general make their presence known for no apparent reason. Maybe some enjoy watching skate tricks. Since nobody ever used injury statistics as a reason for making helmet and pad laws and when all us stat-freaks like me crunched numbers, we found that skateboarding, like I said earlier, is very low on the injury list. A skateboarder would be the last person to sue a city for an injury. Come on, injuries are trophies! The company I used to work for sported the motto "Dedicated to Recklessness." Come on people, skaters don't sue. They may sue each other over trademark infringement, but never for an injury inflicted while willfully skating.

The majority of injuries to a skateboarder's body are afflicted to ankles, hips and wrists. What then, is the reasoning behind head, knee and elbow protection requirements? It doesn't seem like the lawmakers are too concerned about the safety of the skateboarder. Therefore, I freely and confidently call SB 994 a biased city's vehicle for harassment. Or, possibly revenge?

Revenge of the Soccer Moms

This is a story I just can't pass up the opportunity to tell. Forgive me, Scotts Valley and especially to the one city Council member Stephany Aguilar who worked intrepidly for over a decade in the battle to get the skatepark built. I even have a slight compassion for the cops as we know they only work under the direction of the city Council.

Sessions led the way and administered the Tim Brauch Memorial fund which raised $444K for the city skatepark in Tim's name. Out of city funds, a mere $70K was allocated. The skatepark was scheduled to go in on a former airport runway to be shared with a dog park and a soccer playing field. Lots of room. Conservative members of the city and city council fought it hard. After an at least ten-year battle it finally received approval. At the very last city council meeting which was only on the agenda to approve the bid, the soccer moms and dog park people organized a petition to have the size of the 20,000 sq. ft. skatepark reduced to allow for more parking spaces in addition to the 100 already in the plan for the soccer game-goers. The petition was horrible; I had never seen such bias against skateboarders and it got a lot of local press. They claimed a larger skatepark would attract more "undesirables" from out of town among other NIMBY rhetoric and that 20,000 sq. ft. was "gigantic." They did not want the skatepark and this was their final last-ditch effort.

The mayor was cool, and after a 4 hour meeting where over 50 people (including myself) spoke, pretty much said shame on you soccer moms and dog park people. The bid was approved in a vote of 3 to 2. The skate supporters cheered in victory. The two were pissed. One of them actually asked the room filled with skateboarders if they were going to wear helmets, because it's the law. This was the warning; I could tell what was coming next.

The park was finally built and it's an awesome Wormhoudt park everybody around here appreciates. Within a month of being open, a total of 83 tickets and three arrests happened. The cops even hauled away a 12-year-old for skating without a helmet. He ran. Gee, we don't exactly teach our young kids how to act while getting arrested, do we? Around here helmets have never been enforced neither at Derby or the Fun Spot so skaters were not use to this kind of heavy handed enforcement. Skaters from the bay area were getting ticketed left and right, unaccustomed to the helmet law suddenly being strictly enforced.

The cops had a lot of help in their ticketing campaign. The soccer moms and adjoining dog park people were monitoring the skatepark and calling police when they saw someone skating without a helmet or pads. They called police when they saw someone smoking a cigarette, though there is no law for smoking outside. They called the police and city council to report out of town license plates at the skatepark. They were determined to get back at the skateboarders. Funny that it was not a big news story when 20 girl soccer players flushed their socks down the public toilets resulting in a huge plumbing bill. But if a skateboarder looked at someone sideways, he was reported to the cops. Scotts Valley hired an undercover cop to monitor the skatepark. When he spotted helmet and padless skaters he would radio the on-duty cop to come and write tickets. Can you say witch hunt? These tickets after all the various city and county fees attached came to $360. Skaters could conceivably save some money by skating over at the grocery store lot where they use to skate illegally. It is outlawed there, but sports only a $30 ticket.

I went to court with the skaters and their parents. It had been reported in the local paper the day before that Scotts Valley was down four police and facing a 600K+ deficit to the general budget. Yet they paid the salaries of the undercover, the City Attorney, and the ticketing cop to sit in court half a day to prosecute skateboarders!

To this day there have been three closings of the Scotts Valley Skatepark due to graffiti. This isn't your usual run of the mill graffiti, but rather explicit messages to the cops. Could these messages possibly be counter revenge?

The future lies with you, seriously. A Southern California Skatepark group along with the new IASC executive are working towards getting the law amended to remove the pads, drop the 14-year-old age limit, and apply the law to both supervised and unsupervised skateparks. NOT GOOD ENOUGH!

We need SB 994 REPEALED, we need Section 115800 of the Health and Safety Code REPEALED. We need to let SB 994 sunset and we need skateboarding to be put on the HRA list. We need all of you to write to your local state legislature and assembly and make these demands. It must be changed for good! By the time this book goes to press there will be petitions and other information available for skaters, parents, authority figures and everyone else who has been affected by this ridiculous law.

It is said that skateboarders have attitude.

Maybe so, but I wonder which came first, skater attitude or abuse of authority?

“The majority of injuries to a skateboarder's body are afflicted to ankles, hips and wrists. What then, is the reasoning behind head, knee and elbow protection requirements?”

et
SCARECROW

# *I WANT TO BE SOMEONE ELSE, ANYONE*

by Jeff Knutson

Usually, there's this one particular look that they give me and he's doing it right now. It's Dylan, I think. Was that his name? Shit. We're already into the 3rd week of school and I still don't have all the names memorized. What can I say though, five classes at 35 to 40 kids each. I'm probably not doing that bad.

He's still staring at me from the back row, eyes motionless and he's slouching in his desk. He's got this messy-black, retro-new-wave hairdo. In between the rows of desks I spot that he's wearing some skate shoes and the now requisite too-tight black jeans. He keeps staring at me like that, like some life-sized paper cutout torn from the ad-pages of any recent Thrasher - just an illusion, some Hollywood backdrop.

Wait. Shit, was he the one who saw me at Burnside last week while I was pounding that tallboy of PBR? Is that why he's staring? No, I don't think so - I don't think that one was him. Shit, I hope not. I don't think that kid goes to my school.

Anyway, it's not important right now. Right now I'm starting class - today everyone is making their own zine, a project for the next two weeks. They've all been reading books that they've chosen and their zine will relate in some way to their book. But first, I'm giving them a background on zine history and zine culture. I'm even mentioning the zine's significance and relation to both skate and punk culture. It's a little speech I've prepared. This is a cool assignment. These kids don't know how lucky they are. We could have kicked off the school year with grammar lessons and vocab quizzes.

But it's still happening, and I hate it when this happens. I can't tell you how distracting it is trying to talk to a group of people - a group of teenage people - when one of them has some vibe thing going on, just staring at you. It's like silent heckling. I swear, it's so fucked up. I just keep going with my spiel (and I have sworn to keep the teacher-talking and lecture time to an absolute minimum) but before I know it I'm in the daze, that out-of-body public speaking thing.

It happened just last week, too. This girl, this innocent, smart, naove-looking girl all of a sudden shows up to my class in some ass-length mini-skirt. Like she somehow got up that morning and decided that, today is the day for the too-short mini-skirt, today is the day to try on being a teenage huss. Then she somehow decided that sitting right in front of me, in the front row, would be a good thing to do; her knees open just slightly under her desk. Totally inappropriate - how did she sneak past her parents like that? I'm not supposed to notice it, but I can't avoid it. As a responsible adult I'm I supposed to say something to her later - right after class maybe - but then that, well, that would mean that I was looking. And I'll be damned if I'm going to get into that kind of battle. I swore to myself while I stand there blabbering about last week's reading assignment, "If I ever have a daughter she'll never, never..." but that's beside the point because then I realize that I'm doing it; talking about one thing while I'm thinking about another. These types of things happen every day. It's kids being kids; testing things out, what's acceptable, what they can get away with, learning. Sometimes I think my job isn't so much about "teaching" *per se*, as much as being a guide for them. Sometimes I think to myself, "shit, maybe I'm not cut out for this after all."

But today things are going well and I've forgotten all about it. I've got them all going on their zine projects now. I'm all done talking and giving instructions. Everyone is bustling about the room - writing, cutting, pasting, folding, talking - it's a beautiful sight. One girl comes up to me with a handful of cut-out photos, pleading for a pass to go use the photocopier. This is awesome. This is hilarious. I've just created a classroom of thirty-five zinesters.

But then I notice Dylan - he's still just sitting there at his desk, motionless with this sort of snide-smirk on his face, looking right at me. I try looking back at him with some kind of goofy, confused look, but it doesn't seem to register. It's not the usual for him - he's a bright kid. And then it hits me - wait, is he fucking stoned? Hold on, maybe not - I shouldn't jump to conclusions. I can't tell if he's just toasted from a lunchtime joint or if he's actually giving me that one look - the suspicious one they always give me. Either way, it's now gotten to the point where it's kind of creeping me out.

Given that he comes across as an authentic skater - or at least one who actually rides a skateboard - I figure I'll give him the benefit of the doubt. This would explain his look. It's the look I get when they've caught on to me. He's figured out that I'm a skater but he's wondering what the hell I'm doing teaching high school - that must be it. I've seen it before - quite a few times, really. It's not the look of adulation one might expect when finding out that their English teacher skates. Rather, it's a look of suspicion - like a very articulate form of stink-eye; a look that reads: "How dare you. I'm the kid here. Skateboarding is mine and not yours. Just who the fuck do you think you are, anyway?"

It's easy to tell who's a real skater - the ones who actually care about skateboarding - not by what they wear or the scuffs on their shoes, but by observing if they give you this look. I respect them for it, really - it's a valid question. I mean, seriously, who the fuck am I?

I'm a skater and I'm a high school English teacher. I'm 27 years old but people are always telling me I look younger. Once, on my first day working in a new school another teacher was being a total asshole and - in complete seriousness - asked me for my hall pass. Most of my students don't know that I skateboard; most of the teachers I work with don't know either. Most people who skate with me don't know that I'm a teacher - some of them probably wouldn't hang out with me if they knew.

I've been told by high school students, on a number of occasions, that I should fuck off. I have also told lots of cops and security guards to fuck off as well. Twice in my short life as a teacher, students have tried to punch me in the face. I can't tell you how many times I've thought about punching a cop or a security guard in the face, although I've never actually done it.

I don't overtly advertise that I am a skateboarder at work. I'm not trying to be that teacher - the "cool" teacher - I'm not trying to revel in some false sense of popularity that I missed out on when I was in high school. I don't care about any of that. I'm a teacher because I think education - communication in particular - is important, because I think kids are great people to work with, and because I'd much rather spend my days hanging out with teenagers than sitting in some stuffy office somewhere or breaking my back for ten bucks an hour.

Really, I'm just trying to make high school as normal an experience as possible for these kids. I remember how awkward and painful that part of life could be, and I figure maybe I can do something to make that a little bit better for someone. If, in the process of that, skateboarding is discussed and someone labels me as "cool" then so be it. But when all is said and done, at the end of the day, a good number of students that I work with - most of them actually - couldn't care less about skateboarding and whether or not I do it.

The hard part for me is that I continually find myself in situations that test who I am, my ability to live in two very different worlds; one where I am an authority and one where I have been diametrically opposed to authority for the better part of my life.

And today, Dylan, Duncan, Devin - whatever his name is - he's doing that to me. It's almost the end of class now. Somehow a million little things came up - student after student coming up to me with questions - and I've been distracted all period. I'm pretty sure now that he's high. There are serious consequences for being caught high at this school - whether it's pot or anything else: suspension, expulsion, meetings with administrators and parents, weekend classes, prevention programs and all of the unnecessary stereotyping, out-casting and labeling that goes along with these things.

Not to mention the possibilities for parental punishment. You never know when someone's parents are going to just blow it off or, on the other hand, end up beating their kid - just downright abuse because someone at the school had to call home. It could be anything in-between. For some kids most of the normal consequences for something like this are a positive thing. For others I can't imagine anything that would want to make them go off and start getting high even more. All of the unknowns - the idea of being complicit in any of this - make doing my job more difficult every day.

Of course there are other options. I don't have to send him to the office or make some big embarrassing scene in front of his classmates. There's always the after-class one-on-one discussion. Sometimes just knowing that a teacher, some adult figure, has acknowledged that they're high and that they were making a fool of themselves is enough to get the point across. At the same time, as a licensed teacher I'm legally responsible to notify an administrator or the police of any threat to any student's health or safety. Lawsuits can and do happen all the time.

He's totally fucked up beyond belief - I'm positive of it now. I know because I've been there. Granted, I never really got high at school, that wasn't my thing. But I've been in that situation - on the brink, barely able to hold it together - in a public place no less. And no matter how humorous or cool some people might find it, it's no place for a 15-year-old to be. It's really no place for anyone.

I know this because he's not even looking at me now - he's straight-up passed out - eyes still slightly open - a sizeable pool of slobber collecting on the laminant desk under his mouth. It wasn't that look of suspicion and distrust after all. Some of the other kids have taken notice - now they're starting to say things. A few seconds pass but in my head they take forever. It's hard to tell if he's just going to pass out right here in my classroom, and if he's seriously that fucked up, or if he's just going to snap out of it, shake his head together and make it to the next class.

I have to wonder, is it even just pot? What else could he have been doing? Is it his meds? Is he on meds? Was this on purpose? I mean, teenagers are still kids and sometimes they have strange ways of telling us things. Is this some misguided, passive-aggressive way of telling me about some unspeakable thing happening to him at home? It happens.

But then, all of a sudden, out of the blue, he comes to. It's as if he just fell asleep in class and woke up, still looking pretty phased, nonetheless. Sheepish and giggling a bit.

The hard part for me now is to try and interpret what the hell is going on today, to try and figure out what the fuck I'm going to do about it. I watch the second hand on the clock creeping slower and slower while I'm stuck there trying to figure out which version of myself I need to be. And I really have no choice in this one; I am the authority here. But what kind of authority am I going to be? Can I be an authority without being authoritative? It is in moments like this when I think to myself:

*This is exactly why I shouldn't be a teacher;*
*This is exactly why I should be a teacher.*

"Are we to play along in order to remain mentally stable? The person who just couldn't take it anymore is looked at badly - but what was bad was the antagonist. Why blame the reaction?"

## *REALIZING THE LIES*

by Greg Lang

We are out there very tired and extremely ailing yet prevailing strong.

The framework society created is lined with contradictions and concepts to hold beings down. This life of fabricated stress, disease, hunger and hardship is demanding for everyone. There are no specific instructions for anything. In truth there are no real definitions. All you get are a series of norms created by whatever culture you happen to be brought into. Did anyone ever ask if this culture was good enough? Did anyone ever give you a choice to find a more suitable environment? How are you supposed to grow within these confines and contradictions?

Authorities want to know who you are, where you live, and what you are doing here. They ask why you aren't at work, how you make money, and how much you make. Furthermore, in a few moments an authority figure is going to force you to donate money to the system. If you do not conform they will destroy everything you have. They will take your life and home. The astonishing life you worked so hard to find and create will be gone.

Freedom is found in the sub-culture of skateboarding. Independence is the essence of it as well as the public's vindication. Skateboarders do not expect anyone to understand, nor do we believe they can. It is an activity that has to be experienced and offers a unique perspective of one's self.

Of course society is going to try and stop the act of skateboarding. We are the opposition to its rat race. Skateboarding illustrates what a society built in the name of freedom could actually be like. This is a double-bound society, a contest of contradictory rules predestined to everlasting disappointment. In one breath we are told that we are free. Then while riding a skateboard on public property we will be arrested, ticketed, and sometimes placed in jail.

I grew up in a medium-sized city in upstate New York. It is a conservative and pleasant little place nestled up against the banks of the Great Lakes. I share an affinity for it along with the other natives that inhabit its environment. Inside the infrastructure of the concrete jungle is a fantastic monument. It is a wonderful common triangular area where business types enjoy their lunch on hot summer days. One might find pigeons pecking at the stale breadcrumbs and tramps begging or sleeping on benches. Furthermore, it is a great place to people-watch as commuters catch the bus.

The area around the monument is also an ideal place to perform the wonderful art of skateboarding. It contains all kinds of different sized marble ledges that are terraced to form gaps of assorted dimensions. The greatest aspect of this creation is the smooth riding surface. The tile is forgiving to fall on as well as serving to maintain the wooden skateboards. It is a local favorite and at one time skateboarders would frequent its confines regularly.

There was a point when the general public began to recognize skateboarding as a nuisance and the municipality decided to place 'no skateboarding' signs high up on the light posts. These signs were much too high to notice unless one was specifically looking for them. Shortly after the signs were positioned in the area, the local law enforcement began sending patrol cars. Officers who used to pass without batting an eye began to violently harass the teenage skateboarders. Anyone over eighteen was issued a ticket enhanced with uncouth language used for intimidation purposes. There was not one instance when the needs of skateboarders were even considered to be of worth. We were just told to find somewhere else to go. Or worse they would just take us to jail. I was personally arrested seven different times and was in jail until at least 3 a.m. before receiving my consent to bail.

On one specific occasion I was skateboarding there with about five or six friends. It was late in the evening; therefore we would not disturb anyone trying to enjoy the area. The night air was crisp and we were having a wonderful time skating together. Time had stopped in our lives and we were finally free from the confines of school or our jobs.

Sadly for the law this night was no exception and after about 30 minutes a police car drove hastily onto the sidewalk. Anyone who was near the car was obviously scared and jumped for safety because the car was coming directly at us. A few companions panicked and struggled to set their feet in motion and get away.

The officer jumped out of the car exceedingly fast and began screaming, "Stop and get the fuck over here!"

When I looked over he motioned at the group to saunter over to the car. I think everyone froze for a moment before regaining composure. We strolled over to receive a lecture on how we should be living our lives. The officer's voice was reminiscent of a schoolteacher from a Peanuts cartoon; the vibrations would never be taken with any value.

When all is said and done it's the same old routine. You can't skate anywhere within the city limits. If you ask where you can go? You're sent home to play in your driveway. No matter what the age, you are perceived as an undeveloped, ignorant youngster. Additionally, sometimes you are treated like an animal.

Soon we were dismissed. In spite of this the member of our group whose skin happened to be black was given orders to come closer to the officer. Meanwhile, the rest of us were commanded to leave. Just as concerned friends would act we slowly walked a minor distance away. It was to hopefully insure that the well being of our friend would remain unharmed. He was given a supplementary scolding for at least ten minutes before being instructed to abscond.

Once our cohort was reunited with us we curiously asked what the officer had said. He began to laugh and described how the cop felt that his duty was to speak to our friend in a language he thought would be better understood.

The officer said, "If you are ever caught in my turf again I am going to jack your ass up and send you upstate." This was a blatant form of racism on behalf of the police officer and amazingly our friend shrugged it off with no trouble. Afterwards we disappeared and rolled off into the night.

Does it ever end? Is there a time when this stress is lifted? It lingers like a black rain cloud and when there is rain it makes matters worse. When do we get to relax and find some time to let it all roll away? It's not like we are asking for much. The problem is that people are all competing. There is no competition if you're not after something. So now we just sit here in patience and wait for our turn. Go look for a job, register the car, get insurance. Find an apartment. Go out and skate! Find time to paint the bookcase. Find money to pay for all this shit. Find a college to go to, get the transcripts, and pick a major. Go into debt to pay for college, fill out the application, and try to get accepted. Find some interesting classes to take. Now, it is time to make dinner; don't forget to pack a lunch for tomorrow because now you're broke. Try not to spend too much money anyway. Try not to feel bad about buying something if you have any money. Wonder if you look okay and will not be judged by your appearance. Pull up your pants. Don't get frustrated with the horrible drivers out there.

I will ask you: is this how it all begins? Do we all just walk in circles until we find a way to stop? Where will we end up today? That is an easy answer because it's the same place as yesterday. Is skateboarding the only thread that is holding us together? What if we did not have that? Would it be something else? What would the activity have been?

Soon you find out you have been let down for years and misled by someone else's interests. It's all to try and keep you herded inside the fence. The facts are hidden and only those that spend years looking for the keys are rewarded. After that, who is not going to emerge feeling superior to others without a mind? Are we to play along in order to remain mentally stable? Can the mind be pushed so far as to explode given a receipt of ridicule and laughter in return? The person who just couldn't take it anymore is looked at badly - but what was bad was the antagonist. Why blame the reaction?

My questions never stop and answers are hard to find. This can become more or less difficult depending on whom you know. Get into the right category or else. Power is amazing and greed is terrifying. I watch with fixed, wide eyes wondering why society thinks as it does? Nothing has to be the way it is within the framework of society. The skateboarders that are you and I, we define what people want to be.

"Freedom is found in the sub-culture of skateboarding. Independence is the essence of it as well as the public's vindication. Skateboarders do not expect anyone to understand, nor do we believe they can."

# *FLIPPING THE SCRIPT*

by Paul Cote'

As the progeny of old anti-establishment hippie types, my twin brother Chris and I spent a lot of our youth under the radar, ducking away from the authorities so my mom (a former public school teacher) could educate us on her own terms, without having to report monthly to the nearest school board for independent testing. The HRS (Florida's equivalent to California's CPS) would bang on our door almost monthly and demand we register to test or face legal penalties. Consequently, I think I was inbred with a natural predisposition to question authority.

After I fell in love with skateboarding in 1988, our new P.E. hour was devoted to skating the jump ramp in front of the house, and we had a ready excuse if the police ever showed up to scuttle us away: "We're only trying to further our education, officer!"

When we started hitting the streets to hone our skills on stairs and handrails, the same authority figures would inevitably intercede and try to chase us off. I always found myself skating toward the advancing officers instead of away from them; my rationale said we were not guilty of any misdoings, so why give the impression that we are guilty of doing something wrong when skateboarding is a perfectly legal undertaking?

I would gingerly approach the officer and ask the ever-popular and clichıd question, "What seems to be the problem, officer?" I would attempt to take charge of the situation, in my grubby jeans and crooked baseball cap, and that would usually prove to throw ol' flatfoots off their game. I never seemed to be intimidated by them, and never recall having to run from them. They would explain that they got a complaint from a business or administrator or whatever, and that they really didn't give a flying flip either way what we were up to. Most complained that it was a frivolous thing to have reported, and on most occasions they would tell us a good time to come back and skate without having to worry about being hassled.

My pal Nick Matlin used a clever psychological trick he discovered when a Georgia State Trooper pulled us over en route to the I-Level training facility in Tennessee for a big contest. Needless to say it was quite nerve-wracking watching the six-foot-four, flat-topped state trooper in his tan uniform and mirrored sunglasses approach our vehicle. As we exited the vehicle to allow his partner to search the car, Matlin asked the intimidating officer with a Marine Corp sticker on his citation book if he could spare a cigarette. The trooper lit up with him and for a moment they were on the same level: us in our basketball shorts literally hanging under our asslines; grubby, sweaty skaters with mops of hair and a slacker disposition coming from a background that he couldn't possibly relate to.

I came away from most of my encounters with authority with a somewhat renewed faith in humankind, not the sour attitude that most downtrodden skaters come away with. What the majority of us fail to recognize is that if your approach is calm and respectful and at the same time confident that you've done nothing wrong, cops quickly back down and assume their normal roleÖand that is finding any and every way possible to do absolutely nothingÖwhoops, must be my disestablishmentarian side peeking out.

As far as how these types of interactions have influenced my opinions of authority, I have realized that the position of an authority figure attracts exactly those types of personalities that are predispositioned to be corrupted by it.

There are two types of authority figures in my experience. It goes like this: 1) the kid that got beat up a lot in high school and finds a position of power to exact revenge on his/her oppressors: security guards or peace officers of some sort; or 2) the big, kook jock from high school who beat up on the soon-to-be-security guard or peace officer after football practice, that same jock who eventually enlists and goes on a tour of duty or two and gets federally mandated preference in hiring for state and county positions: cops.

Most of the police forces run along the same lines as the military, with a chain-of-command type of structure, making those already trained in that mindstate desirable. In either case it's a bad personality profile to be acquiring these jobs, and most skaters I know could never imagine themselves as the kind of buzzkill personality that could ever aspire to be an officer of the law.

The general populace has failed skaters by not recognizing the creative-expressive aspects of street skating, wherein skateboarders view a building or naturally occurring obstacle much differently than Joe Public. We find a trick to match the spot and perform it, adapting that object in a way unseen before. Society sees waxed-up ledges that stain their four hundred dollar skirts. When they see rainbow-like wallride marks, handrails with red and yellow paint streaks slashed across them and other precious inanimate objects defaced, they equate it with vandalism, and the property owners, usually affluent and held in high regard by the community, find themselves at odds with skateboarders, who are too young and usually too poor to matter to them or their representatives in government. No need to guess who wins that clash of sensibilities.

So where does that leave the lowly skateboarder? Resigned to roaming about the barren landscape as the homeless do, trying to find a hassle-free underground environment where they can set up their obstacles or pour some concrete and make a lot of noise without worrying about finding excuses for the authorities or begging for "one more go at it."

Couple this with the fact that many skateboarders are not yet voting age, and to expect politicians to act out of the interests of a group of the populace that cannot do anything to help them in return is a ridiculous notion at best; it's hard enough to find a politician that even acts in the best interests of their own constituency these days. But all political rhetoric aside, most skateboarders are just not that civic-minded. Unlike myself, they don't attend city council meetings to complain about not having one public skatepark in a town where basketball courts and baseball diamonds abound; instead they are out in the street hunting down new obstacles or perfecting that Cab kickflip over the pyramid hip at a skatepark fifty miles away for lack of a local facility. If they do have a skatepark, odds are it won't have a decent design or professional construction, or prior consultation from actual skateboarders as opposed to playground builders.

When I was given the criteria for this writing assignment, I was asked, "What are the effects of irresponsible authorities on young people?" I thought about the question for a moment, and, being the Zen-utopian thinker I am, I considered the other side of the argument while simultaneously thinking about my own stance on the subject. The other side of the coin presented itself and I immediately thought, "What are the effects of irresponsible skaters on the authorities?"

I think of all the security guards who seemed relieved after I had spoken to them, who told me about the "last group of whippersnappers or hooligans or riff raff" (insert your own antiquated youth reference here) and how they threw their soda cans at them and flipped em' off as they skated away, and I gotta tell ya I kinda feel sorry for the poor, uniformed schmucks. They wear dark-colored poly blend pants that are too tight for them, overdressed in the hot sun, all saddled down with walkie-talkies and clanging keys, usually the social outcasts of society, having finally found a way to retreat from the world and yet still having to contend with throngs of bratty skaters, bloodstreams surging with newly developed hormones and off-the-chart testosterone levels.

I have also met positive examples of law enforcement personnel, the guys who just want to make an honest living. Being a cop is a decent gig; four days a week, twelve hour shifts with good pay and benefits, and I have to admit, most of the cops I have known in my personal life (yes I have been friends with cops) seemed to be pretty down to earth, decent fellas. They would regale me with stories about how they used to skate, always trying to find a way to show me that they are, or at least were, "hip" and "with it." I would tell them about my skateboarding misadventures and they all seemed very fascinated by it.

One guy in particular whom I worked with at Hillsborough County Animal Control, Officer John Schnake, (he was an animal investigator by day and police cadet at night) would tell me amusing anecdotes about the "juvie perps" he had to tackle in the mall parking lot the day preceding. We always got along swimmingly; maybe it was my respect for them and the job they have to do that reflected in how I treated them, and while it's true that most cops go their entire careers without having to unholster their police issue, the reality of clocking in and stepping into potentially life threatening situations on a daily basis is something that most skaters will never have to think about. I have the utmost respect for those in positions of authority who choose not to abuse it, and the inherent risks involved in keeping our streets safer to skate is indeed worthy of praise.

Asking about the effects that irresponsible authorities have had on skaters is necessary, but must also be countered with introspection about the role we play, and how we are perceived by society. We usually don't look the part, but if you dig deeper most skateboarders prove themselves to be intelligent, engaging, creative and well ahead of the average "athlete." Skateboarding introduced them to concepts of creative expression that are hard for a non-skater to recognize, ones that open the mind to be unique and adaptable, with exceptional focus and problem solving abilities...and that lends itself to all walks of life, both physical and intellectual.

Authorities are a product of their environment. I'm quite sure there are a lot of mellow cops in Canada and places outside of the United States with lower street crime statistics. It's funny that some of the safest places to get away with skateboarding are in the sketchiest of neighborhoods, where the cops have much bigger fish to fry than the errant clack and grind of a heated street skating session.

"Asking about the effects that irresponsible authorities have had on skaters is necessary, but must also be countered with introspection about the role we play, and how we are perceived by society..."

"I think most people in authority, at least the ones who exploit it, are intimidators who know when they are able to bring another person down and steal their chi..."

# *DEVOLVE*

by Matt Goodwin

I've got respect for authority, and I see how it can be necessary if it is used the way it was intended. Hell, even communism was a good idea until you put it in the hands of power hungry totalitarians, but the people who seek positions of authority are most often the people who should never have them. Often these are people who were picked on or feel like they drew the short straw in life. They lack the flow of energy needed to keep content and constantly evolve, so they steal energy from other people.

I think most people in authority (well, at least the ones who exploit it) are intimidators who know when they are able to bring another person down and steal their chi. Usually this brings the average person down while making the intimidator feel better, but this is only temporary because a person who can create his own energy will be able to build it back up, while the intimidator has to find another person to knock down.

This is a vicious cycle that will continue to go on as long as bullies, cops, security guards and politicians continue to use their power and social status to bring people down. After all, there are real criminals getting away while another skateboarder receives a lecture and fine outside the grocery store or bank, and these people should take a step back and think about whether a ground-down curb is really affecting anybody. That curb serves a much better purpose when making a group of kids happy for hours and days at a time than it does being just a curb.

A skateboarder sees everyday life in a completely different perspective. If you ever see a skater get excited and it looks like nothing is there, look harder because that hip, handrail or three-stair is somewhere. The world just does not understand that skateboarders make a playground out of the blockades, steps and benches they stroll by every day, usually without giving any of these animate objects a second thought. I have seen a new set of stairs or a new marble ledge light a skater's eye brighter than cop floodlights in your rear view; I have not only seen this but I've felt it first person.

Authority figures have a choice of whether to be cruel or nice, and I understand either way they are just trying to do their job. Although the few nice security guards and police officers I have run into throughout my years of skateboarding have given me some tolerance when it comes to authority, there is the other ninety percent of the time when cruelty was the norm. The following is an account of one of those cruelties when a simple change in attitude from an adult could have changed my whole perspective on authority.

Junior year of high school - my friends and I geared up and met at the heathen's residence for a downtown Phoenix Sunday skate session. About ten of us packed into a few cars; I was rolling in the infamous stickered-up 1970 Volkswagen camper bus that Park Bench ventured all the way out to Phoenix in.

We roll up to Central and Thomas to skate the statue gap, marble ledges and gap to manual pad. Everything goes well and we were far from done, so we skate south down Central, hitting spots up all along the way. We venture into the restricted Deck Park; this spot was famous and we didn't usually get harassed by the police...yet.

We make our way down Central a little bit further, feeling good and popping stairs and gaps as we roll ten deep down the street. We make it to the wall rides at the Bank One building. Now this is a sketchy spot and we were there about five minutes when two cop cars rolled up on the sidewalk like a swat team on a drug bust. We scatter immediately. Nine skaters and all the pigs go one way, so naturally I go the other. I can see they nabbed one of us already, so I book. I'm scott-free walking towards the van when all of the sudden one of those bastards gets on me in a flash, takes my board, tosses it in his trunk, cuffs me and tells me I'm going to jail.

I join my friend already cuffed in the backseat, and they drive us about a mile in the wrong direction (away from the station in the avenues) talking shit to us the whole way. Finally, they pull off to the side of the road to write us tickets, un-cuff us, throw our boards out of the trunk and onto the ground. As we were walking the mile-plus distance back to the van, the cops followed us the whole way in their car, making sure no urethane touched their precious concrete.

I looked at the ticket and it read, "Skateboarding is illegal in the downtown district between Jefferson and Washington." I thought to myself that all those bumper stickers were wrong - skateboarding is a crime. Then I realized that simply because there is nothing I like to do more in this world than push a plank of wood up and down the streets, I am a criminal. Even so, I still look back on this day as positive because the good skate session far outweighed the bad cops, and I also learned a valuable lesson that day: if you get away from the cops, ditch your board in some bushes until the heat is off you.

The injustice I was previously speaking of is not as common anymore because there is less street skating and more park skating going on. We are now in the neat little fenced-off area like any other mental patient or transient is expected to be in. Skateparks were built so cops and security guards could have an excuse to kick us off the streets. Before they would tell us, "get out of here, go somewhere else." Now they have a specific place to tell us to go.

Now I'm not hating, because I am just as guilty of abandoning the streets for these beautiful new cement parks. These parks are popping up so fast and they are built so well down here in Phoenix that I forgot what the concrete at the bottom of a six-stair tastes like. The flavor is completely different; it is like comparing a fine whiskey to a forty of Olde English. One is great but the other just has that classic, perfected taste.

I am not saying street skating is dead and I know it never will be, but with the advent of beautiful, forty-thousand square foot skate parks it is on life support. My point is that kids today are seeing less oppression from authority, oppression that was so common on the streets five to ten years ago; oppression that gave us veteran skateboarders our askew views on authority. This younger generation of skaters is getting more respect because of a new tolerance for skateboarding due to the *X-Games*, full length feature films, Tech Decks and the Tony Hawk Pro Skater video game series.

I salute the kids who still go hit the streets. I know it's been a while for me. I love seeing all the street footage still coming out in videos these days, and I hope this motivates the young and extremely talented generation of skaters out there today. By street skating kids can learn the whole truth and learn to recognize the irresponsible authority figures for who they really are. Then they will see the whole picture a little more clearly and learn who not to trust, and which way to vote to make changes.

My stories of skate harassment do not stop there and that one was pretty cruel, but every story has to have a happy ending, right?

Everett, Washington, the summer of 1996. My fellow thrasher Brown and I were strolling the streets, headed towards a few known spots in downtown Everett. The first two were a quick bust: no problem, we're used to it. Now we were heading down to the last spot we knew of and whad'ya know? There's a cop setting up a speed trap directly in front of the nice waxed ledge. We stroll by nonchalantly, when we catch an inviting smile from the police officer. Paranoid, I get to thinking, "...turn around and skate right by his car" but just as I'm rolling by, he blurts out, "hey that's a nice waxed ledge over there." This cop is fucking with me right? Nope, he gets out of his car and says, "Skate the curb, let's see what you got."

So Brown and I throw down a session on the ledge, while Mr. police officer is clapping and cheering us on. Like any good cop, he got back in his car to go bust some real criminals and let the kids have some fun. As he was leaving he said, "Have fun but don't stay too long, I don't want to get into trouble." So we sessioned for about ten more minutes, respected his suggestion and took off to the next spot.

This was an authority figure in a position to make a decision and he chose to be nice. It took five minutes of his time but I'll remember that day for the rest of my life. If I could somehow extend all of my advice to authority figures that have the daily routine of kicking skateboarders off private properties and the occasional civilian hero who tries to kick us off public property, my advice would be to kick us out peacefully and we're going to leave without a fight, but kick us out like an asshole and there is going to be a war.

Even though the popularity of skateboarding is huge, realize what we have been through, and realize the likely residual feelings still held towards skateboarding by authority figures of today. To these authority figures we are just pests, not young men learning how to be adults! Skateboarding has taught me so much about authority, politics, friendship and true love. Once these authority figures find out how much passion is behind skating they will let up... hopefully.

For when I skateboard I fear nobody, feel no pain, and learn how to work both as an individual and as a team. So I say to the authority figures trying to bring us down - bring it. I would talk more about my views on the most threatening authority figure in the world today, but that is a completely different story.

"This was an authority figure in a position to make a decision and he chose to be nice. It took five minutes of his time but I'll remember that day for the rest of my life."

## *THE NEFARIOUS*

by Nate Sherwood

I have had too many run-ins with police, rent-a-cops, school teachers, violent pedestrians, suburban soccer moms, big city suits and dogs chasing me to write about just one brush with the law, but there is one funny incident that comes to mind.

It was this day at Water Front Park in Portland, Oregon where my homie David and I were skating. There were these horse cops who would patrol the park and basically hassle skaters only - never mind the hypodermic needles on the ground from heroin junkies or the strung out bums all over the place - they loved to bother us, give us tickets, talk smack and all sorts of other shit.

Anyways, David and I both had already accumulated a wad of unpaid tickets for skateboarding. I was fourteen with no I.D. except a bus pass that had the name Jeff Petit on it. I drew that on my bus pass for the sole purpose of giving it to cops who asked for I.D. for write-ups (Jeff Petit was an old skater from Marin who rode for H Street if any of you are old enough to remember that).

Anyway long story short, the cops were coming and I was chill, like, "...cool, another ticket for Jeff, hope he never comes to Portland..." David, not wanting to get caught, thought it would be rad to leave his board and jump into the Willamette, the most dirty-ass river ever. The dude jumped thirty-some-odd feet into the river from a bulk head that was built to dock Navy ships and he fucking swam to the center of the river and climbed the Burnside Bridge. He chilled there in the middle of the cold-ass river chock full of toxic sludge.

The cops trotted up to me and they asked me why I had two skateboards, and I told them one was for when it rained and the other was for when it was sunny. I made up a whole pile of shit about tricks and how one board was better for cruising on sidewalks while the other was better for tricks. They wrote Jeff Petit a ticket, gave me the bullshit lecture and I skated off to Cal Skate hoping Dave would show up. He showed up soaking wet and freezing. I bought the dude a slice

"David, not wanting to get caught, thought it would be rad to leave his board and jump into the Willamette, the most dirty-ass river ever. The dude jumped thirty-some-odd feet into the river from a bulk head that was built to dock Navy ships and he swam to the center of the river and climbed the Burnside Bridge..."

of pizza and some soda and we took the 5 interstate bus home and he made the damn bus stink so bad.

Being a skateboarder and being exposed to constant urban decay you run into a lot of threats in both the suburbs and the city. Dumb-ass janitors in the suburbs at school yards who for some reason love the shitty local school board that pays them six bucks a hour to clean gum and spitballs from lavatories and classrooms more than they love the creative expression of students who use the school or their parents who pay taxes to run it.

In the big city, the dangers ever so present are rent-a-cops or the fiending crackheads who want to jack you for your Bladd or vx1000 in the turbo ghetto. None of these dangers can compare to the magnitude of the police, who strike more fear into my heart than all of the above combined. They are the ones who have a badge and a gun and many love to abuse power anytime they can, to jack your camera or to slam you on the ground, crack your ribs and take you to jail, or fine you which is just the same as mugging.

The world has nefarious humans all over waiting to stamp out self-expression. This has nothing to do with just the United States. Greed and power is the work of all evil in every land. Look at Barcelona; it used to be a skateboarder's Mecca, now I see capped ledges there. I think that we as people should understand: anytime a society values property over human life or health, they have failed.

The nefarious will use every ounce of power they have to make your life harder, and the economy is what defines how a person will act when they stop you for skating. If they just had a pay cut, or better yet were fired, they are looking for a scapegoat. The poor want you dead for cash, viddy-cams, etc. The rich want you gone due to you damaging their wack-ass stale property.

The average traffic fine in the state of California for running a red light is two hundred bucks. I know people who have been fined three hundred and fifty for skateboarding. Now what do you think is more of a danger to society? Skateboarding down a sidewalk that nobody walks on due to the fact you live in L.A. where nobody walks anyways? Or running a red light that could hit a tanker full of gas and burn down four city blocks, kinda like the one I checked out on the news last night?

Police have no mind of their own, and cops have picked on counter culture lifestyles and artists forever. We are easy targets; we never have guns, we are peaceful people. If skaters start to rise up and show them that we are just as dangerous as any hard hitting gangster they would lay off us and go pick on emo people or Morrisey fans. I really think strength is missing from skateboarding as of late. I miss the violence we had before, great minds like Moses Itkonen, Sean Sheffey and Mike V, people who would not get pushed down by security or the law, people who took a stand for their rights as humans. If somebody would have rose up in Germany in 1939 we may never have had to go to war.

There are power hungry people everywhere and they love to fuck with us; that is a global problem. I hear stories of tickets, knobs and jail time in skate Meccas like Barcelona and the Czech republic. Skating is hated on in every land. We are different, like spiders. What is your first impression of a spider when you see it? You want to crush it, right? That is why they want; to crush us. That is why you and me get stomped by the police and they can't understand us - they can't understand our artistic minds, they only love shooting guns, driving big trucks and hoes who like country music. So their world could never see ours.

Creative people have been prosecuted since Socrates drank the hemlock, just as skaters today are faced with the same hate. "They love us when we give them seventy grand in taxes, but will cuff us if we skate on the sidewalk we payed for." Rob Dyrdek told me that and it is true.

Government is owned by huge corporations and lobbies who put money in Congressional pockets. I think the only way we will see the end of our strife or adversity is if we build our companies to the point where we can have some say in our laws and maybe turn some federal penal codes of our cities around, but until Tim Gavin and Don Brown have the power that Halliburton and Shell do, we will not see the great shit we all hope for.

"The average traffic fine in the state of California for running a red light is two hundred bucks. I know people who have been fined three hundred and fifty for skateboarding."

# *SKATEBOARDING MADE ME A BETTER PERSON*

by Scottie Vosburgh

The reason I got into skateboarding was simple: my friend Nick and I (both 11 years old) were aimlessly riding our bikes around and saw kids skateboarding in the parking lot of the grade school I went to.

With nothing else to do, we sat down and watched them for a while. Our interest grew immediately. We decided to bike home and grab our cheap Nash skateboards bought at Toys 'r Us and give skateboarding a try. We went back and those kids taught us how to drop off curbs and how to do the foot motions for an ollie. We must have been trying to ollie for four hours straight with nothing happening except the tail of the board hitting the ground. We enjoyed it though, so we kept riding.

The more I skated, the more I liked it. Even though I could only ride up curbs at the time and my ollie was about an inch, it was still fun. Pretty soon Nick's brother Jon started skating and the three of us became a small crew. We rode our bikes and skated everywhere that summer.

Almost every night our little crew would find ourselves at the same school (one that was located just down the street from my house) with up to fifty skaters. This place was one of the biggest hang-outs I had ever seen for skaters outside of a shop or skatepark. It did not take long for the school to try to put a stop to it, though.

My first encounter with an adult against skateboarding was in my first summer of skateboarding, which also marked the first time that my opinions and beliefs would be challenged. I had been skating for about three months and one day as I was skating at the school, the principal came outside and called me over. She asked me if I had been skating with all of the kids in the parking lot at night.

Without thinking about it I told her I had and she proceeded to give me a speech about how I should not be hanging out with older kids and told me to "please inform them to stop skating on the curbs."

With that she said goodbye in a cheery, grade-school-principal voice and went inside.

At this point, I was still impressionable by both adults and kids who were older than me. On one hand I wanted to follow with what adults said and be a good kid; on the other hand I wanted to be cool, especially with kids that were older than me. I contemplated what the principal had told me. I wondered, "Does she really expect me to tell these kids who were my idols to stop doing something they loved, something that had brought me to like them so much? Why didn't she just do her own dirty work and tell them to stop?"

I also wondered why she didn't want us to skateboard anymore. We weren't hurting anyone or anything. Needless to say that message never made it any farther than my ears. I still think of that principal on occasion when being kicked out of places. The more I think about it the more I realize how fake adults can be to each other and even worse, to children.

In junior high my skate crew grew by one or two people. It was awesome to have more friends that would skate, even though most of them quit as soon as it would get cold. Nick, Jon and I remained a constant crew and the kick-outs from adults became more frequent. Before we knew it, there was a script to these kick-outs that all parties involved would follow, most of the time without even realizing it.

"You have to leave..." a security guard would say.

"Come on, just one more try."

"That's it - I'm going to call the police."

No matter how many times I was kicked out of a place, it always confused me. I just didn't understand why we couldn't skateboard in certain places. I couldn't grasp why people could ride their bikes in the middle of some of the busiest intersections in Chicago yet I couldn't ride my skateboard in an empty parking lot. A lot of other questions started to come into my head that no one could give me a valid answer to.

For high school, my parents decided to send me to a Catholic school. In typing class, my freshman year, I discovered it wasn't just the people kicking me out of places that didn't like skateboarding. Some of my classmates had a problem with it as well. Brad, a rich kid who no doubt still sucks today, drove me to do something I have never done or been taught to do. We were all sitting in typing class when he started to throw Skittles at the back of my head while making fun of me for skating. I immediately jumped out of my chair and pushed his monitor into him as hard as I could.

The teacher intervened before anything else could happen but I could tell that I had hurt Brad three days later when I saw a huge bruise on his stomach in the locker room. The counselor sat me down and had a big, long talk with me about "being poor" and how I "couldn't take it out on other kids." This was, of course, the biggest load of bullshit I have ever heard in my life. First off, my family is not poor. We may not be as rich as most of the kids at that school, but by no means are we struggling to get by. And how does that at all relate to me standing up for myself in the face of blatant bullying, anyway?

I didn't understand why these people had such a problem with me, or why they thought I was poor, or why they thought that people who rode skateboards were synonymous with the mentally handicapped. I realized that day that spending my time outside on my skateboard taught me things that not all people learned, like equality and respect. I started to take notice of people; the people I hung out and skated with all came from different backgrounds: some had money, some didn't, some were of different color and ethnicity, and I hardly had an idea to what my religion was, let alone anyone else's. So I came to the conclusion that I did not want to associate with the people at my school or others like them. Their ideals of popularity, money and a lack of individualism, which they failed to see, were not something that I believed in.

Being kicked out of a spot was as much a part of skateboarding as the hardware was. I started to find that my friends had the same views and attitudes about people that I did. After being denied so many times for just having fun and doing something I love, I started to think that the majority of people sucked and I grew angry. But the more I skated, the more I realized that life shouldn't be spent being angry with people. You should do things that you love and so I continued to skateboard, despite the increasing opposition.

Sophomore year, one day after school, my friend Alex and I where skating in some office complex. I found an old, moldy wooden picnic table in a corner and I climbed on top of it with the idea of just ollieing of the end, but before I could even get to the end, I fell through. Five minutes later the cops showed up. They told me that one of the workers in a building "saw me cursing at the table and beating it with my skateboard." I was arrested on the spot, without concern to my injuries sustained from falling through the table or the truth. I spent the next eight hours sitting in that cell thinking about what had happened before my parents picked me up. Why I was constantly getting kicked out of places and arrested for falling through old picnic tables was never going to make sense to me.

Near the end of high school I noticed that it all comes down to politics: the citizens elect a leader. That leader has control over the law and if the law serves and pleases the citizens, the citizens then re-elect that leader. In this cycle, the underdog or outcast consistently gets stuck up the creek without a paddle. I now understood why we were getting kicked out of places, but I didn't understand why the majority did not like us.

Finally I graduated from high school and the kick-outs actually became few and far between. It turns out when you are some 18-year-old skating by yourself in a parking lot, people don't seem to care as much. It also helps when it's somewhere between midnight and three in the morning.

Our original small skating crew still keeps in touch; we're still friends. Jon is becoming a ripper. There is no doubt that out of the immediate crew he has the most talent. Nick still skates occasionally but has become a tattoo artist and spends a lot of time concentrating on that. I'm in school at Western Michigan University and skating as much as I can. It won't be long until I'm done and I'm going to look for a job in graphics somewhere in the skate industry.

I love the fact that a toy I played with as a child influenced such a huge part of the person I am today. Thinking of who I could have been if I would have never started skating actually scares me a little bit. Contrary to the cries so typical of authority, skateboarding has done anything but ruin my life.

# *THE ART OF DREAM BLOCKING*

by Airto Jackson

In recent years, one of the greatest deterrents towards skateboarding hasn't been the underwhelming desire to see your faced smashed against something while simultaneously being ticketed, though the allure is there. The greatest deterrent is skatestoppers.

Rumor has it that skatestoppers were invented by a Benedict Arnold of sorts from within the skateboard community. At any rate, kudos and a round of applause to him for making skating harder, because that's what it really needed. As if it's not enough to sprain ankles and wrists and knees and toes to start off the day, it's always fun to get to your favorite spot and find it's no longer a spot because it's been blocked.

Not only is it now useless concrete to anyone, but tourists who once considered these slabs the optimum place to hunker down their tired, waddling buns to soak up some of America's blood, sweat and wax are forced to sit at other locations littered with scenery of bridges, flower gardens and buildings. Boring.

Tourists love watching skateboarders; it's a fact. I've seen some manual thing that people get when they come here from distant lands. It says "check the museums" on one page and "local skaters" on all the others. What's to become of these tourists whose only desire is to come to America and bask in our world-renowned rebelliousness?

Skateboarders are right up there with Clint Eastwood, James Dean and the ultimate tattered-robe-wearing, bearded rebel known the world over, yes, I'm talking about the one on high who whispers in our ear to remind us of what we need to do; Obi Wan Kanobi. Sometimes you have to ask yourself what would Kanobi do? Cheers to those who block. In fact, it's such a great idea that it should be considered for other sports.

Imagine how awesome basketball would be if under the rim there were huge hunks of metal positioned so that every time you go up for a dunk, whammo...not only does your team get two more points, but you win a free trip to the emergency room because you came down and broke off pieces of annoying bone inside your ankle. Funtastic!

Not to be outdone, bowling might catch the drift and as a show of support choose to have sniper units placed behind the pin deck willing to knock off a few silent taps to the brain of anyone who throws a gutter ball.

Football would be much better off for having considered making the endzone an actual lava pit. It really keeps the rotation of players on the bench more fluid. Fluidity is the strength behind survival, or as Darwin would've put it, "something, something, something species, blah, blah, adaptability."

Adaptability has always been skateboading's hidden agenda. What better way to celebrate its malleability but to wander like urban nomads across the great expanse of superfun sites and gang ravaged wastelands? So, in reality, if it wasn't for whomever it was that created skatestoppers, skating wouldn't be evolving as fast.

Really, once you've looked at skatestoppers in the right light there's nothing to complain about. Cities spend millions in making what was once useless to many, even more useless to many more. Skateboarders abound and now get to feel the same fun discrimination that other groups have felt for seasons past. Imagine if there were slave ship blockers...where might America be now?

The point is when you're older and you're at the bar with your friends and you're all swapping stories about how you can't remember the dreams you had as a kid because they never came true, you can smile and remember that those pills you swallowed, though tough and bitter, were really blocking your dreams for your own benefit.

"Rumor has it that skatestoppers were invented by a Benedict Arnold of sorts from within the skateboard community. At any rate, kudos and a round of applause to him for making skating harder, because that's what it really needed..."

## *SKATEBOARDING: RAISE THE BAR*

by Anthony Pappalardo

Seventh grade: bad sneakers, bad hair, worse clothes and a jacked up, second hand, waterlogged Gator in my basement.

An oblong cardboard box waits on my doorstep. A square was cut out of the first issue of Thrasher I found. That four-inch square and money order would net me my first real set up.

I flipped through that mag a million times hoping everyday that board would be at my house and there it was finally. If you were willing to wait 4-6 weeks you could get a complete from Skully Brothers mailorder company for about thirty dollars cheaper than the rest so I was patient and it finally paid off.

I cranked the blue Gullwings down, popped the bearings into the 95a Slime Balls, mismeasured the rails and finished the worst grip tape job of all time. It took me five minutes to push my way to this double-sided curb near my house. Five minutes later I rode away from my first true boardslide and I was even cheered on by these cool dudes who drove by in a Monte Carlo yelling, "skate or die faggot!" and threw something that missed me.

If it would have hit me, it probably would have sent me on a downward spiral of substance abuse, chasing women and pissing myself a lot but I just tried to boardslide the curb again. Then this guy who worked at the pharmacy adjacent to the curb came out and told me to leave. I can't lie - at twelve years old or whatever age you are in the seventh grade this was all a pretty big kick in the balls: the wheels I got were way too soft and slid like shit, dudes called me a faggot and I was kicked out of one of the only spots I knew about; that was a rude awakening.

Waking up early on a Saturday and having some coach yell at you while you run laps to win a game that doesn't mean anything is a shitty proposition. In case you didn't know, most of us got sucked into this whole skateboarding shit because we hate being told what to do. And despite wanting everyone to accept how brilliant and creative skateboarders are, we're still a bunch of clowns jumping off shit, farting on stuff, being obnoxious and making people laugh and/or enjoy themselves.

This inspirational haven for degenerates isn't an art form to anyone who's not steeped in it, and skateboarding is either a commodity or a nuisance to authority. Our favorite pasttime takes place in public spaces yet so few of us have the knowledge of our right to these spaces or the impact that could be made by taking an active role in protecting the right to them. Was there a legitimate push to register eligible skateboarders to vote? Why do we know what brand of shoes some pro wears but not if there is any legality to a cop confiscating your board and giving you a ticket?

Skaters and their organizations should continue to challenge the perception of self-absorbed criminals set to bum the world out. We're witnessing an unparalleled boom that's giving skateboarding a chance to do something more than just continue to play cat and mouse with the world. You'd think that a light bulb would go off in someone's head with a six figure bank account, something like, "Holy shit; everyone thinks my profession is filled with a bunch of scumbags...maybe if I did something for the community the world might not think we just fart on each other and swear a lot." Much like a balding number cruncher grinding out a Silver Bullet soft ball game, skateboarding is in denial.

Sorry skateboarding - I'm critical of you, I think you have a tendency to be complacent and lazy. It's harsh, yeah, but you gave me so much and you're letting the world piss on you and treat you like a clown. Just standing for "fuck you" is pretty damn easy, so easy that it's cliché.

There's a greater consciousness of skateboarding's past mistakes and the learning process is giving birth to a new era, but most people still want to be the underdog. They're like Cubs fans that want the team to lose so they'll have something to bitch about. With the profile and power that skateboarding currently has there is so much potential to not only take care of itself and people supporting it, but also to show that we can do more than drop one liners when we feel threatened.

I have other truly shocking stories about harassment but I'd rather forget the time I had to spend a sweet night in Roxbury, MA jail, have a guy with a flat-top tell me I sucked and confiscate my board. We piss people off so much that cities will organize task forces, have cops dress undercover and use force to keep us in line.

## *WHAT DO WE OWE THEM?*

by Jeremiah Liebrecht

I had my first experiences skateboarding in 1986. I was nine years old. At fourteen I had my first experiences with resistance.

In the teenage years I was skating every day with my homies Justin, Bryan (RIP), Carlos, Mason and all of those dudes on a regular basis. Tony Hill, one of the older dudes, got arrested at Birney Elementary for boardsliding a bench. I was into skateboarding, too, and I knew trouble was close behind.

I started getting tickets on the regular, running from cops, heckling security guards...you know all the usual stuff (which I occasionally still enjoy).

The guys I grew up with started getting involved in graffiti, gangs and drugs, and as they started doing time in juvenile hall, a general disdain for authority arose throughout the crew. I learned exactly what the headlights of a late model Ford Crown Victoria looked like; memorized all back alleys in the hood; I wasn't going to be caught for skating.

While most of my friends were being locked up on various charges, I kept skating. Their contempt for the police came through the association of losing their freedom. Mine was derived from a lack of respect.

If you ask my Mom, she'll say all of my problems in school, and to some degree at home, were a direct result of my insatiable need to skate. Instead of homework, I would go skate until late at night then come home and read Engels, or Trotsky. Out on the streets I was getting into heated disputes with security guards that kicked me out of spots.

I've read so many pieces on the dynamic between skaters and authority growing up. As I read in *Thrasher* or *Transworld* and found articles and letters complaining about cops kicking skaters out of spots, I wondered, "Am I rebelling because I skate, or do I skate to rebel?" These lines became blurred. I knew that I skated for fun first of all, and at times the best part of that was running from cops. I had tirades ready for security guards, asking them who's property they were protecting. I'd go so deep as "It's the end of the world soon, who gives a shit if this marble ledge gets scraped up?"

Every skateboarder will have their stories of oppression. Getting kicked out of skate spots can be so minute compared to the everyday injustices perpetuated by these "keepers of the peace." To be honest, a ticket or some minor harassment is nothing but dumb luck - luck, in the sense that if you skate, and you have had less-than-inspiring experiences with policemen, you probably have a better grip on reality than most. Drug epidemics rage through poor neighborhoods. Bombs drop on foreign countries. You should be considered fortunate that a ticket is the sum of your worries.

One thing I did learn as I got older was that the chump security guard was actually a working class dude - probably underpaid with a family - it seemed increasingly pointless to harass them. Cops, on the other hand, I viewed as ex-military jock assholes that got off on violence and fucking with kids that could be doing so much worse.

In the past few years, I personally, have become complacent. I realize now that you can question authority and never get the answer you're looking for. If you enjoy exercising futility, fight the government.

What it really boils down to is, know your enemy. Is the working class security guard really worth spending your energy screaming at because you didn't get that front smith on video? Is it worth risking your freedom to fight when that punk, thug, jock or cop tells you to leave a spot? The bottom line is that these people are not in power. They just enforce it, and the systematic harassment is ongoing. Are they singling out skaters? I cannot imagine a recreational activity that has more legal restrictions on its practice. Amidst homelessness, the war on drugs, gangland murder, the war on terrorism, natural disasters and thoughts on how to boost tourism, skateboarding poses no real threat to the ruling class.

What I've shared here is just a little bit of my life; my association of skateboarding and my lack of respect for authority. I do not really believe that they are born of each other. I managed to stay out of jail and have not been locked up for skating, except one resisting arrest.

The powerful rich don't care if you skate or not unless it concerns their profit margin. Municipalities equally don't give a shit. Sure they'll build a skatepark, to corral you into one place, then dictate to you what protective gear you'll wear while you use their space. Tickets given for pads are probably distributed more than for skateboarding in a business district.

We live in the most free country in the world. We should not be quarantined to the skatepark we're supposed to be so grateful for, while Officer Asshole writes yet another ticket for not strapping pads and a helmet. While he'll justify that he's just looking out for your safety, he'll be the first to crack you in the head with a baton for assembling to resist unjust policy.

What do we really owe them, that we should be complacent to their rules?

"...despite the impersonal connotations of the vocabulary used to embody this concept, such as the state, the courts, the government and the law, the exponent is always a person..."

# *ON AUTHORITY*

by Nimal

The word "authority" implies power; an overwhelming power, but one that denotes a sense of objectivity, impersonality, and even fairness along with its grandeur. Yet, strangely, the authority we come to know in this society bears none of these qualities when examined.

The authority we are most familiar with is the local policeman. Some aren't too bad and possess a semblance of the three qualities above. However, this analysis is about the others, and in all fairness, the majority.

Your standard policeman is a complicated specimen. On attaining his position he begins to mull its meaning and the ideas of 'authority' and 'power' which he possesses. On doing this he undergoes a profound metamorphosis of identity. He soon becomes obsessed with his position's implications and what he believes his badge imbues him with. The authority vested in him becomes a defining aspect of his identity and, as such, the process of megalomania begins.

He quickly develops an unfounded sense of superiority to others. He singles out those he can get away with pushing around or those he believes to be inferior because of his racism: Blacks, aliens, skateboarders anyone deviating from the social norm.

His megalomania and delusions of grandeur unlock his latent and suppressed human instincts. As the gorilla demonstrates its dominance over other males in the band through rape, so the policeman attempts. He talks to the honest skateboarder or nonconformist with pure disdain, ensuring his nightstick is in plain sight when you talk back. His nightstick is long, hard and intimidating, a representation of his power over you...it becomes his symbolic penis that he will bludgeon you with if you get too obstinate; pure domination analogous to the gorilla's propensity. Do we even need to get into the implications of his pistol?

Is the bad cop's abuse of power directed toward some greater metaphysical cause such as preserving the peace or upholding the law? Or is it a selfish desire to build up one's own ego by pushing someone with impunity? When the person pushes back, we see the full blown primitive behavior of this policeman. His attempts at domination become his redemption, his outlet and his obsession.

As is obvious, the abusive policeman's actions are in clear contrast to what anyone would call for in a 'democratic society' and the great, yet many times ignored, idea of 'majority rule, minority rights.' These policemen is allowed to carry out flagrant violations of civil rights on nonconformists simply because he can.

The fact that skateboarders harm no one and break no laws, but simply utilize the very public amenities that their own tax money subsidizes, matters little when compared to the monumental prejudice of the policeman and the public.

At a certain level the rights of the minorities, however harmless their actions, become ignored. Mrs. Brown down the street will tell her bourgeois husband, "thank heavens those dirty skateboarders are gone..." unknowing this is antithetical to the very ideals of the republic in which she lives.

In the end the rights allocated to us come down not to what is written on a piece of paper named the Constitution, but from the prejudices of the people we live amongst. All those perceived as 'different' or 'deviant' become the object of this discrimination as they are the groups who receive indifference from the public in sight of such egregious treatment. The abusive policeman might as well defecate on the Bill of Rights, while others watch on.

But a discussion of authority would not be complete without touching on the macroscopic. Does the gargantuan hierarchy that controls this pawn of a policeman display these same characteristics of carnal domination? Indeed, it does. Despite all the academic claptrap and studies of the causes of the first World War, in reality it is not too difficult to realize that it became nothing more complex than a dick-measuring contest between the leaders of the European powers.

The very existence of authority implies domination, and despite the impersonal connotations of the vocabulary used to embody this concept, such as the state, the courts, the government and the law, the exponent is always a person; a person with the same proclivities to intolerance, megalomania and rape as your average gorilla or psychopath.

## *SKUNK NAMED PURPLE*

by Lizzie Lee

In 1977 on the island of Bali a fortuneteller looked into my eyes and told me that I am on this Earth to be a "healer." I never really believed in fortune telling, but I never forgot the word 'healer.' I don't dwell on it, nor do I live my life striving to heal. It just happens in my everyday life at the shop.

In the general public skaters are looked down upon. There's a stigma with the mainstream populace about skaters. I see it everyday. Dunno why? So, I guess it's not cool? Who cares because we're happy. It shows on our faces. One can feel the good vibe and energy when entering into the shop.

Perhaps this is my mission in life to make people happy and feel good about themselves through the little skate shop on Geary called the Purple Skunk. I can't quite pinpoint it. Like I said, I don't dwell on it. I just go with the flow and enjoy the ride.

I grew up with solid family values and a good foundation. I am third generation Chinese born in America. My parents worked very hard in the 50's running a small grocery store in the Western Edition district in San Francisco to provide us with a comfortable life and a good education. They taught me to appreciate life to the fullest and not to take anything for granted. I am an extension of my parents that I have great respect for.

Twelve years ago a new chapter in my life started. I gave birth to a little skate shop named the Purple Skunk where I became a mom, sister, and auntie...even a 'dude' to many. The accordion gate is pushed back, the key unlocks the door and the open sign is clicked on. Another day at what most people would call a toyshop. I call it a melting pot of life experiences. Everyday is different like a soap opera on TV. There is no set routine or script because the customers that walk through the door set the tone of the day.

There are several avenues I could have taken to live out my destiny in life. I chose to be a small business owner of a skateboard and snowboard shop.

I don't know who chose who, but I do know that I don't regret what I am doing for one second. Life is a constant learning whirlpool to better one's self and grow. No money could ever buy the experiences I have had in the twelve years of business through my customers and my extended family.

When the doors first opened in 1993, children from the age of eight to twelve walked in with curiosity to discover a friend for life - their first skateboard. Their wooden friend doesn't talk back. It's with you for as long as you want it to be. Kick it, flip it, roll it - it will always be an extension of one's soul. This is what has touched me because to this day, the same kid that walked in as a boy is visiting as an adult, still sharing and keeping me updated on what is going on in his life.

My staff and I have created a *joie de vivre*, youthful and happy environment for all ages and genders. We greet everyone that walks through the door. To exist for skaters that are in their 40's, 50's & 60's is like discovering the fountain of youth for them. What a great feeling that is! To see and feel one's passion for skating even enlightens my own enthusiasm for life.

To many the Skunk is a place where one can call home because there is no other place to hangout at for the moment. We were looked upon as the lawbreakers or troublemakers even though we're far from it. Just because we skated in front of the shop or sat on the curb smoking cigarettes, that made us bad? We're as normal as normal can be. Who stereotyped skaters or skate shops as being gnarly or scary? Funny how a friendly "hello" or "make yourself at home and let me know if I can do anything for you" can flip a customer's perception on skaters.

It took closing down for a few days to recognize the impact that the little skate shop on Geary had on the community. I didn't grasp how influential we were to the neighborhood until March this year. After all, I sometimes feel like the oddball shop because we're just a little different amongst the restaurants, banks and other businesses in the neighborhood. A little?

We papered the windows to do some remodeling. The neighborhood and customers freaked. They thought the Skunk was closing down. We never heard the end of it - "Are you closing down, you can't leave, where are you going, are you moving"? I was touched beyond words. The Skunk is here to stay for generations to come.

I remember an incident sometime back when a parent from Mill Valley visited the Skunk for the first time. He was on a mission to purchase a skateboard for his son's birthday. I could see he was reluctant because he had no clue about skating. I do recall him saying that he thought skaters were like dropouts, losers in life or punks. After several minutes into conversation and educating him on what his son was interested in, he changed his whole persona on skaters. He honestly thanked us for our time, for opening his eyes to not pass critical judgement on skaters. Chalk it up for total respect both ways.

Like they say "if you can't beat them, join them!"

I see a challenge, perseverance and drive on kids' faces that only encouragement will give them confidence in. You can always hear laughter during the day. How healthy is that? Very.

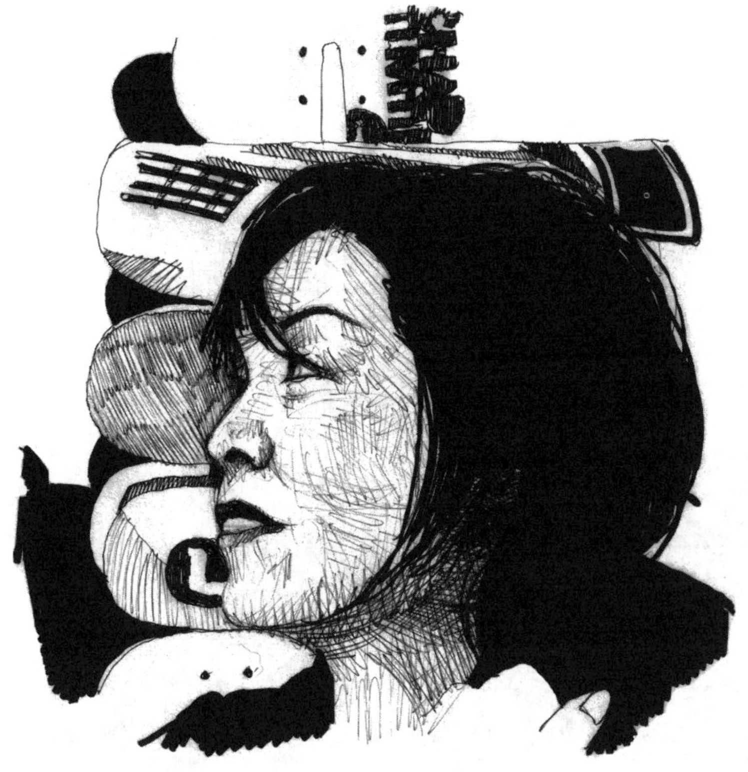

"In the general public skaters are looked down upon. There's a stigma with the mainstream populace about skaters. I see it everyday. Dunno why? So, I guess it's not cool? Who cares because we're happy. It shows on our faces."

"The weird cop, who I have always assumed was hopped up on speed, was freaking out, cussing at us, saying we're going to prison, running around and generally acting like a complete idiot..."

# *FUN WITH COPS*

by Joey Young

This is the true story of what happened to myself and some of my friends one cold night in San Francisco; our encounter with authority. I have not changed any of the names so if you're in here, sorry. I do not place blame on any of the participants. The police officers involved were doing just as many (if not more) drugs than (as) us. We did make some mistakes, but overall it was a very interesting experience.

In order to understand the progression I'm going to start a few months earlier on a visit to a friend's house in Minnesota. Dave was a handy person, with a bunch of cool tools in his barn. He had carved some pipes out of deer antler using a drill and a saw. I thought it was pretty cool so I made one too, although that day the power was out in his barn and I had to carve my pipe by hand. So, pipe in pocket I said 'so-long' to Dave and headed back to the city living my dream as a derelict skateboarder.

Months later I was living on a couch, packing my bags. The following morning I was to leave on a train headed for the small town of Visalia to visit my girlfriend, Dannelle. I had to get to bed early since the bus to the train station leaves the Ferry Building at 6 a.m.

In addition to myself the apartment was filled out with Luke, Sam, Cuervo and Jerry, who had just broken his leg. We decided to go out for a late night session. We drank some more Tequila and headed out the door, leaving Jerry, who was still in a lot of pain, with the rest of the bottle.

We headed over to the Federal Building, which was being rebuilt. Everyone has seen photos of the outside of the building, but before it was completed and skatestopped you could also skate the inside courtyard, on top of the banks. The layout was amazing. Granite hips everywhere. I was just about to launch a frontside ollie off of one of the banks, really concentrating of getting a good smack when I noticed there was a cop car looking at me. I quickly turned around and pedaled the opposite direction around the building, right into another cruiser.

Before I knew it I was face up against a wall in handcuffs. I tried to talk calmly to my captors, but all I got back was, "If you call me 'dude' one more time I'm going to put you in jail." There were three police officers; two men and a woman. The man who had my face pressed against the wall was acting very strange, the first thing he did was reach into my pocket and grab my deer antler pipe.

"Oh-Ha," he blurted. "Narcotics!"

He seems overjoyed. The woman was more calm, trying to be our friend obviously in the hopes of one of us saying something incriminating. I never had a chance to meet the third cop; he took off as soon as we were sitting three across in the police cruiser. The weird cop, who I have always assumed was hopped up on speed, was freaking out, cussing at us, saying we're going to prison, running around and generally acting like a complete idiot.

I was figuring we would head downtown to the police station or something, but instead we pulled around the Federal Building and into the hidden garage located in the basement. We were searched, had to turn in all our belongings and put in a little cell. Around this time they started asking my friend, Sam, why he didn't have an I.D. on him. He didn't want to tell them he was from Canada and here illegally so he just kept saying he forgot it at his apartment. This was before the big scam and deportations were not as common back then, but still, I was worried. Drug Cop was pacing back and forth really getting crazy with Sam, and the poor Canuck really didn't have any legs to stand on. They let Sam call his roommates and eventually Drug Cop had enough and announced he didn't have time to deal with some juvenile delinquent who didn't carry an I.D. so they might as well let him go. Sam, who was in the sketchiest situation, inches from deportation and no credible defense, was let go first. Funny.

A few hours of boredom later, Luke and I are joined in our cell by this college kid, who had gotten too rowdy at Fisherman's Warf. The officer standing outside laughed that he was wearing a skate shirt and they put him in with us. He did have a Quicksilver t-shirt, as many drunk college kids do, and proceeded to pass out in the corner. By this time I had given up hope of catching my train in time. Hours pass and we are moved to another cell, I am glad to hear we are now in the release cell.

Luke and I spend a good four hours in the release cell along with the drunk college kid, who has by this time sobered up enough to stand. Finally we are led out, they make us sign some papers and we get all our possessions back, minus my deer antler pipe. We also get a note that we are to come to the main police station downtown and pick up all our previously confiscated skateboards...bonus! We are officially released around three in the morning. It's pouring rain. We walk home, get inside, I set my alarm for five and fall asleep, bummed that I lost my good pipe.

"The officer standing outside laughed that he was wearing a skate shirt and they put him in with us. He did have a Quicksilver t-shirt, as many drunk college kids do, and proceeded to pass out in the corner..."

"With luck, communities will repeal their "no skateboarding" laws, labeling them as antiquated as slavery or prohibition. For that to happen, however, we need skateboarders as authorities..."

# *ROLL FOR OFFICE*

by Matt Derrick

I had my first taste of skateboarding in 1986. One autumn afternoon I went to a friend's house after school and rode around on his banana board while he tried to ollie on his Nash Executioner. I was instantly hooked, and I couldn't stop thinking about skateboarding on the ride home or before I went to sleep that night.

Skateboarding became illegal in my town about a week later.

I was appalled that something as innocent as skateboarding could be considered a criminal activity, and I instantly acquired a distaste for local authorities. I often wonder if this is really the case, however. Did authorities' attitudes towards skateboarding forge my rebellious spirit, or did my rebellious spirit choose skateboarding? I was a pretty well-behaved kid before skating, and for the most part, still am (other than skating itself). Did skateboarding help me to view the world differently?

In effect, I became a 12-year-old outlaw. I would never look at a police officer the same way again. Where once the badge held at least some level of respect to me, it became a symbol of "The Man" telling me what I could or could not do. I refused to believe that skateboarding was a bad thing. In turn, I came to feel that the people who were telling me that it was bad must have been wrong.

When NWA's "Fuck the Police" came out, I related to the song, as many other skaters did. The only reason my suburban self felt some shared sense of frustration with Compton gangbangers was the alienation I felt as a skateboarder.

When a police officer pulls you over for skating a curb in an unused parking lot, you can't help but be resentful. Surely there are more serious crimes being committed than skateboarding, even in the small town I grew up in. Why are skateboarders so persecuted?

There is something innately rebellious in the act of skateboarding in that there is a distinct lack of rules and regulations.

Where competitions are involved, you will likely see a few *ad hoc* panels or committees formed, but they are the exception, not the rule. There is no proper way to ride a skateboard; it's entirely up the individual. People have opinions about what looks good, or what is considered cool at the time, but they're just that - opinions. If somebody wants to do a "non-traditional" trick, it's still completely valid skateboarding, even if the masses may deem it uncool. If a baseball player wants to run the bases backwards, then the player is playing wrong. In skateboarding, breaking the rules is practically encouraged, whether through inventing new maneuvers, performing tricks on new terrain, or even in a more societal manner, such as living a nomadic or party lifestyle.

This can be hard for some people to relate to. Most things in our culture come with instructions; skateboarding encourages the individual to write their own instructions, to be one's own coach.

Skateboarding continually re-interprets its surroundings and adapts them for progressive purposes. This is a type of rebellion as well. Redefining a bench as a 'skateboard obstacle' is symbolic of a refusal to accept facts at face value. Whether conscious or not, the trespassing that so often accompanies a day of skateboarding is a rebellion against ideas of private property.

One reason parents may object to skateboarding is that it's not usually performed in a contained area. A kid can tell his mom that he's going to the YMCA to play basketball, but if he tells her he's "going skating," she doesn't know where he'll be. He might not even know himself; he may just cruise around and see what he finds.

Skateparks offer a different scenario. A skatepark can be a training ground of sorts where one can practice moves and develop skills. If properly designed, they can offer idealized terrain to entertain skateboarders and challenge their abilities. There are limits to this scenario, however.

Skateboarding began in the streets. The skateboard evolved from roller-skates and the box-crate scooter hybrids that came from them. Their first function was as a transportation device. To use a skateboard is to go somewhere on it. As a logical extension, the more you ride it, the more you see of your surroundings. The more you see of your surroundings, the more fun stuff you find to skate on. This hardly seems threatening, though the precariousness of early skateboards led the general populace to think of skateboarding as dangerous. Tricks soon followed.

Initially tricks were culled from gymnastic or figure skating sources: balance tricks, spins and the like. Later, the influence of surfing and the invention of the urethane skateboard wheel led to more fluid, dynamic tricks, often incorporating angled or transitional surfaces, such as empty swimming pools.

The infiltration of empty swimming pools is the start of much of skateboarding's outlaw image. Clearly, skating someone's pool without permission is trespassing, and possibly destruction of private property as well.

The growing popularity of skateboarding (and entrepreneurs' desire to make money off of it) led to the first wave of skateparks. Developers tried to make surrogate pools and contained areas for skating. For the first time, skateboarders had a place of their own to skate. Unfortunately, also for the first time there were rules to skateboarding. As most, if not all, of the first skateparks were private, you had an admission fee to pay. You also had to wear shoes, pads, and a helmet. For skateboarders who were used to riding by their own rules, this was hard to swallow.

Of course, many skateboarders bitterly accepted the rules and skated the parks. Having access to unique terrain led to new tricks and a general advancement of the activity. With the advancement came more rules, though, and many skateboarders couldn't accept them. Tired of being told when and how to skate, people started doing skatepark tricks outside of the parks, on the free and lawless streets.

Skateboarding was again back in the streets where it had started, with new tools at its disposal. The ollie revolutionized skating by allowing a rider to jump up curbs, down stairs, or over obstacles. Soon benches, handrails, cars, walls and just about anything else was a potential place to skateboard. This led to the current state of affairs, with skateboarding outlawed in many communities, and often seen as a menace to the smooth operation of society in general.

The unlimited potential of street skateboarding led to unprecedented levels of popularity, and coupled with greater media exposure, skateboarding is showing no signs of slowing down. Accordingly, many communities, afraid of damage to property and an unfounded fear of personal injury lawsuits, have been building skateparks to contain skateboarding.

If properly designed and built, a skatepark can be a fun and challenging place to skate. All too often, though, communities build little jails, rather than satisfying skateboard environments. Tour the country and you'll find that most skateparks are located on the fringes of town. Often, they're located directly next to the police station. In addition, they're frequently fenced in, adding to the sense of being imprisoned. Adding insult to injury, a great number of skateparks are poorly constructed, prefabricated pieces of junk. Rarely are the skateboarders trusted with the design and construction. This leaves the skater with a choice: skate the not-very-fun, fenced in, designated area with full pads, usually, or resume skating in the streets, where now when the skateboarder runs into authority, they tell him to go to the local skatepark.

How, then, can the skateboarder and society peacefully coexist? Ultimately a few things need to happen.

Communities with a skateboard population need to build good skateparks that will challenge and satisfy skateboarders. This is best done by working with the local skateboarders and listening to what it is they want. Also important is to hire the most capable builders, who will often be the skateboarders themselves. A skateboarder will know nuances of design and construction that would not be obvious to a non-skater.

Skateparks alone are not the answer. Skaters will always skate the streets; it's a fun, non-polluting means of commuting, and an entertaining pastime. Provided it's done relatively safely, riding a skateboard should never be illegal. Given the creative nature of skateboarders, sometimes they will do tricks on things. This may or may not be destructive or trespassing.

Skateboarding is not a crime, but breaking stuff is. In that case (as much as I hate to admit it) the skateboarder should be held responsible. If I'm skating on your step and I break it, that's my fault. What really bothers me is having to be worried about getting arrested for simply riding home (which has happened).

I feel that in time, society will realize that the act of skateboarding is not criminal. Criminal acts can be committed while skating, and they should be handled accordingly, but the activity itself should not be to blame. My hope is that with the enormous amount of skateboarders today that is many generations deep, slowly the perceptions of skateboarding will change. With luck, communities will repeal their "No Skateboarding" laws, labeling them as antiquated as slavery or prohibition. For that to happen, however, we need skateboarders as authorities.

"Skateparks alone are not the answer. Skaters will always skate the streets; it's a fun, non-polluting means of commuting, and an entertaining pastime. Provided it's done relatively safely, riding a skateboard should never be illegal."

## *SUSPECT DEVICE*

by Richard Hart

The U.S. authorities' recent paranoid penchant for terrorist threats butted heads with my ongoing paranoia of the U.S. authorities the other day.

I was only going to get tax forms. Like a good resident alien, I went to the San Francisco Federal Building and put my metals through the detector.

"I am only here to get tax forms," I said.

"OK, sir... that cell phone, does it have a camera?"

"Er...no" I muttered, eager to get out of there as quickly as possible. I mean, I never use the camera, but it seems you aren't allowed one in government buildings.

"Let me see it, sir"

"Oh, a camera. Yes, it has one of those. I thought you said... er...something else."

I was glared at as I checked in my camera phone and threatening one-inch keychain Swiss army knife.

"Don't lie!" he yelled at my back as I went to get the forms.

I find it very confusing just finding the right tax forms, being a 'self-employed photographer.' For some inexplicable reason, I knowingly choose to torture myself each year by doing my own taxes; getting more and more frustrated as the questions begin to contradict themselves, and that in order to answer 6b you find you must first answer 17c. I shout, I throw pens, I play punk rock records and curse the IRS and the mothers that bore them.

I was looking for the form which makes you calculate the percentage of the floor space of your home which is used for your business (and thus the percentage of rent which you may write off as a business expense) when the metal detector guy entered with a cop the size of a telephone booth.

"Please come with us, sir," he bellowed.

Everyone in the room turned and looked at me.

"Er... well, I just need the form with the bedroom percentage and the..."

"COME-WITH-US-SIR..."

I was escorted into the hallway. There were more uniforms out there. One of them held up my phone.

"What is the meaning of this, sir?"

"It's...for making phone calls?" I ventured. I wasn't trying to be clever; I didn't quite understand the question.

"This, sir..." he jabbed the back of the phone while confiding to his fellows.

"He's lied to us once already".

I looked at the back of the phone and words failed me. I was fucked. I have, you see, a friend who is an artist. His room is always an inch deep in scraps of paper and strips of tape, most of them with words and phrases scrawled all over them. When we lived together, I was forever finding sentences attached to my clothing. I walked around all day once with 'THE PENIS IS A HUMMINGBIRD' stuck to my back. Anyway, a couple of weeks before this, I had been enjoying a cup of tea with him when I found a scrap of tape from some half-finished piece stuck to my elbow, and I transferred it to the back of my cell phone.

It said: 'THIS JOKE WILL BLOW YOU UP'.

"What is the meaning of this, sir? Is this meant to be funny? Because we don't think it's very funny."

I thought about trying to explain the Monty Python sketch which, I presume, was the reference point for the offending sentence: the one where a guy writes the funniest joke in the world; a joke so funny that anyone who hears it laughs to death or simply self-combusts. Somehow, though, I didn't think any of these steely-faced patriots were familiar with the work of Cleese and company.

"Don't you think you're being a little... paranoid?" I gently suggested.

"No, I do NOT, sir. We take this kind of thing very seriously..." (places hand on gun) "very seriously indeed."

"How many terrorists write 'THIS IS A BOMB' on their bombs?" I thought, but I judged it unwise to inquire. Then began the lengthy process of establishing my identity.

"I can't believe they let him in the building without a California I.D." the Booth remarked to a woman that looked like Goebbels.

"These are easy to fake," he added, checking my UK passport.

I was getting really freaked out. Another cop told me to "stop moving around so much...I don't want to have to handcuff you."

I felt much like one does when walking through Customs at the airport. You know you haven't done anything wrong, but under the suspicious glares of the uniforms, you begin to feel that maybe you have, after all. Have you?

I desperately wanted to show them the third page of my passport because there's a stamp on it from Malaysia dated September 11th, 2001. Aside from the fact that I didn't know how to drive and thus had no driving license, the Booth was also skeptical that I didn't know how tall I was or how much I weighed. Should I know these things? I have managed alright so far in life without this knowledge. I mean, I know what size clothes I wear. That's all I've really needed thus far. The last time I weighed myself, I was about seven stone, I remember, but that was in primary school in England. Probably no good. I wanted to guess, but I was drawing a blank on which measure of weight is used in America.

Eye color and hair color, though...those I had down. No worries. Blue, brown. I was now eager to cooperate. He was still convinced that my passport was fake, though. It had proven good enough for about fifty of the world's immigration personnel, but not for this crew-cut brute. Eventually someone on the other end of his walkie-talkie gave my description.

"Six foot one, something-or-other pounds, brown hair, eyes."

"Ha! Brown eyes!" Booth was triumphant, smiling. He had me. I thought for a minute he was going to high-five Goebbels.

"Oh, wait - brown hair, *blue* eyes..." the voice corrected itself. You know how apes get that sad expression sometimes?

This whole time, even though I knew I harbored no aspirations of blowing anything up; I was increasingly scared that they would find some unpaid skateboarding tickets on record somewhere. I have received several over the years, but usually I would give the names of obscure 80's vert skaters because I had no California I.D. I have had tickets written out to Monty Nolder and Steve Schneer, but I couldn't recall if there were any unpaid ones in my real name.

Well, if there were, they didn't find them; and at long last, reluctantly, disappointingly, they had to let me go.

But not before taking a Polaroid of me "to put on the wall next to the picture of Saddam" Booth said.

"Only joking..." Ha ha. Yes, got it. The simian has a sense of humor after all. This year, I did my taxes more grudgingly than usual.

"They are intimidated because we role in packs of ten or more, and everyone in that pack is usually from a different ethnicity. It's beautiful to us, but not to them, so they react with force..."

## ***ASS BACKWARDS***

by Karl Watson

One of my strongest memories of skateboard harassment dates to when I was fourteen years old, hanging out at Embarcadero with my board in my hand. These two cops arrested me for just having a skateboard on the premises. This was my first time being arrested. I remember being extremely upset since I was innocent, so I started talking shit back to the cops, which wasn't a good idea. At the station, one of the cops handcuffed me to the bench, and then flat-out hit me. I really felt it, too. Keep in mind this was a grown man hitting a little, scrawny, 14-year-old kid. I couldn't believe it!

So about a week later my mother and I tried to press charges, but it was funny because every one of those cops that witnessed the incident suddenly got amnesia and said they didn't see a thing.

I already knew authority and American society were crooked, and this further showed me that American society is one big joke. America values property over life; our president even said he would not fight global warming because it might "damage the economy."

Authority figures really should be nicer and not have such egos. I feel the reason they are typically so harsh is because when they see a skater, they see a free person who usually doesn't want anything to do with mainstream America. They are intimidated because we role in packs of ten or more, and everyone in that pack is usually from a different ethnicity. Its beautiful to us, but not to them, so they react with force because that is the only way they were taught to act. In other countries they are more lenient when it come to fines and going to jail, but for the most part they don't like skateboarders all around the world.

If you treat someone hostile with kindness they usually calm down - and hopefully they won't give you a ticket.

"...on a Saturday afternoon and there would be fifty or sixty skaters there and people just hanging out with no shirts on drinking 40s."

# *ALL ROADS LEAD TO EMB*

by Lee Smith

I guess the first memories I have of skateboard harassment are from skating at the Embarcadero.

In the beginning, we would skate there all the time and no one cared. It's amazing to think that in the early nineties you could go down to EMB on a Saturday afternoon and there would be fifty or sixty skaters there and people just hanging out with no shirts on drinking 40s. I could never imagine this happening these days.

I really don't think it became a big deal until the Hyatt started complaining, because all the skaters were going inside the hotel to use the bathroom all the time...this was because of all the beer consumption, of course.

I'm sure the last thing the police wanted to worry about was skateboarders, but after the Hyatt complained enough times, they started to do something about it. Along with that, they started taking notice of all the other things that were going on with the skaters: fighting, drinking in public, graffiti and just mayhem in general.

I mean, the Hyatt is big business.

It's hard to say who is right in this situation. I wouldn't want somebody tearing up my house if I were to ever buy one (hopefully one day); would you? Being a skater myself, I want to say that we are right and that they have no right to throw us out of our beloved Embarcadero. However, I also know that we caused so many problems there that it's silly not to expect it. But no matter what, the police have no right to punch 14-year-old skaters in the face while they are handcuffed to a bench for skating.

Think about it from the other side: skateboarders hate rollerbladers because they wax the shit out of curbs and ledges to the point of danger. We don't like bikers because their pegs tear up the ledges, but in reality what they are doing is no different from what we are doing. They're having fun doing something that is not accepted by normal society. We dis bikers and rollerbladers so much because we're not thinking of the feeling they get from what they do as they ruin our precious spots. So how can skateboarders expect "normal" American society to care about what they do?

To me, the best interaction with authority is no interaction. If I'm not allowed to skate somewhere, I generally don't go there. The last thing I want to do with my time is listen to some dickhead tell me what I need to be doing with my life, and all that "why am I in this neighborhood when I live in another part of the city" bullshit. If I have an encounter with the cops or security guards I don't say anything, and if I am questioned I answer clearly, honestly and to the point. Trust me, no matter how good of an argument you have for them about how "we are not criminals and there are drug dealers down the street," they are not going to understand. Save your breath and keep it moving. That's the ultimate form of rebellion in my opinion.

The police need to improve their interactions with everybody these days, not just skaters. In my experience, in the eyes of the police, everybody except other police officers is a criminal.

They don't treat people with respect. They bark orders at you even if you haven't done anything wrong. You can't even ask them a question respectably without them wanting to arrest you for "being a wise ass." The police need to realize that just because there are some really messed up people in the world, not everyone is like that; especially not people going out and skateboarding.

As for security guards and those types, I understand that they have a job to do, but I have no idea why they act as if the property they are protecting is their own. When they come to kick you out of a spot they are often so aggressive and full of angst it is incredible.

Just ask the skaters to leave and that's that. Some skaters like to mouth off and I understand that could get annoying; actually it's annoying to me as well. Be cool, do your job, tell us to leave, we'll go quietly and come back later, and we can do it all over again. The skaters are giving them something to do besides sit on their asses, but maybe that's why they are mad...?

It seems that power and authority are always used in ways they shouldn't be...from your boss at work to the police and security guards, government, the church and so on. We don't need to get into examples, there's not enough time in the world.

It all boils down to money. Money is obviously more important than human life these days. Right now I've discovered that there is 150% more freedom in Western Europe and I'll leave it at that.

## SAVE YOUR BREATH

by Mike York

Getting chased out of EMB by police running full speed at me at fourteen years of age was pretty traumatic, and that made me feel distrustful and unsafe when I'd see police after that.

This influenced me to get by any way possible without hurting anyone. What I mean by that is: if I'm breaking the law or doing something illegal that I feel in my heart isn't, or shouldn't be, then I'm gonna do it without feeling the least bit bad or guilty about it.

When encountering a police officer, just give the respect you would give to a sergeant or general in the army. The word "sir" usually does the trick. Police like that respect. I see kids trying to be smart-asses to the cops, or they try and break off a piece of knowledge to the cops, who could care less about what they're talking about and got better things to do than to listen to you. So save your breath boys!

What should authority figures do to improve their interactions with skateboarders? Don't interact with us. As for a positive example of authority, well, I thought the NYPD was pretty raw on 9/11. They came through.

People are harsh because they think that we are vandalizing property, that we have no respect, that we are trespassing, loitering or lurking around. They're not understanding the bigger picture that skateboarders have in their mind.

I don't think that the skate spot is valued more than a human being or life itself. I think it's more of a misunderstanding from their point of view and our point of view, because usually the skateboarder values the handrail, curb and block more than the people who are kicking us out. That's our skate spot and we want it to be good so that we can skate it. Holla!

America is quick to put a label on you and throw you into a category. So if you are a skateboarder who is black, white, Filipino or Korean, you're still a "skateboarder" kind of like members of a gang are always "gangsters." Have you ever seen *Colors*? There were white crips, black crips and Mexican crips, but the keyword was "crips."

In other countries that I have travelled to and experienced, the people seemed to not really trip on the skateboarders. Like in Barcelona; we were skating this spot and the police pulled up and looked like they were about to harass us, but instead walked up to these two ladies with dogs in the park and gave them tickets for not having their dogs on leashes. The cops turned around and looked at us before they got back into their car. They gave us a smile and a wave then drove off.

I thought that was the shit.

## *THE LEGAL HYPOCRISY OF SKATESTOPPING*

by Chris Long

Stories of mistreatment from authority are standard in skateboarding, and at the risk of sounding redundant I decided not to elaborate on any of them for this essay, instead choosing to focus specifically on one isolated expression of the ongoing conflict between skateboarders and society.

We've all noticed them, but the non-skating individual often has difficulty in discerning their function: aesthetically incorrect knobs screwed tightly around the edge of a bench or ledge, abrupt clamps fastened every few inches along a handrail or awkward-looking gouges routed into the edges of brick, stone or concrete slab. To the untrained eye they invite confusion, but the skateboarder instantly piques their insidious design - all are forms of a heinous fad known as skatestopping.

First off, the average person overlooks the potential benefits of having skateboarders around at weird times. Skaters are out there observing late night scenes, and no doubt many a soldier out there has seen some kind of real crime go down while they were out skating. It is not uncommon to hear a skater tell of how he or she witnessed some crazy crime. One time three friends and I nabbed some junkie guy who robbed a lady at a store - then they kicked us out for skating the bench afterwards!

The main objection to skating is often damage - but it would take just as much effort to put angled iron down the entire length of a school ledge than ugly, unaesthetic brackets or clamps. In fact, angled iron as a damage solution would actually be compliant with the Uniform Building Code, and in many cases it would be a viable compromise where everybody comes out on top. It takes years to get a park built, when a ledge can be angle-ironed in a weekend. The school district would curb their damage problem, the skateboarders would have a perfect ledge that would never grind down, nobody would ever have the awkward sensation of sitting down on a skatestopper and if the ledges were near the P.E. area kids could even skate for physical education. It would probably raise their grades.

The skatestopping concept was definitely born of true demand and in all honesty, skaters gotta admit that occasionally spots do get trashed beyond repair. In this aspect I can side with the frustrated business owner. If my sole proprietorship was a little upscale, foo-foo restaurant and it was like a make-or-break scenario where I needed every customer I could get, the last thing on Earth I would want would be a bunch of squatter-looking skater pirates hanging around the front door smoking cigarettes and hucking themselves down my stairs, especially the breed that enjoys making off-the-cuff comments at random, mainstream customers who typically don't take well to any aberrance from normality.

The stopper concept receives more praise than it actually deserves, especially on the websites of their manufacturers. The majority of the skatestoppers in production prevent virtually one form of street skating: hubba or handrail. There are dozens of skateboarding movements that cannot be as easily stopped by architectural modifications, and there are many spots that cannot be stopped due to their inherent geometry or historic significance (pristine marble ledges surrounding a civic courtyard is a good example). Last but not least, if the stoppers do anything at all, they simply encourage skaters to continue their search for viable spots elsewhere - usually on to the next school, courtyard or business district - leaving the roots of the problems unaddressed.

Fact of the matter is, skateboarders and business owners are being mistreated by a common enemy, namely the apathetic, disinterested or otherwise unwilling park officials, council members and city planners whose civic responsibility is to meet the needs of the people. That firms such as Intellicept, Ravensforge and SkateAbate exist demonstrates the failure of local communities to accurately interpret the recreational preferences of their constituency.

A quote taken from SkateAbate's website reads, "It is an aspect of our legal system that anyone who is injured by their own fault (the skateboarder) or no fault of their own (innocent bystander) can seek monetary compensation for their injuries, pain and suffering from the owner of the property where the injury occurred." Isn't this absurd law the true root of America's public space problems?

Skateboarders have long spited the presence of killjoy knobs and clamps intended to quell skating and prevent damage. To clarify, *skatestoppers* is a brand name and registered trademark of Intellicept, a San Diego County based firm that dominates the skatestopping market along with two other manufacturers: Seattle's Ravensforge and SkateAbate of Encinitas, California. All three of their websites denigrate skateboarding and place the entirety of the blame for the problems on us.

These firms sell products to stop what can on occasion be an illegal activity - skateboarding. Technically, the only time skating is illegal is when it's done in the vicinity of an ordinance against it or against the direct orders of an officer or property owner. However, here's an interesting twist: selling and applying skatestopping products can often be an illegal activity itself.

Although I must admit they are premature and I do need to check sources, recently I made a few discoveries in the world of code enforcement that may yield leverage for skaters to lean on in their hatred of skatestopping. Many states are required to comply with a piece of legislation known as the *Uniform Building Code*. The UBC is the most widely adopted building code in the world and like most laws, most states have their own particular interpretations, but the UBC is generally adhered to in most American cities.

We find language to the effect of the following: (See section 1003.3.3.6) "The surfaces of all handrails must be smooth and free from sharp edges or corners." It would seem that the application of skatestoppers is in stark violation of this clause, wouldn't you think?

Our local County of Ventura Code Enforcement representative Liz Cameron had never heard of such a question in her fifteen years on the job. "My son skatesÖ" she said. "This is actually a pretty interesting question..." While the UBC conflict question remained unanswered, Liz also brought up an interesting secondary point. United Laboratories is a firm that tests new products for possible code violations. Of the three companies mentioned, I couldn't find any public information stating that their skatestopping products are registered with United Laboratories, either.

Companies such as Ravensforge, Skate Abate and Intellicept do not work towards the true solution, which is adequate accommodation of skateboarding. Nor do they bother to even mention the potential UBC hassle to their customers. They merely delay the necessary action and thus divert energy and funds from where they're needed most. I would like to invite these companies to work towards better solutions, or to begin the implementation of skate-friendly solutions in 'public domain' type places. Furthermore, recreational planners could plan standard skateable ledges with angle-iron and ample flat concrete in upcoming parks and CIP projects. Such amenities greatly reduce the burdens of street skating and their usage should be covered under state law just as any other recreational activity being performed at the park. There are plenty examples of cooperative solutions - true solutions that keep kids skating and out of dangerous situations - as opposed to lining the pockets of hate.

There is a strong and urgent need for skaters to do two things: a manufacturing firm with sufficient drive, skateboarding commitment and professionalism needs to develop skate-friendly forms of damage solution systems. Such a firm could analyze each problem area and look for methods of proactive solutions - for example, a beach boardwalk scenario such as the now defunct 'pits' in Venice could have easily been angle-ironed and declared a skate-friendly zone.

So it appears there are two potentially major strikes against those who supply skatestopping products: non-UL approval and UBC code violation. As far as Liz could see, companies such as Ravensforge, Skateabate and Intellicept who manufacture non-UL approved products designed specifically for applications that violate UBC codes are breaking both UBC compliance and local legislature. I didn't notice any seal of UL approval on their websites. In many and most cases, skateboarding is not necessarily illegal, but unwanted.

The irony is beautiful. In their zeal to uphold the law they end up breaking it. As it turns out, the tagline from skateplaza.com's website is true: *skatestopping is a crime*. What I would like to see happen is a formal reprisal to these three companies in particular from the Uniform Building Code committee, as in the majority of cases they are as equally guilty of lawbreaking as we are.

Any good lawyers out there?

"A quote taken from SkateAbate's website reads, 'It is an aspect of our legal system that anyone who is injured by their own fault (the skateboarder) or no fault of their own (innocent bystander) can seek monetary compensation for their injuries, pain and suffering from the owner of the property where the injury occurred.' Isn't this absurd law the true root of America's public space problems?"

## *ANOTHER KIND OF AUTHORITY*

by Travis Jensen

I met Joel Costello through a mutual skateboarding buddy in the summer of '93. I was 14 and Joel was 15. We were both going into ninth grade. Joel had dyslexia and was held back a year as a kid. The two of us went to different schools. I lived on the eastside of Milwaukee and Joel lived on the Southside, about fifteen minutes away by car.

Joel had more natural talent on a skateboard than anyone in Milwaukee. He could shred any terrain: streets, ramps, pools, etc. He had style and would pull the most difficult tricks almost effortlessly and with ease. Joel, in my opinion, definitely had what it took to make it big in the skateboard industry.

Joel was the first guy in our little skate crew to smoke weed and drop acid. The rest of us didn't experiment with that stuff until a few years later. I remember one Saturday that summer, Joel met up with all of us downtown and told us he had dropped two hits of acid before leaving his house. He was so fucked up that he could barely even push straight on his board. He had no business being out skating. However, when we went to one of our usual spots, the three-up-three-down behind the Milwaukee Courthouse, Joel decided that he was going to try and crooked grind the thick, gold ten stair rail in front of the main entrance.

The first couple of tries Joel made at crooked grinding the rail were straight suicide attempts. He was falling so hard I could barely stand to watch. Each slam made me wince. But then, on the fourth or fifth attempt, Joel started locking into the trick and a few tries later he pulled it. I couldn't believe it. He stuck it clean, too. It was a textbook crooked grind.

Back in '93, crooked grinding a ten stair rail was nothing short of amazing, especially when the individual doing it was frying off two hits of acid. Word of this crazy stunt spread through town in no time and Joel was a legend amongst the Milwaukee skateboard community.

Most skaters my age and older will agree when I say San Francisco was the Mecca for skateboarding in the early to mid 90s. San Francisco housed some of the best spots in the world and a host of big name pros called the city home. Joel knew that San Francisco was where he needed to be to make it big in skateboarding. He wasn't going anywhere with skateboarding in Milwaukee and he knew that.

That following summer, the day after school let out, Joel packed his bags and hitchhiked to San Francisco. He was only 16. We all thought he lost his damn mind. Joel and I talked about moving to there together after graduating high-school, but he couldn't wait that long. He asked me if I wanted to join him early. I thought long and hard about it, but ultimately decided to wait until after I finished school. I figured I owed that much to my folks.

Joel called me a couple of weeks after he left. He said the journey out west was crazy, but he made it in one piece. He was living with an Art Academy student in the Tenderloin and paid $100 a month to crash on the floor. Joel also said he landed a part-time gig bussing tables at an Italian restaurant in North Beach.

"How's the skating going?" I asked him.

"I skate EMB almost everyday," he replied.

"The other day I kickflipped the Gonz and tomorrow I'm gonna try and 360 flip it. I know I got that shit."

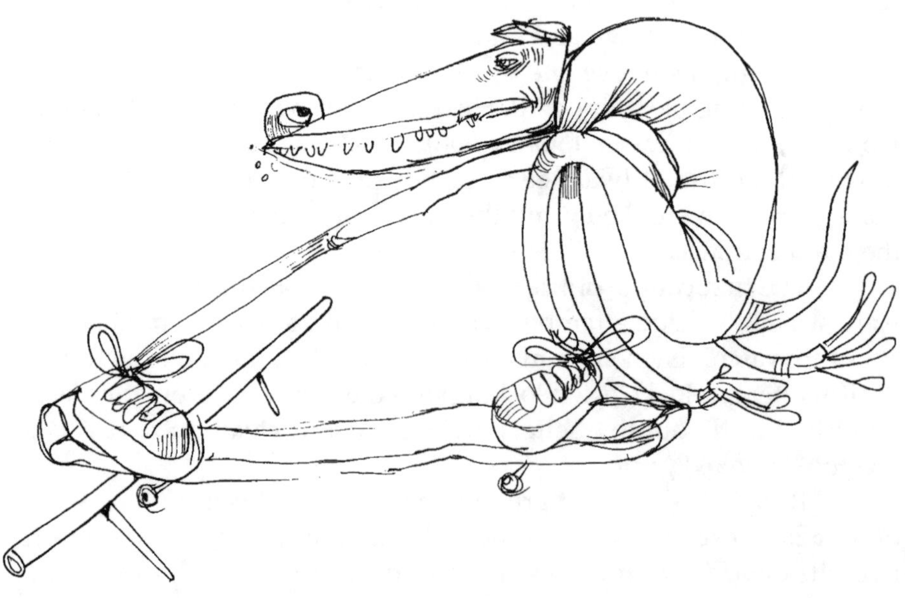

Joel and I talked until his calling card ran out of time and we were disconnected. After that, I didn't hear from Joel again. I had no way of getting ahold of him. I kept expecting to see him pop up in the magazines and videos, but he never did.

I moved to San Francisco the day after graduating high-school in June of '97. It was almost three years to the day since Joel had left. I rented a room for $100 a week in the Tenderloin on Ellis and Jones. I asked every skater I met if they knew Joel Costello. A few guys said they did, but they had no clue of his whereabouts.

As luck would have it, I ran into Joel while skating Union Square my third week in the city. He was very surprised to see me. The two of us caught up with one another over a cig on one of the benches aligning the exterior of the park. He said he hadn't been skating much and that he had been through a lot over the last three years. That was obvious just by looking at him. He had big, dark circles under his eyes and his teeth looked like they were beginning to rot. He said he was crashing with a friend over on 6th and Market, which, like where I was staying at the time, was one of the seedier neighborhoods downtown.

"Hey," he said, looking down at my old board. "You wanna buy a deck? I have a brand new one I'll sell you for $10."

I desperately needed a new board and $10 was a hell of a deal.

"It's gripped and everything," he added.

"What kind of board is it?"

"A Stereo...Chris Pastras."

"I'll take it."

"Ok, let's bounce to my crib then."

"You don't wanna skate for a little bit first?"

"Naw, let's go now."

Joel and I left Union Square, bombed down Powell Street past all the tourists, and skated up Market to 6th. He lived on the corner above Tulan's Vietnamese restaurant. Joel's place had no bathroom and no kitchen. There was a jail-cell sized living area, a closet, a sink and mirror combo, and a small window that overlooked 6th Street. The place reeked heavily of body odor, feet, and Vietnamese food. There were two dirty mattresses on the floor and one swivel chair. That's it. They had no other furniture.

"Where's your roommate?" I asked.

"Working or something."

Joel handed me the deck and I gave him $10.

"You got any tools I can use to hook this shit up?"

Joel dug around in the closet for a couple of minutes and revealed a screwdriver and a wrench.

I took a seat on the swivel chair and began disassembling my old board.

Joel said, "I'll be right back, ok?"

"Where are you going?"

"The store."

I had already finished assembling the new board by the time Joel returned. Once inside, he locked the door, latched the chain, and took a seat on the floor with his back up against the wall. Then, much to my surprise, from his pocket he pulled out a small baggie and a dirty glass pipe. The baggie contained what appeared to be two crack rocks. Although I'd never seen the stuff in person, it didn't take a rocket scientist to figure out that's what it was. Joel then proceeded to pack the bigger of the two rocks into the pipe.

"You got a light on you?" Joel asked, patting his pockets down. "I think I lost mine."

It took me a minute to respond. I was in shock that my old friend was getting ready to smoke crack in front of me like it was no big deal. This explained the dark circles under his eyes and his rotting teeth, I thought. This was also probably the reason he was in such a hurry to sell me that board for so cheap. He needed a fix.

Joel asked me again, "Can I get that light off you, bro?"

I handed him the lighter.

Joel put the pipe in his mouth and fired it up. He took a fat hit, choked a few times through his nose, and then exhaled. A smile came over his face and he closed his eyes and tilted his head back up against the wall.

"What's it feel like?" I asked him.

"It's the best feeling in the world, man. Almost like a full body orgasm. You wanna hit?"

"Naw, I'm straight," I replied.

He shrugged his shoulders and proceeded to smoke the rest of that first rock. Then, once that rock was dusted, Joel packed up the second rock and smoked it to the face. The small baggie was now empty.

"How long have you been smoking that shit for?" I asked.

"Almost two years."

I chilled for a couple of minutes while Joel enjoyed his high, but soon decided it was time for me to get out of there. The whole situation sketched me out. I was disappointed in Joel, but at the same time felt sorry for him.

I asked Joel, "You wanna go back to Union and skate?"

"Naw, I'm gonna chill here. I got shit to do."

> "Joel had more natural talent on a skateboard than anyone in Milwaukee. He could shred any terrain: streets, ramps, pools..."

"You sure?"

"Yeah, but I'm down to skate tomorrow. You wanna meet up at Union?"

"What time?"

"Five."

"Sounds good. You got a number I can reach you at?"

"Naw, the phone is disconnected. I'll be up there, though, don't worry." I gave Joel a pound and then left. I didn't even feel like skating after that. I was just glad to get the fuck out of there.

I showed up at Union Square the following day about a quarter to five. I waited for Joel for almost two hours, but he never showed. I should have figured as much.

Nearly a week went by and I still hadn't run into Joel, so I decided I would stop by his house to see if I could catch him. I rang a few different buzzers until I got the right one.

"Is Joel home?"

"Who's this?" A muffled voice scowled through the speaker.

"This is his friend Vince."

"Joel doesn't live here anymore."

"Do you know where I can find him at?"

"Naw," the muffled voice replied, and then hung up.

Close to two years went by before I finally ran into Joel again. It was '99 and I was on Upper Haight shopping for music at Amoeba with a friend. Joel was sitting on the sidewalk with his back against the wall outside of Ben and Jerry's ice cream shop. Goddamn he was in bad shape. His hair was natty, he had scabies on his face, his clothes were dirty and torn, and he smelled awful. It was obvious he had been living on the streets for quite some time.

"Joel?" I said to him.

He looked up at me with a blank expression. He was so far gone that I don't even think he recognized me at first.

"It's Vince, man!"

He looked up, smiled, revealing a mouth full of rotten teeth, and then started laughing to himself.

"I'm fucked up," he said, rubbing his hands through his natty hair. I didn't know what to say.

"Can I get a cig off you?" He asked me.

I gave him my whole pack.

"You can keep 'em," I said.

"Right on, bro. You gotta light?"

I handed him my lighter and he fired up one of the smokes. He took a big pull, closed his eyes, exhaled, and then started coughing and wheezing. It sounded like he had a severe case of bronchitis.

"Where are you staying at?" I asked him.

"Here and there."

I studied Joel for a minute as he smoked. I couldn't believe how awful he looked. I didn't know what to do or say.

"Can I borrow a couple bucks off you?" He asked.

I was working in a mailroom downtown at the time making $12 an hour, which wasn't much for San Francisco, but I got by. I had a little over $30 in cash on me and I handed it all over to him. Joel shoved the money in his pocket. Then I wrote my number down on a party flyer I picked up while shopping at Amoeba.

"Here's my number," I said, handing Joel the flyer. "Give me a call if you ever need anything."

The conversation with Joel was difficult. I wasn't getting anywhere with him. It was obvious he didn't want to talk to me. He responded to all my questions with simple yes or no answers. I tried forcing the conversation for another couple of minutes, but then decided it was pointless. He was too far gone.

Before parting ways, I reminded Joel to call me if he ever needed anything. Joel half-nodded his head and my friend and I walked off down Haight. As expected, Joel never called me.

On New Years Eve day of '02, I was riding the 38 bus home from work. My supervisor let me leave a couple hours early. I was living out in the Richmond District. As the bus stopped at the intersection of Geary and Polk, I saw Joel exiting the liquor store on the corner. I quickly pulled the stop chord, jumped out of my seat, and hollered at the driver to let me out the back door. I leaped down the three stairs of the bus and ran to catch up with Joel who was now walking up Polk towards Post.

"Joel!" I yelled.

He didn't hear me, so I yelled again, this time much louder.

"JOEL!"

He stopped and turned around. By the looks of him, it was obvious he was still homeless. He was carrying nothing but an old, raggedy blue backpack. Talking with Joel, I could tell he wasn't high. He seemed very depressed.

I asked him, "Are you still smoking that shit?"

"I haven't smoked yet today. I wanna quit and get my shit together. That's my New Year's resolution."

I don't know what came over me, but right then and there I decided that I was going to take Joel home with me. I had a roommate, but he was out of town for the holidays and wouldn't be back for a couple more days.

"C'mon," I said. "You're coming with me."

"Where are we going?"

"You're gonna stay with me for a few nights. My roommate's out of town."

"Naw, its cool, man, I got things to do."

"I insist."

Reluctantly, Joel agreed to come along. I gave him bus fare and the two of us jumped on the Geary bus headed out to the Avenues.

Back at my house, I gave Joel a new change of clothes and shoes. Then I helped him buzz his natty hair and told him to take a shower. He cleaned up pretty nicely.

I treated Joel to dinner that night and later on we hooked up with some of my friends and went to a house party over in Hayes Valley. We didn't get home until almost 4:00 a.m. Joel stayed on the couch and woke up the next morning after sleeping only five hours and said it was the best night of sleep he had in years. I cooked Joel breakfast and the two of us spent the remainder of the day reminiscing our youth and watching old skate videos.

Later that evening, maybe around 8:00, I noticed Joel was starting to get really antsy. He couldn't sit still and was chain smoking cigarettes. He said he needed some alcohol to calm his nerves. I let him drink the few beers I had in the fridge. He put them down one after the other.

The two of us went to bed around midnight. About an hour later, I heard Joel shuffling around in the living room, so I got out of bed to see what he was up to. He was fully dressed and had his backpack slung over his shoulder.

"Where the fuck are you going?" I asked him.

"To the store. I need some Pepto. My stomach's fucked up."

"I'll go with you."

"Naw, it's cool. I'd rather be by myself right now."

Joel left his backpack at my house to prove that he would return. I waited on the couch for him for over an hour, but he never showed. I knew he wouldn't. The backpack sat on the living room floor for two days until my curiosity finally got the best of me and I decided to take a peek inside. I unzipped the bag and the foul stench it unleashed about made me gag. It smelled like a vast bouquet of body odor, shit, piss and stale booze. I then tied an old t-shirt around my nose and went to the kitchen for the cleaning gloves.

Once I was properly geared up, I started pulling out the contents of the bag one by one. What I found about made me sick to my stomach. Buried underneath a heap of dirty clothes, I discovered a plastic bag filled with condoms. I knew right away what they were for. Joel was whoring himself out for money to buy crack with, which also explained what he was doing on New Year's Eve on the corner of Geary and Polk, an area notorious for young male prostitution. Disgusted, I shoved the bag of condoms back in the backpack, zipped it up, and dumped it in the trash behind the house.

I decided it was time for me to call Joel's parents and let them know what was going on. This was something I should have done a long time ago, I thought, as I picked up the phone, dialed 411, and asked the operator for the number. Joel's mother answered the phone on the third ring. I introduced myself and started to explain the seriousness of her son's addiction. She interrupted me mid-sentence by saying that she and her husband hadn't talked to Joel in over three years and they no longer considered him their son. He had put them through too much hardship, she said. She didn't want to hear what I had to say and refused to let me finish. Then, in a threatening voice, she warned me to never call her house again and hung up the phone.

Later that night, for the first time since I was a little kid, I knelt down at the bedside and prayed. I didn't know what else to do. The drug had absolute authority over Joel's mind, body, and soul.

"...for the first time since I was a little kid, I knelt down at the bedside and prayed. I didn't know what else to do."

"For me skateboarding has always been about the freedom of just riding and doing your own thing...so how could I not get into it with authority?" -Gary Cease

## *TO COMPLY OR NO COMPLY*

by David Wallace

I could tell you about all of my crazy experiences, but instead this is all I have to say:

If you're skating around town and somebody tries to take your skateboard or tells you that you can't skate somewhere because there are signs saying not to, try to comply with them nicely by saying, "Sir (or M'am) I was skating along having such a great time that I just didn't see the sign."

If it's a cop be cool 'cuz they can do whatever they want and you definitely don't want to get a ticket or get your board taken.

To comply or no comply?

My advice is always to comply: unless you have no choice.

**end.*

# contributor bios

etnies
SLAP
GO VEGETARIAN
NOT A CRIME
Coors
ABCK02
ZERO
STEREO
PornStar
one
SANTA CRUZ

**CHRIS LONG** began writing creatively around Detroit, Michigan and grew up skateboarding in southern California, where he formed Funnotfame Productions in 2003.

An accomplished author, screenwriter, journalist, editor and publisher, Chris has been writing for over twenty years. Since 2001 Chris has been a member in good standing of the Writers Guild of America, west. He has scripted series and screenplays for NBC and Disney and his work has also appeared in the LA Times, Ventura County Star, Ojai-Ventura Voice, VCReporter, *SLAP Magazine, Thrasher, Concrete Wave* and skatenerd.com. Diverse interests create deep story wells and his writing span includes youth culture, skateboarding, health, philosophy, short stories, essays, science, politics, religion, the paranormal, tech, editorials and more. Chris is always looking to write for the screen and is working on his fourth title, *Bats in the Belfry: Towards Clarity in the Origin of Life Debate.*

An avid skateboard enthusiast, Chris stills films and skates for fun. In the 1990's Chris founded VSIC, now a 501(c)(3) non-profit group dedicated to supporting skateboarding in Ventura County. Together with Pat Tafoya, VSIC has been successful in persuading the city of Ventura to build a new skatepark, and partial proceeds from sales of *No Comply: Skateboarding Speaks on Authority* are donated to that effort. funnotfame.org/rebuild

Chris bids love to all his Friends and Family, and would like to thank God, Mom, Dad, the beautiful Alexis, Ladell, Zach, Uncle Ted, Tommy, the Bavero family and Five Points. Shouts out to Steven, Katie, Skye, Daniel, Erin, Stitch, Scooter and Jay. Also my cousin Jason McComb, Claudia Verdugo and Aunt Marcie, who all are in the movie *Jarhead*. Also the late: Spot, Skate Street, T. Garrety, Aunt Donnelle and my grandmothers(RIP).

Chris' special thanks for this project go to Travis Jensen, Dale Dreiling, John Fleming, Albert Cole and all the contributors.

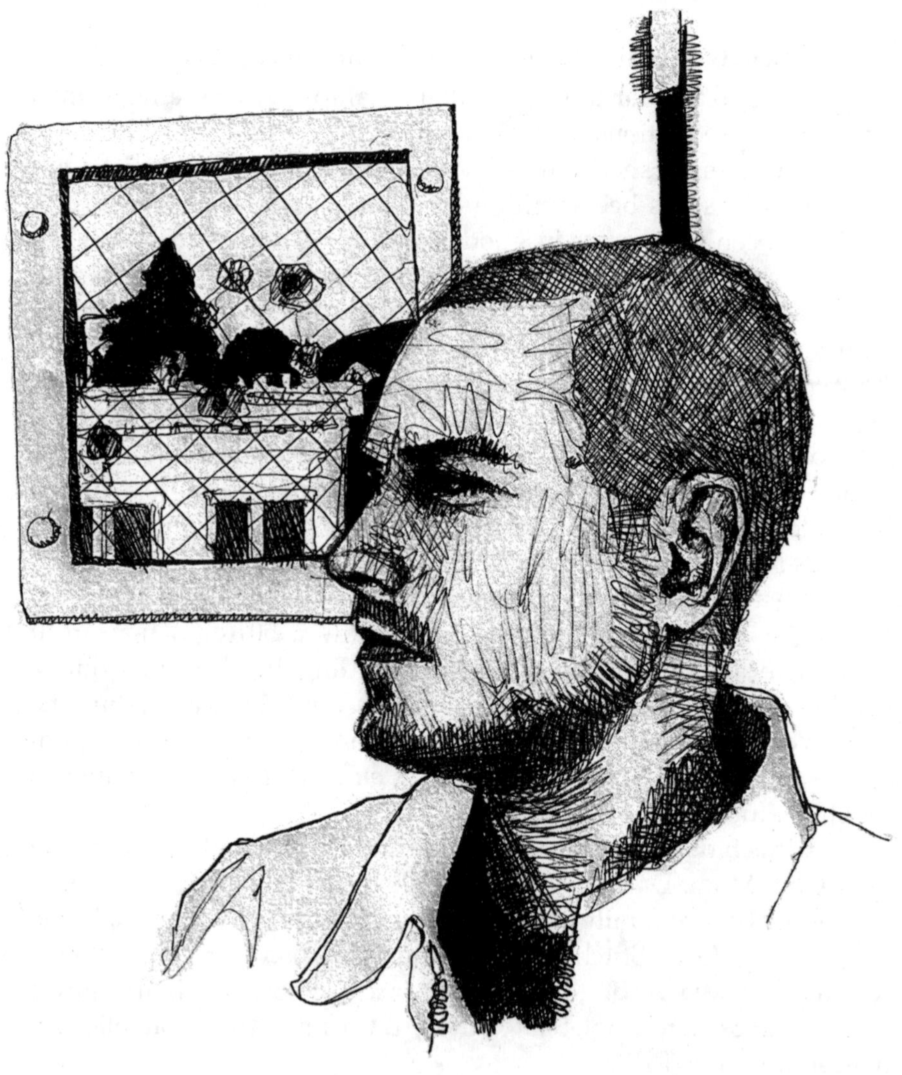

**TRAVIS JENSEN** was raised in Milwaukee, Wisconsin where he attended public school. Travis moved to San Francisco in 1997 where he developed a passion for writing. Travis' first book, *Left-Handed Stories*, was released in June of 2004 and was instantly considered an underground classic.

Travis' work has appeared in Perian Springs Literary Journal, Clout Magazine, Vapors Magazine, Beckett Baseball Monthly, Section 'M' Magazine, Etc. Magazine, SLAP Skateboard Magazine, Mesh Magazine, STAF Magazine (Spain), and Versus Magazine among others. When not writing, Travis enjoys skateboarding, going to flea markets on the weekends and studying the paranormal.

Travis is 26 years old and currently lives in San Francisco where he is working on his third book, entitled *Welcome to San Franpsycho*, scheduled for release sometime in 2006.

Travis would like to thank the following people: All of the *No Comply* contributors, Eva Dancel, mom, dad, Chris Long, The Purple Skunk Family, Big Wigg Loc', Isaac Mckay-Randozzi, Jag and Katie, Ando @ FTC, Joe and Lauren @ Asita Recordings, Jenn @ Giant Peach, Garet O'Keefe, Wes Roisum, Andrew Schoultz, Madeline Borne, Adek, Ellay Khule "The Rifleman", Brian Tucci, Al Partanen, Brian Brophy @ Mesh Magazine, Chris Pastras, Snoopy Snow Cone Man, Sean Goldchain, Riddlore, Mimi, Lori Spears, Danae, Leland and Mary, Juan @ STAF Magazine, John Trippe @ Fecalface.com, The Benhamida family, OG Hugh-Emc, Fritz Clap, Sonny Barger, Cellski, Cocoa, Mounaim, Najia, Alfredo and Gilda Puccio, The Hamburger Eyes Crew, Chris @ Clout Magazine, Bill Kaschner, and everyone else that's helped me along the way. THANKS!

You can read more about *Welcome to San Franpsycho* and other projects Travis is working on at sfmasher.cjb.net.

**DALE DREILING** is a multi-media artist working primarily through drawing, painting, screen-printing, collage and sculpture. His works often mix two or more of these disciplines. In addition to visual art, he is also involved in several writing and music projects.

The subject matter of his work is derived from personal experience, whether first hand or observed from the outside. Visually, his inspiration is pulled from the urban environment. Images of anonymous strangers, celebrities, personal friends and all of their situations, architecture, signage, mass-media communication, industrial/technological by-products, alcohol and drugs fill his compositions. Themes of destruction, conflict, escape, contemplation, simple joys and resolution are consistent threads in his work.

Previous venues range from galleries and museums to open public spaces. He has exhibited in group and solo shows in Ventura, San Diego, Oakland, San Francisco, Los Angeles and New York City.

Dale has designed for Upper Playground, Steady-6, Root Tone Music and Funnotfame; also for the independent label/no label musical artists Deepakalypse and the Kamikaze Collective, Glass and Ashes, Order of Operations and Ronin Grey.

Raised in Ventura, California, Dale Dreiling is a graduate of the San Francisco Art Institute and he currently resides in Seattle.

Inquiries regarding art purchases, commissions, freelance design and illustration can be made at: dale@funnotfame.org

Also at: daledreiling.org

**Airto Jackson** is age 28. He was born in Texas and currently resides in San Francisco, California where he skates and writes.

**Ando Caulfield** is a skater and freelance photographer, currently residing in San Francisco where he and his friends run FTC Skateboards. You can check Ando's work at andosf.com

**Anthony Pappalardo** spent years jumping around with a guitar at your local VFW hall under the guise of a band, and has been rolling on urethane religiously since the age of twelve. He attended Massachusetts College of Art and his writing has appeared in SLAP Magazine, Alternative Press, Magnet, Law Of Inertia. He recently traded evil Boston for Brooklyn, NY and a ring around the finger of the girl of his dreams: Mrs. Tara Pappalardo.

**Blair Alley** was born in San Diego. He grew up with Ocean Howell and Willy Santos. The guy has more cameras than the CIA and loves scoring a holga cheap. Blair currently lives in Pacific Beach and has a degree from UC Berkeley in Fine Art. He has had his hand in the game for over fourteen years and is not slowing down anytime soon.

**Bob Kronbauer** is a photographer/designer/writer/idea-haver. He spent the past few years in Los Angeles working in Girl Skateboards' Art Dump and is currently residing in Vancouver where he runs his independent clothing label, Crownfarmer. Bob's first book of photography, *Beach Glass,* was released last year by Holy Water of London. Online at crownfarmer.com

**Brian Tucci** is a professional skater hailing from Washington DC who spends his time staying creative and off the grid. Look for his model on Circle A Skateboards.

**Brock Essick** was born in 1975 in Ojai, California. He currently resides in Winchester, California where he teaches art and raises his two children. When not working he creates, reads, writes, remodels his home and rides his skateboard on any and all terrain.

**Brown** enjoys wrenching on muscle cars, reading, music and throwing the ball for Karma Dog. He can be found around Phoenix, usually with a beer and smoke in hand trying to find someone to skate street with. brown12345@gmail.com

**Chris "Wez" Lundry** is a PhD Candidate in Political Science at ASU where he lectures in Political Science, History and Southeast Asian Studies. He has published his own skate zine, Pool Dust, since 1988. He is a staff writer and photographer for Thrasher and his work has also appeared in Maximum Rock 'n' Roll, Flipside, Razorcake, Fiz, Juxtapoz, SLAP, Poweredge, *Life and Limb,* the *Encyclopedia of the Developing World,* and elsewhere. He is married to (and tolerated by) his lovely wife, Meg Watjen.

**Clarkie** is a skateboarding advocate currently fighting to change California's absurd pad laws. You can learn more about the cause at her ever-informative skate website. realskate.com

**Corey Daniel** is a lifelong skater who currently skates and migrates as much as he can. Corey would like to thank Friends.

**Darin Bendall** is a lifelong artist and skater from Beaver, Oklahoma who currently lives in Japan for inspiration. He still can't walk down the street without seeing an imaginary skater shredding everything. bendall.biz

**Dave Franklin** has been shooting photos since his dad let him use his camera as a child in Papua New Guinea. He now resides in San Francisco as a freelance photographer and also produces the Underskatement Film Festival with his friend Andreas Trolf. forgivemegod.com

**Dave Miller** was born and raised in Milwaukee, Wisconsin and has been skateboarding since the junior high days. He continues to stay creative with his music.

**David Wallace** can often be found ripping the Camarillo park with Corey, Calvin, Adam and the rest of the lurkers.

**Erik Olsen** is a lifelong skater and skate photographer who has contributed to several companies and skate media. Erik's skills are currently employed by SLAP Magazine.

**eTHOS** originally hails from Oklahoma and is currently living between Brooklyn and Chicago. He grew up on the Osage Reservation and draws much of his influence from the haunting images of old Indian graffiti which dominated the area. Much of that influence is reflected in the primordial nature of his work which depicts the struggle between nature and man.

**FERRIS PLOCK** is an artist living in the Western Addition neighborhood of San Francisco. He grew up in the Bay Area, amusing himself with comic books, graffiti, hip-hop and Chevy Impalas. His work has been featured in XLR8R magazine, Mad Mixer magazine, Tokion magazine, Quarter magazine, Freedom Book and flavorpill.com. He has shown work in NYC, Seattle, New Orleans, Tokyo, London, Paris, Dublin and in cities all across California. ferrisplock.com

**FRANK ATWATER** is more comfortable skating a pool than most people are walking. A veteran professional, his board is available through Old Star Skateboards. His other sponsors include Grind King, Oust Bearings and Funnotfame Productions.

**GARET O'KEEFE** is a happy father who was born and raised in Berkeley, California, where he surfs, skates and practices law.

**GREG LANG** obtained his first skateboard at two and has spent the last fourteen years leading a life that places him in constant situations of conflict. He has lived on both coasts and in between on the quest of his skateboard dream, the all-consuming search for knowledge and its counterpart, wisdom. Greg currently lives in Philadelphia, continuing that pursuit at Drexel University in the Anthropology program.

**ISAAC MCKAY-RANDOZZI** currently resides in San Francisco where he lurks at art shows, works, skates and take pictures. He's a proud member of the notorious Silly Pink Bunnies. His photos and writing have been featured in Hamburger Eyes, MESH magazine, Fecalface.com, Crownfarmer.com, GetUnderground and Maybe Magazine.

**ISMAEL BENHAMIDA** graduated from UC Berkeley with a degree in Chemical Engineering. He is a math wizard who currently skates and resides in Menlo Park, California.

**Jafon "Jay" Hakkinen** was born and raised in San Francisco. He owns and operates Receiver, a boutique design studio and art gallery. receiverstudio.com

**Jeff Knutson** compiled and edited *Life and Limb: Skateboarding Writes From the Deep End* along with his friends in 2004. He currently resides in Portland, Oregon where he enjoys skating, writing and teaching high school.

**Jeremiah Liebrecht** is a 28-year-old skateboarder and sound engineer who currently lives and skates in San Francisco, CA.

**JTRD** is lucky and also known as Jeremy Henderson. He was born in Long Beach, and in the early 80's he moved to NYC to learn art fabrication where he later became pro for Shut Skates. JTRD is a forefather of skateboard art in the vein of Neil, Gonz, Natas and Lance. He portrayed a young Salvador Dali in *Dali by Dali* and has worked for many greats from Morley to Longo to Basquiat.

**Jessie VanRoechoudt** is a professional skater who spends most of her time traveling, skating and writing. Jessie currently has a model with Rookie Skateboards and she has been a contributing writer for Kingpin Magazine (Europe), Transworld Skateboarding Business and other skate-related publications. Jessie is on the Distinguished Alumni List at San Francisco State University and currently writes a column for Skateboard Trade News. She is also a freelance photographer.

**Jim Gray** is a professional skater who owns ABC Board Supply and spends his free time skating local parks while thinking of ways to improve skateboarding in general. Jim is a member of IASC. skateparkcoalition.org

**Joey Young** lives in Fresno CA, with his wife Dannelle and daughter Lydia. He skates for Working Class Skateboards in addition to being the editor in chief of Paying In Pain skate zine.

**Joshua J. Feldman** works as a race car tech and is currently pursuing a teaching degree. Josh is a master skateboarder and has been flowed by several companies including Shorty's and Emerica, and was a co-founder of Persona Skateboards. His current sponsors are Five Points and Funnotfame Productions.

**JOHNNY "BURRITO" RODRIGUEZ** has been skateboarding for twenty years. He currently resides in Ventura, California where he works, skates and continues to make art. John skated for Shorty's back in the day; check his part in the first Church video.

**KARL WATSON** is a professional skateboarder and freelance artist currently residing in Los Angeles. His current sponsors include I-Path, Organika, Venture Trucks, Jessup and LRG Clothing. He was born in Oakland, California and has spent sixteen years acquiring knowledge on his skateboard.

**KEIR K. JOHNSON** resides and grew up in the Washington DC metro area and has long been part of the ever-changing skateboarding scene in the city. Keir graduated from the University of Maryland with a BA in American Studies and released ten episodes of his original hiphop/skateboarding television show *Two Zero Two TV* on public access in San Francisco between 2004-05. His writing has appeared in TheForgottenCity.com, the Wall Street Journal, Thrasher Magazine and Unkut.com. keirjohnson@yahoo.com

**KEN GOTO** was born in Tokyo in 1976. At the age of ten he moved to Kawaguchi city; at fourteen he began skateboarding. In 1997 he moved to San Francisco, where he began taking photos, eventually earning a degree in photography from San Francisco City College. His work has appeared in SLAP, Thrasher and Skateboarder; he has also shot for DVS, I-Path, Real, Chocolate and others. kengotophoto.com

**KEVIN MCHUGH** is 20 years old from Toronto, Ontario. He currently attends the University of Toronto majoring in English and Urban Geography. He started skating in high school and has great interest in architecture, in particular its relationship with skateboarding. Kevin plays hockey, goalie, for the University of Toronto and other leagues.

**LEE SMITH** is a professional skateboarder. He is currently living in Barcelona and probably enjoying every minute of it. His board is available through Santa Cruz Skateboards.

**LELAND B. WARE, JR.** was born March 5, 1975 in Atlanta, Georgia. He now resides in San Francisco. Leland started skating in 1983.

**LIZZIE LEE** is the proud owner of Purple Skunk Skateboards on Geary Blvd. She lives in San Francisco, currently in the pursuit of life, liberty and happiness. purpleskunk.com.

**MARC JOHNSON** is a currently studying both microcosm and macrocosm, anticipating the impending planetary shift into 4D with a joyful anxiety quite like that of skateboarding.

**MARK WHITELEY** is the editor-in-chief/writer/photographer at SLAP Magazine. He received his art degree with honors from UC Santa Cruz. He is currently married with a new daughter and his skateboarding roots are old enough to buy beer legally. He gave us his measurements but that's none of your business.

**MARK WHITAKER** is a skateboarding photographer and resident of Oxnard, California. A graduate of Brooks Institute of Photography, he spends his free time documenting the local skate and music scenes.

**MATT DERRICK** lives in San Francisco where he runs DLXSF with his friends. Matt keeps heavily involved in the local skate scene and spends his free time making music.

**MATT GOODWIN** is a resident of Scottsdale, Arizona where he spends his time working, skating the fabulous desert parks and hanging out with friends. He is an aspiring death metal singer (Carpe Noctem) in his spare time and he also maintains a website of the local skate crew: geocities.com/nspskate

**MICHAEL BROOKE** was born in Leeds, England and was sadly not old enough to attend the Who concert. He moved to Canada with his family in 1972 and started skateboarding in 1975. Michael attended college in Toronto where he graduated with a BA in Applied Arts (radio & television). mbrooke@interlog.com

**MIKE YORK** is a professional skateboarder who currently resides in Los Angeles, California. His board is available through Chocolate Skateboards.

**NATE HOOPER** was born and raised in San Francisco. He spent most of his early years drawing, skateboarding and getting himself into a lot of trouble. He later went to art school to pursue painting and photography in Pittsburgh, Pennsylvania and then London, UK. He currently lives in San Francisco, working as a graphic designer for Ordinary Kids (ordinarykids.com), freelancing, painting, and taking photos. Nate has shown his work all over America, in the UK and France. natehooper.com

**NATE SHERWOOD** is the Fidel Castro of skateboarding. He was exiled from his native Portland to San Diego, CA for being too outspoken to the mindless sheep that grazed there. He is now living in a remote location, training a guerrilla camp full of free-thinking skateboarders to fight the circumcised state of mind that has been accepted as the norm in skateboarding. (words by Ross Mallard)

**NIMAL** is currently a student living in San Diego where he studies computational biology. He is 20 years old and hopes to work in the field of bioengineering with applications for medical treatment. Although trained in the physical sciences, he also has a deep interest in the social sciences, especially history.

**PAUL COTE'** grew up in Florida and first fell in love with skateboarding in 1988. He is also a freelance artist who enjoys skating, writing, reading and the dissolution of craving.

**PAUL URICH** currently lives in San Francisco. He is 31 years old and enjoys surfing, skating and making art. You can check out some of his work at fecalface.com

**RICHARD HART** was lured from England to California in the mid-90's, all because of skateboarding. Now he enjoys shooting photographs, writing, drawing and buying records.

**ROB BRINK** was given his first Vision Shredder 2 complete in 1989 and has since accumulated a vast knowledge of skateboarding. Rob holds a master's degree in writing and is a prolific contributor to various skate media who spends his free time skating flatground and red curbs late at night. robbrink.com

**RORY PARKER** writes some rather hilarious columns for Automatic Magazine. He currently lives down south where he surfs, skates and writes freely.

**SATVA LEUNG** is a professional skater. He currently resides in San Francisco and can be found DJ'ing at local clubs and their subsequent afterparties. He is also a freelance skateboarding videographer, currently working on an independent project.

**SKATER DAVE** has been skateboarding for over 25 years. He currently resides in Ventura, California where he manages Five Points Skateboards. A lover of transition, Dave is also a freelance artist and costume designer.

**SCOTTIE VOSBURGH** picked up skateboarding at the age of 11 and is pursuing a degree at the University of Michigan.

**STEVE KANG** is a lifelong skateboarder and professional footwear designer whose clients include Circa, Emerica, 88 Footwear, Reef and Nadia. Steve currently resides in Orange County, California. His other hobbies include MX, snowboarding, masonry and foos-ball. Steve holds a bachelors degree in applied science from Design Engine, Utah.

**YONG-KI CHANG** was born in Seoul, Korea and moved to Oahu, Hawaii at the age of three. Yong-Ki found his first love on the day of his 12th birthday when Mom took him to get his first skateboard. Currently 32, Yong-Ki is happily engaged to Sylvia while running The Solitary Arts, Inc. with Geoff McFetridge, distributing Hessenmob Skateboards and also works by Greg 'PNUT' Galinsky through Equal Distribution. In addition, he enjoys time at the neighborhood skateshop Purple Skunk, and is attending SFSU full-time in the Marketing department.

**hority:** (authority) *n., pl.* **-ties** **1. a.** the 'er to command, enforce laws, exact lience, determine or judge. **b.** a person or ıp invested with this power, i.e. government. 'reedom or right granted to another. **3.** A ic agency or corporation with administrative ers in a specified field, i.e. *The Port ıority.* **6.** Power to influence or persuade lting from knowledge or experience.

**hority:** (authority) *n., pl.* **-ties** **1. a.** the 'er to command, enforce laws, exact lience, determine or judge. **b.** a person or ıp invested with this power, i.e. government. 'reedom or right granted to another. **3.** A ic agency or corporation with administrative ers in a specified field, i.e. *The Port ıority.* **6.** Power to influence or persuade lting from knowledge or experience.

**hority:** (authority) *n., pl.* **-ties** **1. a.** the 'er to command, enforce laws, exact lience, determine or judge. **b.** a person or ıp invested with this power, i.e. government. 'reedom or right granted to another. **3.** A ic agency or corporation with administrative ers in a specified field, i.e. *The Port ıority.* **6.** Power to influence or persuade lting from knowledge or experience.

**hority:** (authority) *n., pl.* **-ties** **1. a.** the 'er to command, enforce laws, exact lience, determine or judge. **b.** a person or ıp invested with this power, i.e. government. 'reedom or right granted to another. **3.** A ic agency or corporation with administrative ers in a specified field, i.e. *The Port ıority.* **6.** Power to influence or persuade lting from knowledge or experience.

**hority:** (authority) *n., pl.* **-ties** **1. a.** the 'er to command, enforce laws, exact lience, determine or judge. **b.** a person or ıp invested with this power, i.e. government. 'reedom or right granted to another. **3.** A ic agency or corporation with administrative ers in a specified field, i.e. *The Port ıority.* **6.** Power to influence or persuade lting from knowledge or experience.

**hority:** (authority) *n., pl.* **-ties** **1. a.** the 'er to command, enforce laws, exact

**2.** Freedom or right granted to another. public agency or corporation with administr powers in a specified fi *The Authority.* **6.** Power to influence or pers resulting from knowledge or experience.

**authority:** (authority) *n., pl.* **-ties** **1. a** power to command, enforce laws, e obedience, determine or judge. **b.** a perso group invested with this power, i.e. governm **2.** Freedom or right granted to another. public agency or corporation with administr powers in a specified field, i.e. *The Authority.* **6.** Power to influence or pers resulting from knowledge or experience.

**authority:** (authority) *n., pl.* **-ties** **1. a** power to command, enforce laws, e obedience, determine or judge. **b.** a perso group invested with this power, i.e. governm **2.** Freedom or right granted to another. public agency or corporation with administr powers in a specified field, i.e. *The Authority.* **6.** Power to influence or pers resulting from knowledge or experience.

**authority:** (authority) *n., pl.* **-ties** **1. a** power to command, enforce laws, e obedience, determine or judge. **b.** a perso group invested with this power, i.e. governm **2.** Freedom or right granted to another. public agency or corporation with administr powers in a specified field, i.e. *The Authority.* **6.** Power to influence or pers resulting from knowledge or experience.

**authority:** (authority) *n., pl.* **-ties** **1. a** power to command, enforce laws, e obedience, determine or judge. **b.** a perso group invested with this power, i.e. governm **2.** Freedom or right granted to another. public agency or corporation with administr powers in a specified field, i.e. *The Authority.* **6.** Power to influence or pers resulting from knowledge or experience.

**authority:** (authority) *n., pl.* **-ties** **1.** power to command, enforce laws, obedience, determine or judge. **b.** a pers group invested with this power, i.e. govern **2.** Freedom or right granted to another. public agency or corporation with administ powers in a specified field, i.e. *The*

er to command, enforce laws, exact
ience, determine or judge. b. a person or
p invested with this power, i.e. government.
reedom or right granted to another. 3. A
ic agency or corporation with administrative
ers in a specified field, i.e. *The Port*
*ority.* 6. Power to influence or persuade
ting from knowledge or experience.

**hority:** (authority) *n., pl.* **-ties** **1. a.** the
er to command, enforce laws, exact
ience, determine or judge. **b.** a person or
p invested with this power, i.e. government.
reedom or right granted to another. **3.** A
c agency or corporation with administrative
ers in a specified field, i.e. *The Port*
*ority.* **6.** Power to influence or persuade
ting from knowledge or experience.

**hority:** (authority) *n., pl.* **-ties** **1. a.** the
er to command, enforce laws, exact
ience, determine or judge. **b.** a person or
p invested with this power, i.e. government.
reedom or right granted to another. **3.** A
c agency or corporation with administrative
ers in a specified field, i.e. *The Port*
*ority.* **6.** Power to influence or persuade
ting from knowledge or experience.

**hority:** (authority) *n., pl.* **-ties** **1. a.** the
er to command, enforce laws, exact
ience, determine or judge. **b.** a person or
p invested with this power, i.e. government.
reedom or right granted to another. **3.** A
c agency or corporation with administrative
ers in a specified field, i.e. *The Port*
*ority.* **6.** Power to influence or persuade
ting from knowledge or experience.

**hority:** (authority) *n., pl.* **-ties** **1. a.** the
er to command, enforce laws, exact
ience, determine or judge. **b.** a person or
p invested with this power, i.e. government.
reedom or right granted to another. **3.** A
c agency or corporation with administrative
ers in a specified field, i.e. *The Port*
*ority.* **6.** Power to influence or persuade
ting from knowledge or experience.

**hority:** (authority) *n., pl.* **-ties** **1. a.** the
er to command, enforce laws, exact
ience, determine or judge. **b.** a person or

public agency or corporation with administra
powers in a specified field, i.e. *The*
*Authority.* **6.** Power to influence or pers
resulting from knowledge or experience.

**authority:** (authority) *n., pl.* **-ties** **1. a**
power to command, enforce laws, e
obedience, determine or judge. **b.** a perso
group invested with this power, i.e. governm
**2.** Freedom or right granted to another. 3
public agency or corporation with administra
powers in a specified field, i.e. *The*
*Authority.* **6.** Power to influence or pers
resulting from knowledge or experience.

**authority:** (authority) *n., pl.* **-ties** **1. a**
power to command, enforce laws, e
obedience, determine or judge. **b.** a perso
group invested with this power, i.e. governm
**2.** Freedom or right granted to another. 3
public agency or corporation with administra
powers in a specified field, i.e. *The*
*Authority.* **6.** Power to influence or pers
resulting from knowledge or experience.

**authority:** (authority) *n., pl.* **-ties** **1. a**
power to command, enforce laws, e
obedience, determine or judge. **b.** a perso
group invested with this power, i.e. governm
**2.** Freedom or right granted to another. 3
public agency or corporation with administra
powers in a specified field, i.e. *The*
*Authority.* **6.** Power to influence or pers
resulting from knowledge or experience.

**authority:** (authority) *n., pl.* **-ties** **1. a**
power to command, enforce laws, e
obedience, determine or judge. **b.** a perso
group invested with this power, i.e. governm
**2.** Freedom or right granted to another. 3
public agency or corporation with administra
powers in a specified field, i.e. *The*
*Authority.* **6.** Power to influence or pers
resulting from knowledge or experience.

**authority:** (authority) *n., pl.* **-ties** **1. a**
power to command, enforce laws, e
obedience, determine or judge. **b.** a perso
group invested with this power, i.e. governm
**2.** Freedom or right granted to another. 3
public agency or corporation with administr
powers in a specified field, i.e. *The*

er to command, enforce laws, exact ience, determine or judge. **b.** a person or p invested with this power, i.e. government. reedom or right granted to another. **3.** A ic agency or corporation with administrative ers in a specified field, i.e. *The Port ority.* **6.** Power to influence or persuade ting from knowledge or experience.

**hority:** (authority) *n., pl.* **-ties** **1. a.** the er to command, enforce laws, exact ience, determine or judge. **b.** a person or p invested with this power, i.e. government. reedom or right granted to another. **3.** A ic agency or corporation with administrative ers in a specified field, i.e. *The Port ority.* **6.** Power to influence or persuade ting from knowledge or experience.

**hority:** (authority) *n., pl.* **-ties** **1. a.** the er to command, enforce laws, exact ience, determine or judge. **b.** a person or p invested with this power, i.e. government. reedom or right granted to another. **3.** A ic agency or corporation with administrative ers in a specified field, i.e. *The Port ority.* **6.** Power to influence or persuade ting from knowledge or experience.

**hority:** (authority) *n., pl.* **-ties** **1. a.** the er to command, enforce laws, exact ience, determine or judge. **b.** a person or p invested with this power, i.e. government. reedom or right granted to another. **3.** A ic agency or corporation with administrative ers in a specified field, i.e. *The Port ority.* **6.** Power to influence or persuade ting from knowledge or experience.

**hority:** (authority) *n., pl.* **-ties** **1. a.** the er to command, enforce laws, exact ience, determine or judge. **b.** a person or p invested with this power, i.e. government. reedom or right granted to another. **3.** A ic agency or corporation with administrative ers in a specified field, i.e. *The Port ority.* **6.** Power to influence or persuade ting from knowledge or experience.

**hority:** (authority) *n., pl.* **-ties** **1. a.** the er to command, enforce laws, exact ience, determine or judge. **b.** a person or

public agency or corporation with administr powers in a specified field, i.e. *The Authority.* **6.** Power to influence or pers resulting from knowledge or experience.

**authority:** (authority) *n., pl.* **-ties** **1. a** power to command, enforce laws, e obedience, determine or judge. **b.** a perso group invested with this power, i.e. governm **2.** Freedom or right granted to another. public agency or corporation with administr powers in a specified field, i.e. *The Authority.* **6.** Power to influence or pers resulting from knowledge or experience.

**authority:** (authority) *n., pl.* **-ties** **1. a** power to command, enforce laws, e obedience, determine or judge. **b.** a perso group invested with this power, i.e. governm **2.** Freedom or right granted to another. public agency or corporation with administr powers in a specified field, i.e. *The Authority.* **6.** Power to influence or pers resulting from knowledge or experience.

**authority:** (authority) *n., pl.* **-ties** **1. a** power to command, enforce laws, e obedience, determine or judge. **b.** a perso group invested with this power, i.e. governm **2.** Freedom or right granted to another. public agency or corporation with administr powers in a specified field, i.e. *The Authority.* **6.** Power to influence or pers resulting from knowledge or experience.

**authority:** (authority) *n., pl.* **-ties** **1. a** power to command, enforce laws, e obedience, determine or judge. **b.** a perso group invested with this power, i.e. governm **2.** Freedom or right granted to another. public agency or corporation with administr powers in a specified field, i.e. *The Authority.* **6.** Power to influence or pers resulting from knowledge or experience.

**authority:** (authority) *n., pl.* **-ties** **1. a** power to command, enforce laws, e obedience, determine or judge. **b.** a perso group invested with this power, i.e. governm **2.** Freedom or right granted to another. public agency or corporation with administr powers in a specified field, i.e. *The*

er to command, enforce laws, exact ience, determine or judge. b. a person or o invested with this power, i.e. government. eedom or right granted to another. **3.** A c agency or corporation with administrative ers in a specified field, i.e. *The Port ority.* **6.** Power to influence or persuade ting from knowledge or experience.

**ority:** (authority) *n., pl.* **-ties** **1. a.** the er to command, enforce laws, exact ience, determine or judge. **b.** a person or o invested with this power, i.e. government. eedom or right granted to another. **3.** A c agency or corporation with administrative ers in a specified field, i.e. *The Port ority.* **6.** Power to influence or persuade ting from knowledge or experience.

**ority:** (authority) *n., pl.* **-ties** **1. a.** the er to command, enforce laws, exact ience, determine or judge. **b.** a person or o invested with this power, i.e. government. eedom or right granted to another. **3.** A c agency or corporation with administrative ers in a specified field, i.e. *The Port ority.* **6.** Power to influence or persuade ting from knowledge or experience.

**ority:** (authority) *n., pl.* **-ties** **1. a.** the er to command, enforce laws, exact ience, determine or judge. **b.** a person or o invested with this power, i.e. government. eedom or right granted to another. **3.** A c agency or corporation with administrative ers in a specified field, i.e. *The Port ority.* **6.** Power to influence or persuade ting from knowledge or experience.

**ority:** (authority) *n., pl.* **-ties** **1. a.** the er to command, enforce laws, exact ience, determine or judge. **b.** a person or o invested with this power, i.e. government. eedom or right granted to another. **3.** A c agency or corporation with administrative ers in a specified field, i.e. *The Port ority.* **6.** Power to influence or persuade ting from knowledge or experience.

**ority:** (authority) *n., pl.* **-ties** **1. a.** the er to command, enforce laws, exact ence, determine or judge. **b.** a person or

public agency or corporation with administr powers in a specified field, i.e. *The Authority.* **6.** Power to influence or pers resulting from knowledge or experience.

**authority:** (authority) *n., pl.* **-ties** **1. a** power to command, enforce laws, e obedience, determine or judge. **b.** a perso group invested with this power, i.e. governn **2.** Freedom or right granted to another. public agency or corporation with administr powers in a specified field, i.e. *The Authority.* **6.** Power to influence or pers resulting from knowledge or experience.

**authority:** (authority) *n., pl.* **-ties** **1. a** power to command, enforce laws, e obedience, determine or judge. **b.** a perso group invested with this power, i.e. governn **2.** Freedom or right granted to another. public agency or corporation with administr powers in a specified field, i.e. *The Authority.* **6.** Power to influence or pers resulting from knowledge or experience.

**authority:** (authority) *n., pl.* **-ties** **1. a** power to command, enforce laws, e obedience, determine or judge. **b.** a perso group invested with this power, i.e. governn **2.** Freedom or right granted to another. public agency or corporation with administr powers in a specified field, i.e. *The Authority.* **6.** Power to influence or pers resulting from knowledge or experience.

**authority:** (authority) *n., pl.* **-ties** **1. a** power to command, enforce laws, e obedience, determine or judge. **b.** a perso group invested with this power, i.e. governn **2.** Freedom or right granted to another. public agency or corporation with administr powers in a specified field, i.e. *The Authority.* **6.** Power to influence or pers resulting from knowledge or experience.

**authority:** (authority) *n., pl.* **-ties** **1. a** power to command, enforce laws, e obedience, determine or judge. **b.** a perso group invested with this power, i.e. governn **2.** Freedom or right granted to another. public agency or corporation with administr powers in a specified field, i.e. *The* er to command, enforce laws, exact ience, determine or judge. b. a person or p invested with this power, i.e. government. reedom or right granted to another. 3. A ic agency or corporation with administrative ers in a specified field, i.e. *The Port ority.* 6. Power to influence or persuade ting from knowledge or experience.

**hority:** (authority) *n., pl.* **-ties** **1. a.** the er to command, enforce laws, exact ience, determine or judge. **b.** a person or p invested with this power, i.e. government. reedom or right granted to another. **3.** A ic agency or corporation with administrative ers in a specified field, i.e. *The Port ority.* **6.** Power to influence or persuade ting from knowledge or experience.

**hority:** (authority) *n., pl.* **-ties** **1. a.** the er to command, enforce laws, exact ience, determine or judge. **b.** a person or p invested with this power, i.e. government. reedom or right granted to another. **3.** A ic agency or corporation with administrative ers in a specified field, i.e. *The Port ority.* **6.** Power to influence or persuade ting from knowledge or experience.

**hority:** (authority) *n., pl.* **-ties** **1. a.** the er to command, enforce laws, exact ience, determine or judge. **b.** a person or p invested with this power, i.e. government. reedom or right granted to another. **3.** A ic agency or corporation with administrative ers in a specified field, i.e. *The Port ority.* **6.** Power to influence or persuade ting from knowledge or experience.

**hority:** (authority) *n., pl.* **-ties** **1. a.** the er to command, enforce laws, exact ience, determine or judge. **b.** a person or p invested with this power, i.e. government. reedom or right granted to another. **3.** A ic agency or corporation with administrative ers in a specified field, i.e. *The Port ority.* **6.** Power to influence or persuade ting from knowledge or experience.

**hority:** (authority) *n., pl.* **-ties** **1. a.** the er to command, enforce laws, exact ience, determine or judge. **b.** a person or

public agency or corporation with administr powers in a specified field, i.e. *The Authority.* **6.** Power to influence or pers resulting from knowledge or experience.

**authority:** (authority) *n., pl.* **-ties** **1. a** power to command, enforce laws, e obedience, determine or judge. **b.** a perso group invested with this power, i.e. governm **2.** Freedom or right granted to another. public agency or corporation with administr powers in a specified field, i.e. *The Authority.* **6.** Power to influence or pers resulting from knowledge or experience.

**authority:** (authority) *n., pl.* **-ties** **1. a** power to command, enforce laws, e obedience, determine or judge. **b.** a perso group invested with this power, i.e. governm **2.** Freedom or right granted to another. public agency or corporation with administr powers in a specified field, i.e. *The Authority.* **6.** Power to influence or pers resulting from knowledge or experience.

**authority:** (authority) *n., pl.* **-ties** **1. a** power to command, enforce laws, e obedience, determine or judge. **b.** a perso group invested with this power, i.e. governm **2.** Freedom or right granted to another. public agency or corporation with administr powers in a specified field, i.e. *The Authority.* **6.** Power to influence or pers resulting from knowledge or experience.

**authority:** (authority) *n., pl.* **-ties** **1. a** power to command, enforce laws, e obedience, determine or judge. **b.** a perso group invested with this power, i.e. governm **2.** Freedom or right granted to another. public agency or corporation with administr powers in a specified field, i.e. *The Authority.* **6.** Power to influence or pers resulting from knowledge or experience.

**authority:** (authority) *n., pl.* **-ties** **1. a** power to command, enforce laws, e obedience, determine or judge. **b.** a perso group invested with this power, i.e. governm **2.** Freedom or right granted to another. public agency or corporation with administr powers in a specified field, i.e. *The*

er to command, enforce laws, exact ence, determine or judge. b. a person or invested with this power, i.e. government. eedom or right granted to another. **3.** A c agency or corporation with administrative ers in a specified field, i.e. *The Port ority.* **6.** Power to influence or persuade ting from knowledge or experience.

**ority:** (authority) *n., pl.* **-ties** **1. a.** the er to command, enforce laws, exact ence, determine or judge. **b.** a person or invested with this power, i.e. government. eedom or right granted to another. **3.** A c agency or corporation with administrative ers in a specified field, i.e. *The Port ority.* **6.** Power to influence or persuade ting from knowledge or experience.

**ority:** (authority) *n., pl.* **-ties** **1. a.** the er to command, enforce laws, exact ence, determine or judge. **b.** a person or invested with this power, i.e. government. eedom or right granted to another. **3.** A c agency or corporation with administrative ers in a specified field, i.e. *The Port ority.* **6.** Power to influence or persuade ting from knowledge or experience.

**ority:** (authority) *n., pl.* **-ties** **1. a.** the er to command, enforce laws, exact ence, determine or judge. **b.** a person or invested with this power, i.e. government. eedom or right granted to another. **3.** A c agency or corporation with administrative ers in a specified field, i.e. *The Port ority.* **6.** Power to influence or persuade ting from knowledge or experience.

**ority:** (authority) *n., pl.* **-ties** **1. a.** the er to command, enforce laws, exact ence, determine or judge. **b.** a person or invested with this power, i.e. government. eedom or right granted to another. **3.** A c agency or corporation with administrative ers in a specified field, i.e. *The Port ority.* **6.** Power to influence or persuade ting from knowledge or experience.

**ority:** (authority) *n., pl.* **-ties** **1. a.** the er to command, enforce laws, exact ence, determine or judge. **b.** a person or

public agency or corporation with administra powers in a specified field, i.e. *The Authority.* **6.** Power to influence or pers resulting from knowledge or experience.

**authority:** (authority) *n., pl.* **-ties** **1. a** power to command, enforce laws, e obedience, determine or judge. **b.** a perso group invested with this power, i.e. governm **2.** Freedom or right granted to another. 3 public agency or corporation with administra powers in a specified field, i.e. *The Authority.* **6.** Power to influence or pers resulting from knowledge or experience.

**authority:** (authority) *n., pl.* **-ties** **1. a** power to command, enforce laws, e obedience, determine or judge. **b.** a perso group invested with this power, i.e. governm **2.** Freedom or right granted to another. 3 public agency or corporation with administra powers in a specified field, i.e. *The Authority.* **6.** Power to influence or pers resulting from knowledge or experience.

**authority:** (authority) *n., pl.* **-ties** **1. a** power to command, enforce laws, e obedience, determine or judge. **b.** a perso group invested with this power, i.e. governm **2.** Freedom or right granted to another. 3 public agency or corporation with administra powers in a specified field, i.e. *The Authority.* **6.** Power to influence or pers resulting from knowledge or experience.

**authority:** (authority) *n., pl.* **-ties** **1. a** power to command, enforce laws, e obedience, determine or judge. **b.** a perso group invested with this power, i.e. governm **2.** Freedom or right granted to another. public agency or corporation with administr powers in a specified field, i.e. *The Authority.* **6.** Power to influence or pers resulting from knowledge or experience.

**authority:** (authority) *n., pl.* **-ties** **1. a** power to command, enforce laws, e obedience, determine or judge. **b.** a perso group invested with this power, i.e. governm **2.** Freedom or right granted to another. public agency or corporation with administr powers in a specified field, i.e. *The*

SKATEBOARD
ROLLER SKATING
AND
BICYCLE
RIDING
PROHIBITED
SLOW!